Victorian Cemeteries and the Suburbs of London

This book explores how Victorian cemeteries were the direct result of the socio-cultural, economic and political context of the city, and were part of a unique transformation process that emerged in London at the time. The book shows how the re-ordering of the city's burial spaces, along with the principles of health and hygiene, were directly associated with liberal capital investments, which had consequences in the spatial arrangement of London. Victorian cemeteries, in particular, were not only a solution for overcrowded graveyards, they also acted as urban generators in the formation London's suburbs in the nineteenth century. Beginning with an analysis of the conditions that triggered the introduction of the early Victorian cemeteries in London, this book investigates their spatial arrangement, aesthetics and functions. These developments are illustrated through the study of three private Victorian burial sites: Kensal Green Cemetery, Highgate Cemetery and Brookwood Cemetery. The book is aimed at students and researchers of London history, planning and environment, and Victorian and death culture studies.

Gian Luca Amadei is an independent academic researcher, design journalist and lecturer at the Royal College of Art in London.

Routledge Research in Planning and Urban Design

Routledge Research in Planning and Urban Design is a series of academic monographs for scholars working in these disciplines and the overlaps between them. Building on Routledge's history of academic rigour and cutting-edge research, the series contributes to the rapidly expanding literature in all areas of planning and urban design.

Economic Incentives in Sub-Saharan African Urban Planning
A Ghanaian Case Study
Kwasi Gyau Baffour Awuah

Street-Naming Cultures in Africa and Israel
Power Strategies and Place-Making Practices
Liora Bigon and Michel Ben Arrous

Identity in Post-Socialist Public Space
Urban Architecture in Kiev, Moscow, Berlin, and Warsaw
Bohdan Cherkes and Józef Hernik

Sustainable Urban Futures in Africa
Edited by Patrick Brandful Cobbinah and Michael Addaney

Smart Design
Disruption, Crisis, and the Reshaping of Urban Spaces
Richard Hu

Victorian Cemeteries and the Suburbs of London
Spatial Consequences to the Reordering of London's Burials in the Early 19th Century
Gian Luca Amadei

For more information about this series, please visit: www.routledge.com/Routledge-Research-in-Planning-and-Urban-Design/book-series/RRPUD

Victorian Cemeteries and the Suburbs of London

Spatial Consequences to the Reordering of London's Burials in the Early 19th Century

Gian Luca Amadei

NEW YORK AND LONDON

Cover image © Historic England

First published 2022
by Routledge
605 Third Avenue, New York, NY 10158

and by Routledge
2 Park Square, Milton Park, Abingdon, Oxon, OX14 4RN

Routledge is an imprint of the Taylor & Francis Group, an informa business

© 2022 Gian Luca Amadei

The right of Gian Luca Amadei to be identified as author of this work has been asserted in accordance with sections 77 and 78 of the Copyright, Designs and Patents Act 1988.

All rights reserved. No part of this book may be reprinted or reproduced or utilised in any form or by any electronic, mechanical, or other means, now known or hereafter invented, including photocopying and recording, or in any information storage or retrieval system, without permission in writing from the publishers.

Trademark notice: Product or corporate names may be trademarks or registered trademarks are used only for identification and explanation without intent to infringe.

Library of Congress Cataloging-in-Publication Data
A catalog record for this title has been requested

ISBN: 978-1-032-01516-3 (hbk)
ISBN: 978-1-032-01518-7 (pbk)
ISBN: 978-1-003-17893-4 (ebk)

DOI: 10.4324/9781003178934

Typeset in Sabon
by Deanta Global Publishing Services, Chennai, India

To all the wonderful people I encountered in my life, who brought me here. They made my journey worthwhile.

Contents

Acknowledgements   ix

Introduction   1

1   **Health**   9

   1.1 Metropolitan sepulchre   9
   1.2 Overcrowding   13
   1.3 Ordering the dead   19
   Bibliography   27

2   **Identity**   30

   2.1 Landscapes of remembrance   30
   2.2 The business of burying the dead   36
   2.3 Architecture and legacy   41
   2.4 Rational minds   50
   Bibliography   56

3   **Suburbs/Kensal Green**   59

   3.1 Metropolitan picturesque   59
   3.2 Testing ground   66
   3.3 A new suburb   80
   Bibliography   86

4   **Suburbs/Highgate**   90

   4.1 The village at the edge of the metropolis   90
   4.2 Gravestones and vistas   95
   4.3 New hospitals and clean air   103
   Bibliography   117

5 Suburbs/Brookwood and Woking   121

   5.1 Waterways and brick yards   121
   5.2 Cemetery and town   125
   5.3 New century, new beginning   138
   5.4 The Woking residential estates   141
   5.5 Conclusions   150
   Bibliography   152

6 Rethinking   157

   6.1 Open spaces   157
   6.2 New alternatives to earth burial   162
   6.3 Future visions   168
   6.4 Conclusions   171
   Bibliography   173

Index   177

Acknowledgements

This book would not have been possible without the help of so many people in so many ways. It was also the product of a large measure of serendipity, fortuitous encounters with people, places, documents and artefacts that inspired me.

My editors at Routledge and particularly Kate Schell, Sean Speers and Jyotsna Gurund. The team at Deanta, and in particular to Immaculate Nancy Antony, for all the support with the copy-editing process. All the staff at The British Museum, London Transport Museum, British Library, Royal Institute of British Architects and Historic England that granted me permission for the use of their images.

Dr. Brain Parsons, Dr. Lindsay Udall and John Clarke for their supportive feedback while working on the manuscript draft. The amazing staff at the British Library, London Metropolitan Archives and Woking History Centre. Prof. Gordana Fontana Giusti, Dr. Vincent Miller, Prof. Don Gray, Dr. Ruth Richardson, Dr. Tordis Berstrand, Dr. Anja-Karina Nydal, Dr. Julie Rugg, Dr. Ruth Penfold-Mounce, Prof. Leonie Kelleher, Prof. Andrew Saint, Sarah Mann, Joao Guarantani, Vicky Richardson, Kendal Robins, Niamh Tuft, Kate Le Versha, Aras Amiri, James Tyson, Dario Lombardi, Jenny Jones, Jenny White, Corinne Julius, Dr. Krista Bonello Giappone, Gwen Webber, Mami Sayo, Ryoko Uyama, Dr. Amir Hommasi and Dr. Anna-Stiina Wallinheimo, Ben and Andrea Ellis, Angela and Colin Baird, Simona and Raffaella Semprebene – thank you all for your care and availability that I will always remember.

My parents, Anna Maria and Romeo Amadei, for their support and encouragement. My brother Andrea Amadei and the rest of my amazing family as they patiently followed the progress of my writing. Chris and Gina Ellis, for their enthusiastic support and passion for my research. Special thanks to Tim Ellis, a light bearer, all the way through this project.

Introduction

The tragic context of the COVID-19 pandemic has brought a new awareness of mortality, health and wellbeing as well as questions about how to design for spatial distancing. Alongside this, a renewed appreciation for outdoor spaces made experts and communities look at the connection between public health and urban design with different eyes. During the lockdown periods, for many Londoners living in small flats or not having access to nearby parks, Victorian cemeteries became a destination where to walk, think and reconnect with nature and, through their vistas, to the city itself. Besides the fact that most of London's Victorian cemeteries have now almost reached capacity in terms of burial space, they are still relevant to the functioning of the city. For example, for the preparatory work for the High Speed 2 (HS2) railway project (connecting London to Birmingham), the remains of 50,000 graves in the vicinity of London's Euston Station have been reinterred in Brookwood Cemetery (as reported on the RailStaff website on the 17 September 2020). Along central London, the HS2 project is also going to change the area in the vicinity of Kensal Green Cemetery, where a new railway station is planned to be constructed. London's first suburban Victorian cemetery is going to be a key feature in the local masterplan for its landscape, architecture and cultural contribution to the social history of London. Highgate Cemetery and Brookwood Cemetery are also about to receive some crucial changes to both preserve their natural landscape and enhance their offer as cultural destinations for visitors.

Cemeteries are often perceived only as repositories of human remains, and funerary architecture functions as a marker of our respect and a memory holder to those that we once loved who have moved beyond their physical life. When they were first introduced, suburban Victorian cemeteries were designed as gardens of rest, but also as destinations for day trippers. They were a new feature for the city, a new iteration of urban life, that wove together and bridged between the city and the wilderness at the rural fringes of the city. Their relevance to today's urban life is multifaceted and complex, as they are both open spaces yet consecrated grounds. The presence of nature makes them look like parks, yet they are places of rest, contemplation and reflection. They are located in some stunning spots, once on the fringes of

DOI: 10.4324/9781003178934-1

London, that still retain visual connections with the city and beyond (Kensal Green with its views as far as Surrey Hills, Highgate and its views across London or West Norwood with its view of St. Paul's Cathedral).

The introduction of suburban cemeteries had a series of consequences that affected the life of the city then, and still to this day. This book points out the boldness and experimentation that private enterprises took upon themselves to address the consequences to health challenges such as cholera pandemics. The creation of new suburban cemeteries was a massive exercise in problem-solving, which also prompted the central government at the time to take action by validating private enterprises initiating the new suburban cemeteries. This book takes those early examples of private cemeteries that manifested in the once semi-rural areas in the outskirts of London, and highlights how their influence radiated beyond their boundary walls, and affected the formation of the built environment in their vicinities. Ultimately this book is interested in integrating the existing knowledge of London's early Victorian cemeteries by highlighting their unexpected contribution to the suburban development of the capital. The intention is to clarify that cemeteries were not only burial solutions but receptacles of new ideas, and those ideas are still of inspiration to us today.

I decided to focus on the early private cemeteries because what emerged in the surroundings of Victorian cemeteries were not planned in the way we understand urban planning or master planning today. These built environments were new and different from anything seen before, and alongside the new cemeteries they formed a new visual idiom that was unprecedented. Alongside this, I also selected them for the following reasons:

1. They were the first ones that attempted to address and resolve the issue of burial shortage;
2. They formulated a new typology of cemetery that combined funerary architecture and nature in a new way;
3. They formulated a new typology of business and new rules to use the cemeteries that influenced death culture in Victorian London;
4. They were privately owned and therefore more complex, as the companies behind them were both attempting to resolve a problem related to public health but also wanting to have some commercial returns for their investments. This created tension in the way they were perceived by the public;
5. The companies that owned them exercised their powers differently in relation to the local context and surroundings where their cemeteries were located;
6. In each individual case the arrival of the cemetery was a character-defining moment.

I used the points outlined above as the criteria to identify the three case studies cemeteries – Kensal Green, Highgate and Brookwood – that form the focus of this book, and will provide a complex and diverse set of insights. Although the research gathered here is not a comprehensive study of London's early Victorian cemeteries it offers a new insight on how each site connects with its immediate surroundings and particularly with institutions, parks, residential developments and other relevant site-specific conditions and buildings. I have preferred to approach each chosen site in its context, as each cemetery became part of a larger socio-cultural and spatial urban network.

At the time of their inception, Victorian cemeteries attracted the interest of private investors and the attention of the press and media, far more than any other contemporary equivalent to date. London's Victorian cemeteries are a constant reminder of a time when death culture held a high place in society and urban life. Their architecture, landscapes, funerary architecture and even boundary walls, were – and still are – examples of pioneering urban infrastructure, innovation in stylistic language, as well as construction and mechanical engineering. However, their impact and future consequences on their immediate surroundings over the years was not anticipated at their inception by their founders and promoters. This book studies the spatial consequences that occurred when a new cemetery was implemented in an area: a kind of "ripple effect" but at an urban scale. It will also look at Victorian cemeteries as places onto which attitudes towards death are projected – as they are not only receptacles of bodies, but also ideas. Often early Victorian cemeteries were located in out-of-town areas that were mostly rural, or with a low density of inhabitants. However, because of their distance from city transport routes, it was important to keep them directly connected to the city. As we will see later, in some instances, the new cemeteries were implemented – as in the case of Kensal Green Cemetery – along main transport routes that connected them to the city. In other instances, they complemented the existing context and built an environment, as in the case of Highgate village. The locations for the new cemeteries were chosen considering that the dead needed to be away from the city for sanitary reasons. However, the urbanisation process took hold of those areas around the cemeteries, and by the end of the nineteenth century, as the cemeteries were getting filled with new graves, so the areas around them built up with churches, housing, libraries, parks and new transport links. Eventually, the living and the dead were, once again, close to one another.

The history of London's Victorian cemeteries has indeed been widely researched already from many interesting perspectives that give depth and value to these large gardens of death. In the process of reviewing the relevant literature, however, I realised that most studies concentrated solely on the Victorian cemeteries themselves, as individual architectural objects, landscapes or institutions, rather than study them in the socio-cultural context of their local built environment. James Stevens Curl and Christopher Brooks both address in their studies the cultural value of these spaces and have voiced concerns over the deteriorating state of architectural heritage in these cemeteries. Historian Richard Etlin clarifies the use of vegetation and landscape in Victorian cemeteries, while Julie Rugg provides a comprehensive study on the reasons behind the establishment of early Victorian cemetery companies. Ruth Richardson and Elizabeth Hurren both approach the Victorian cemeteries along a specific trajectory through medical and social history. Anthony Giddens more broadly questions the invisibility of death in modernity as part of the process of individualisation in contemporary society, which is symptomatic of how it structured and commodified many aspects of human life, including death. The influence of these works is strong in this field of study, and this book intends to contribute to the existing scholarship on London's early Victorian cemeteries to widen the scope of their interpretations and understanding.

The current status of London's Victorian cemeteries is one of the themes that contemporary scholars have been addressing in recent years, particularly the poor conditions of the historical monuments and graves and the emotional and physical disconnection between society and cemeteries. Historians such as James Stevens Curl and Christopher Brooks, who researched extensively on Victorian architecture and death culture, identify the roots of this problem in the physical and psychological "distance" between society and death. It is this emotional detachment that, in their opinion, produces a lack of understanding of the intrinsic socio-cultural values of the cemetery by contemporary society. For Brooks, this has been one of the reasons for the "destruction" of the cemetery in contemporary culture by neglect. This emotional detachment has direct consequences for the conditions of historical cemeteries, as they are not fully perceived by contemporary society as part of a shared cultural heritage, as in the case of other historical sites or buildings. Paradoxically, most of London's Victorian cemeteries are now fully integrated into the urban fabric of the city, and part of densely populated areas, yet local communities are only partially aware of the conditions and destiny of these historical cemeteries.

Another reason for this emotional detachment from cemeteries is to do with the physical distance of communities from these resting places. Architecture writer Ken Worpole and Julie Rugg first addressed this issue in their report "The Cemetery in the City" (1989). The research assesses the burial needs for London and identifies that the capital's inner districts do not have a suitable stake of land-holdings dedicated to burial spaces, therefore people are often buried far away from where they lived. The origins of the problem rest primarily with the restrictions set in place by burial laws, which, in Britain, forbid the reuse of old graves for new burials. Worpole and Rugg advocate that a change in the laws that regulate the reuse of graves in existing cemeteries could alleviate this problem. Research connected with this issue has also identified that most Victorian cemeteries are now gridlocked into the urban fabric of London. This condition restricts their possibility for expansion; therefore new burial space has to be identified farther away from these existing cemeteries and urban areas. However, this will cause more emotional displacement and distance between society and cemeteries.

Worpole, in his 2003 publication titled *Last Landscapes* also identified that there is a lack of engagement of contemporary architects and planners in applying their skills to the identification of new designs for cemeteries. The author criticises the fact that architects in the modern world have created new kinds of buildings and innovative structures; however, they have not created anything original when it comes to cemeteries. At present, Victorian cemeteries such as Brookwood and Highgate, in particular, are experiencing a new surge of interest, as they are undergoing major redesign of their landscapes, wayfinding signage and upgrading of their existing service buildings. These projects will also provide new spaces where to host education programmes, events (such as talks and lectures) as well as temporary exhibitions. This is a very recent development, which may lead the way for other privately owned cemeteries to be upgraded and considered as part of the cultural strategies of urban development, like other infrastructure and services.

The history of London's Victorian cemeteries is so entangled with many aspects of the city's rich past, that I think some initial acknowledgements could help the direction of travel on this journey. It is indeed evident from the existing research on the subject that the cultural shift in the attitude towards death, initiated in Victorian times, has deeper roots in social studies. Some of the principles of Victorian society were based on capitalism, promoting aggressive individualism, class division and segregation. All of these were strongly concentrated in London at the time and influenced the re-ordering of the city's spatial arrangement, including that of its cemeteries in line with health and hygiene concerns. This book, however, as mentioned earlier, is not primarily concerned in tracing the evolution of Victorian funerary culture, the history of the landscape or indeed the history of urban planning. Instead, it is interested in identifying a trajectory across the complex power-relations established between those forces that ultimately influenced the construction of the new city, and that include: politics, economics, socio-cultural context, transport infrastructure, architecture, planning and history of medicine. I trust that by adopting this methodology of research, I will bring to light new evidence and new knowledge to expand the existing research on the subject, and clarify the contribution that Victorian cemeteries made in the shaping of modern London. Previous and simultaneous to researching Victorian cemeteries, I have also been studying the history of the urban development of London, history, transport infrastructure, socio-cultural context, medical history, economy, philosophy and politics. Therefore my interest lies in understanding the power-relations established between these areas of study. These aspects have influenced my interpretations of the history of Victorian cemeteries; however, the relations between the history of cemeteries, medical history and urban expansion have predominated.

6   *Introduction*

The sources of evidence consulted in the course of my research are numerous; they include key literature – including the ones mentioned above – in the form of books, manuscripts, pamphlets and online resources as well as maps, plans, surveys, prints, drawings, inventories and accounts from several archives and libraries. I have also drawn from contemporary journals, newspaper magazines, auction particulars and a range of manuscripts and published maps, surveys and topographical views of London and its environs. Occasionally, where documentation is lacking for metropolitan examples of certain aspects of the Victorian cemeteries, I have explored these aspects regarding other cemeteries outside central London or indeed Britain. I have likewise included a variety of illustrations, which although not precisely contemporary with the cemeteries which are discussed, can nonetheless be seen as useful and relevant because of the unchanging circumstances. I deliberately did not attempt to make this project a comprehensive study that will cover all the Victorian cemeteries, but I hope it will provide an opportunity for reflection on the changes that were taking place at the time in the capital and their relevance to urban and socio-cultural studies.

The narrative of the book unfolds over six parts. Each one of them approaches the topic of Victorian cemeteries from a different thematic angle through a timeline spanning between the 1830s and the early 1900s. In **Chapter 1** (Health), I provide an overview of the historical context of early nineteenth-century London and explain how and why the conditions of its burials at the time gained the attention of the medical profession, central government and private entrepreneurs. Furthermore, I also explain here how the unique combination of poor living conditions, high urban density, mismanagement of burials and a sensationalist press activated an unprecedented transformation of London's burial spaces, which eventually manifested itself in the form of the early Victorian cemeteries. As we will see, this complex situation instigated visionary solutions that, although impressive for their aesthetics and functions, were either too expensive or required too much time to be implemented. However, more practical and immediate solutions started to be implemented to address the urgent issues and solve the problems, at least in the short-term.

In **Chapter 2** (Identity), I present some insights into how cemetery companies organised and structured new cemeteries for their commercial purposes, establishing new administrative procedures for burials and funerals. Companies also utilised architecture and landscape design as an aesthetic vocabulary that conferred them a distinctive individual style. In this chapter I also highlight how the cemeteries were a new typology of open spaces that were privately owned but accessible to the public, and they were considered symbols of progress and civic pride in terms of public health, respectability and decency. Their presence in the outskirts of London not only contributed to put on the map areas that were otherwise less known by Londoners but also became an outpost of urban civic life.

Taking as a starting point the opening of Kensal Green Cemetery in 1833, in **Chapter 3** (Suburbs/Kensal Green) I observe how the presence of a cemetery in Kensal Green, in a virtually rural area on the edges of London, contributed to the character and development of the suburb. More specifically, this chapter looks at what happens when a new cemetery is established in a rural and agricultural area with virtually no industry or other features apart from very good transport connections to and from London as well as to the industrial heart of the country.

In **Chapter 4** (Suburbs/Highgate) I elaborate on what happens when a cemetery is established in an area that has already a distinguished identity defined by its history and topography and relationship to the city – a place where the local community has power and authority in deciding what developments will take place in the area. The cemetery there contributes to enhancing the identity of the place by preserving open spaces and green areas.

Taking as a starting point the implementation of a new cemetery in Brookwood in 1854, in **Chapter 5** (Suburbs/Brookwood), I study what happens when a cemetery is established in a rural agricultural area that has a modest industry and the cemetery company has control over the land beyond the cemetery itself. The great transport connections to and from London both by water and later by rail could have provided an opportunity for a fast development, however things were slower than expected (as market forces and the public were not ready). Nevertheless, the presence of the cemetery contributed to the growth of local industries that already existed in the area.

Finally **Chapter 6** (Rethinking) looks at how, towards the end of the nineteenth century, the perception of Victorian cemeteries started to change as they were filling up and the problem of burial shortage reappeared. The shift in perception of earth burial at the turn of the century connected with the necessity to retain open spaces. It will also look at how, as a response to the need to preserve open spaces, alternatives to earth burials started to be considered. Lastly it will touch on how new visions of the future, although apparently cohesive and holistic in their approach, refrained from addressing the disposal of the dead.

Indeed cemeteries must have had, to some extent, an active role in shaping the character of London and its unique identity. But what type of relationship did Victorian cemeteries have with their immediate surroundings? What came to exist in their proximity and why? Were they the bearers of new socio-cultural opportunities? Were they convenient for the development of trades connected with the cemeteries themselves? How were they perceived by the local communities? Can we say that they inform the "genius loci" of their locality when considered within the broader context of the area where they exist? Were they always valued, as we do now, as green open spaces? These are some of the questions this book is addressing with the ambition of providing a fresh new perspective on Victorian cemeteries as activators of urban change, whose effects radiated beyond their boundaries.

There is no doubt that London's early Victorian cemeteries were experiments that reframed not only death culture but also redefined the relationship between the city's urban centre and its rural surroundings. They pioneered new architecture aesthetics, landscapes and administrative structures that effectively systematised the burial processes and its connected rituals. The aims and ambitions of their creators were clear: modernise burial processes and rituals by making them safer and dignified for the urban context and society. The coming of the cemeteries was welcomed as a sign of civilised progress and decorum in terms of sanitary and public health that reflected Victorian social values. The cemeteries also embodied forward-thinking, in terms of social reforms, technical and scientific innovation that – combined with access to natural resources and capitals – literally transformed London into a powerhouse of change.

1 Health

1.1 Metropolitan sepulchre

In 1824 architect Thomas Willson devised the design for a metropolitan sepulchre in the shape of a 94-storey-high pyramid that would have provided space for five million Londoners, where: "they may repose in perfect security, without interfering with the comfort, the health, the business, the property, or the pursuits of the living" ("The Pyramid Cemetery" 1834, 389–90). The ambitious challenges of achieving large-scale constructions and engineering projects are indeed part of human history, however, in the nineteenth century, it reached new peaks. The introduction of mechanisation, combined with access to prime resources and minerals, allowed engineers and architects to explore construction ideas and concepts at an unprecedented scale. Willson's landmark pyramid was to be located away from London's congested urban centre in a prominent elevated position on Primrose Hill, overlooking north London. Covering an area equivalent to the size of Russell Square, this intriguing monolith was intended to provide the equivalent of 1,000 acres of burials, by occupying a relatively small footprint of 18 acres. The rigorous yet repetitive inner structure was made up of an extensive number of equal vaults aligned and stacked towards the tapering top of the pyramid. Designed to attract investors, Willson's pyramid had an estimated cost at the time of £7 million (Loudon 1829, 214). The Pyramid General Cemetery Company was in charge of the initiative and intended to charge £50 per vault to parishes or directly to individuals (Arnold 2006, 86–7). Willson detailed his ideas in all their technicalities to make the building function. He envisaged external stairs along each side of the pyramid, hydraulic-powered lifts and ventilation systems to deal with decomposing content in his building. Willson's pyramid was higher than St. Paul's dome, featured an astronomical observatory at its apex and was toppled by a granite obelisk (389–90). Willson's megastructure was to be built in bricks and clad in granite. The visionary architect visualised his scheme in a set of evocative architectural drawings that included elevations and sections of his pyramid (see Figure 1.1).

DOI: 10.4324/9781003178934-2

Figure 1.1 The metropolitan sepulchre designed by Thomas Willson. Section Drawing. 1829. © London Metropolitan Archives (City of London).

In 1829, discussing Willson's scheme in one of his articles, the horticulturist, journalist and writer John Claudius Loudon hinted at how complex the possibility to find the ideal solution to the question of London's dead was:

> For London, we would establish two or three burial-grounds, of some hundreds of acres each, a few miles in the country, on the poorest soil, and planted as an arboretum, according to the natural system. But even this we do not think adequate to the wants of an increasing population.
>
> (214)

Willson's vertical cemetery didn't manage to attract the attention of investors, firstly because its cost was very high and secondly the construction and completion could have taken at least 20 years (Curl 2001, 36). London needed a more realistic solution that could be implemented in a shorter time frame ("The Pyramid Cemetery" 1834, 389–90). Loudon, commenting, at the time, on Willson's scheme, reiterated the urgency to act on the question of burial provision. He stated that "no public improvement is more wanted than the removal, in Britain, of burial places from the cities to the country" (Loudon 1829, 214). This was not new though, as Christopher Wren first advanced that solution – after the 1666 Great Fire of London – placing London's dead beyond the urban boundaries. Wren's plan, as we know, was not implemented, and the question over the future of London's burial spaces was left, for the time being, unanswered (as quoted by Bibby in the Historic UK website on 19 January 2020).

Future burial spaces, however, were not only to be of impressive monumental scale, in the city's landscape, but they also needed to be well connected to the rest of the city and via transport networks. Willson was not alone in scoping for possible design solutions for the ultimate burial of the future. In France, too equally visionary architects started to draw together solutions that addressed the future provision of burials for Paris. Some ideas were presented already at the Grand Prix of 1799 where a variety of monumental forms were explored at large scale, just like Willson's one. A design proposal by French architect Jacques Molinos also devised a pyramid-shaped building as the landmark feature to the "Field of Rest" cemetery to be built on Montmartre in Paris. Molinos' pyramid was less grand in scale (only 23 metres high) and contained the cemetery chapel and crematorium (Etlin 1984, 280). As part of the scheme Molinos also designed four mortuary stations for the gathering of the corpses before being transported to the actual cemetery (1984, 273–80). The sanitary issues of how to remove the bodies from private homes were key to his proposal. The core centres of cities such as London or indeed Paris were too overcrowded and needed to be relieved in ways that would allow people to live, work, be connected and carry on with their lives. These schemes provided a substantial and

12 Health

Figure 1.2 Design for a "Champs de Repos" in Paris: section through the central pyramid by Jacques Molinos. 1799. © RIBA.

unprecedented rethinking of burial solutions but also investigated how they could be bridging the existing urban fabric of the city to the countryside (see Figure 1.2).

Although Willson's proposal was criticised at the time, for its imposing scale and for not being technically well resolved, it made the public realise how urgent and complex the question of burial provisions was for an ever-expanding metropolis. Most importantly, Willson's scheme underlined the urgent need for a realistic solution to be implemented to resolve the issue. Beyond attracting investors, Willson's design for a metropolitan sepulchre attracted the attention of the sensationalist press and public imagination. Indeed the scale of Willson's scheme addressed, in such a bold way, the issue of London's burial provision ahead of its future expansion. Its form and function must have stimulated people's imagination about the fantastical visions of London's future metropolitan life to come. Considering that at the time earth burial was the most common practice to dispose of human remains in England, Willson's earthless vertical cemetery was unprecedented. His imaginative scheme still retains its intrigue today. In 2019 Willson's drawings were one of the main attractions at the exhibition "The London That Never Was" hosted by the London Metropolitan Archives (LMA). Commenting on the nature of the imaginative visions of a London of the future that never materialised, lead curator and LMA assistant librarian Jeremy Smith, explained that: "Lots of designs were done as fantasy pieces and were never expected to be built" (Buxton 2019). In one of Willson's existing visualisations of the pyramid, the structure is depicted in isolation with no living presence or indeed a funeral cortege in sight or indeed views of London in the distance. Despite this, Willson's pyramid proposal is still to this day an audacious idea that states the design ambition and pioneering thinking of the architect, and it is a project that, through scale and form, instantly visualises the complex spatial relationship between the city and its dead.

1.2 Overcrowding

The reasons that brought London's burials to a critical tipping point in the early nineteenth century are many, it is impossible to single out just one as responsible for the dramatic change. Indeed, events such as the Industrial Revolution in England as well as the political changes taking place across mainland Europe brought a radical change in the way the urban space of cities was questioned, understood and indeed designed (Vidler 2011, 16–7). Schemes such as Willson's pyramid were one way to frame the issue of burial by drawing public attention to it and address the scale and urgency of the matter due to the fast-growing population of London. In the late eighteenth century, the exodus from the countryside to the city transformed the British economy from mostly agricultural to industrial. In London alone, between 1800 and 1900, the population of London grew from just under one million to 4.5 million ("Report of the Medical Officer of Health for London County Council" 1900, 1). The change was so vast that it had dramatic and unprecedented repercussions on the capital's urban environment. What may have just worked well up to the late eighteenth century such as roads or housing stock quickly became inadequate and obsolete. Fresh new solutions were needed to cope with the fast-growing numbers of urban dwellers.

The socio-cultural context of nineteenth-century London was driven mostly by the rational laws of trade and commerce and set the ground for scientific and medical research and technological innovation. This approach to change and progress was also endorsed by philosopher and social reformer Jeremy Bentham, who formulated the "greatest happiness principle". Bentham's theory, outlined in his *An Introduction to the Principles of Morals and Legislation*, published in 1789, advocates the greatest happiness for the greatest numbers. Bentham viewed medical and scientific research as the application of his philosophical theory into a reality that, in his opinion, would benefit society. It was for this reason that he decided to donate his body to science. Although Bentham is recognised as the leader of the so-called Philosophical Radicals and, in particular, Utilitarianism, his research interests also incorporated the theory of law, ethics and politics. For Bentham, each human being naturally attempts to pursue (what they perceive to be) happiness in life and is not able to grasp the implications of their individual choices on a large scale. Bentham believed that the legislator had the duty to intervene and harmonise this process and reach a balance between the private and the public interests (Russell 2008, 698–700).

This principle had a strong impact on shaping the politics and legislative reformation in early nineteenth-century Britain. However, the unprecedented conditions were far more complex and unpredictable than Bentham's theoretical framework. Effectively there was no cohesive plan that could deal with the consequences generated by the unprecedented fast-growing numbers of urban dwellers. Some of the basic functions of London, such as getting produce to markets and outlets were just as complex as getting access to clean drinking water, or decent shelter or indeed providing suitable burial space to Londoners. In his book *Cities*, author and photojournalist John Reader looked back at the history of cities and the ecology of urban environments. Talking about nineteenth-century London, Reader explains that:

> Keeping the city fed was a huge undertaking – but not one that was centrally controlled, or pre-planned, or growing at a predictable rate. It was growing organically, powered by the economic dynamics of the city itself, regulated by the mechanism of supply and demand, driven by the entrepreneurial instincts of businessmen with an eye on the profit margin.
>
> (2005, 128)

The priorities of the market forces at the time prevailed over those of the otherwise fragmented social fabric of London, overruling even ethical issues such as the disturbance of burial grounds in the name of progress. In his book *Endangered Lives: Public Health in Victorian Britain*, historian Anthony Wohl offers another explanation for this issue as in his view "the early and mid-Victorians were, quite simply, pioneers faced with a set of problems that were novel not only in their form but in their magnitude" (1984, 3).

The unprecedented population growth put a major strain on the city's graveyards and other infrastructures at large (roads, sewage, housing). Indeed, there was no contingency plan either that addressed the provision of housing or burials, therefore solutions emerged, as suggested by Wohl, as and when needed, without a long-term plan but as a quick response to an emerging issue that could also provide a financial return to investors. London, in this respect, was a case of its own, as, unlike other British industrial cities and regions whose economies depended on specific trades or raw materials, London's diverse economy facilitated an endless source of varied job opportunities, from casual work to banking. Although London's service economy largely exploited casual, cheap and part-time labour, the commercial success generated by trade with the imperial colonies created middle-class jobs in shipping, banking, investments and insurance. The affluence of the burgeoning middle classes in turn required workers in construction and transportation, as well as in the crafts and artisanal trades, such as tailoring and dressmaking, in addition to retail (Porter 2000, 187). Unlike the trade patterns in other cities, London counted among these many small businesses that offered a variety of services. For this reason, these trades were vulnerable to seasonal and cyclical changes. Owing to London's fragmented service economy and the high turnover of labourers, the influence of the trade unions was particularly weak in the capital.

The lack of cohesion apparent in the labour market was also mirrored in the geography of the city, as London didn't have a clear centre (Dyos 1982, 40–3). Instead, the city was formed by autonomous districts, which were regulated by local administrations and legislations. The tangled bureaucracy of these local authorities, combined with the absence of a central government to oversee and coordinate the overall expansion of the city, eventually allowed London to grow into a gigantic sprawl (Porter 2000, 186). Although London's scale and the complexity of its local administration made it a difficult place to navigate, its social geography was very clear as the volume of casual labour created high levels of class mobility and fractured the sense of community (Dyos 1982, 40–3).

However, the effects of high density were connected with poor sanitary conditions (homes, factories, public spaces). The existing inner-city graveyards were not able to cope with the high death rate of the city, and soon became inadequate and a risk to the public health or people living in their proximity. The conditions of London's graveyards at the time were recorded by George Alfred Walker in his 1839 book *Gatherings from Grave-Yards; Particularly Those of London*. Here, the London-based surgeon assembles a thorough investigation and reports on the conditions of the capital's graveyards. Walker lived in Drury Lane (between Covent Garden and Holborn), a street where there was a graveyard too. It was thanks to his tenacious research that the grim evidence of London's churchyards was placed under public scrutiny. His publication not only established a direct connection between the poor conditions of the city's burials and the public health of citizens, but also addressed the lack of sensitivity, decency and solemnity on questions concerning the disposal of the dead in Victorian London.

Walker also revealed that the practice of exhumation, which for a long time (before the introduction of the Anatomy Act 1832) had been associated with the illegal trade of corpses for anatomical studies, eventually diverted to a more established form of business. In one instance, Walker includes extracts from an article published in the *Morning Post* on Monday 14 October 1839 reporting about the conditions of the burial grounds behind Globe Fields Chapel near Globe Lane in Mile End, owned by an undertaker. The article reveals that bodies buried in the most prominent and popular part of the graveyard were exhumed and relocated to a more secluded site after an estimated four to six weeks. This practice was carried out regularly to free-up the more desirable burial plots for new funerals and possibly charge customers more for interments in that particular area of the graveyard. As the corpses in an advanced state of decomposition were exhumed, their coffins were dismantled and the wood and nails sold. According to Walker, human bones were also traded (1839, 199–200). Quoting from another article extracted from *Quarterly Review* (no. XLII, 380), Walker reports that "tons of human bones every year are sent from London to the North, where they were crushed in mills constructed for the purpose and used as manure" (218). In another instance, Walker describes the shocking situation of a graveyard near where he lived, in Drury Lane (see Figure 1.3). Here, the topography was affected by the piling up of corpses and coffins: "The ground was subsequently raised to its present height level with the first floor, and in this superstratum vast numbers of bodies have, up to this period, been deposited" (162).

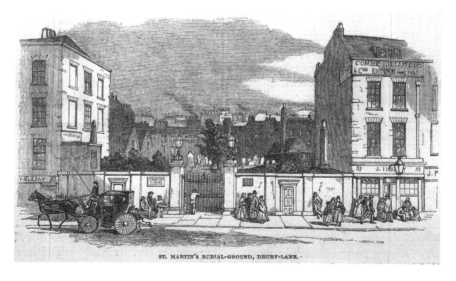

Figure 1.3 Illustration of St. Martin's Burial Ground in Drury Lane, London from the article "Intra and Extramural Interments" published in *The Illustrated London News*. 15 September 1849. Author's Collection.

In pointing out the hazards to public health that the churchyards represented, Walker was driven by two factors – firstly, by his professional commitments as a doctor, in wanting to improve people's health and living conditions; secondly, he was moved by his philosophical convictions as a follower of Bentham's Utilitarian thinking, which, as we previously saw, asserted the greatest good for the greatest number of individuals. The year Walker's *Gatherings* was published, however, Highgate Cemetery was opened for burial and became London's third new cemetery after All Souls Kensal Green Cemetery, which opened for burial in 1833, and by West Norwood Cemetery in south-east London in 1837. Despite these new private cemeteries gradually emerging on the scene, for Walker nothing had particularly changed in the inner part of the metropolis. Although not explicitly stated in his text, Walker wasn't keen on the new cemeteries springing up in the suburbs of London. Their burial plots were intended to attract the wealthy and aspiring Victorian middle classes, but out of reach for London's working classes and the poor.

The picture of London that emerges from Walker's book is that of a city where graves are filling every urban interstice available – a city that is very close to the descriptions found in Charles novel *Bleak House* (1853), where the author describes a churchyard as "pestiferous and obscene, whence malignant diseases are communicated to the bodies of our dear brothers and sisters who are not departed" (130). To reinforce his point, Walker includes comparative studies on the condition of cemeteries in Paris, and in France generally, that illustrate how far behind London was in comparison to other European capitals. In the years following the publication of his book, Walker's reputation grew as he carried on disseminating his findings by writing reports in newspapers denouncing the poor state of London's graveyards. He also gave talks on the subject across the country. *The Leicester Chronicle* on Saturday 21 August 1847 published a review on one lecture (the fourth of a series on the subject) Walker had delivered earlier that month on how hazardous intramural burials were to the health of the public. On that occasion the author warned parents in the audience that "however injurious a deteriorated atmosphere might be to a full grown up adult, it was infinitely more so to children, who perished weekly by the thousands" (4). Walker's work was still mentioned in magazines in the early 1850s. An article appeared in *The Lady's Newspaper* on Saturday 19 March 1853 which praised Walker for being a "benefactor to his country" for succeeding in bringing to the attention of the Parliament and the public "a mass of evidence of the most varied and alarming description" (184).

Prior to Walker, the inadequate maintenance of the graveyards was a reality so embedded in the everyday that no one attempted to address and resolve, but instead tried to ignore it. London's medical community, of which Walker was part, saw the conditions of the graveyards as morally disrespectful to the dead as they were to the living. The growing trade of corpses used for medical training purposes also contributed to the further deterioration of London's graveyards. Before 1832, anatomy in Britain was not legally regulated, therefore the supply of corpses available for anatomical study was unreliable (Southwood Smith 1827, 34). Most corpses available to medical schools or private anatomy theatres for dissection came from the courts, the bodies of those condemned to death and dissection. The shortfall was provided by body snatchers or "resurrection-men", who often dug up freshly buried corpses, exacerbating the precarious state of London's overcrowded graveyards. Eventually the legalisation of anatomy was only partly supported by anatomists, as they feared restrictions on their activities by government-implemented laws (Bates 2010, 90).

One anatomist who campaigned for legislation to regulate the provision of bodies to medical schools was Thomas Southwood Smith, Bentham's private doctor and a follower of the philosopher's school of thought. Coincidentally, it was Southwood Smith who, on 9 June 1832, publicly carried out the dissection of Bentham's corpse, just weeks before the Anatomy Act came into force on 19 July 1832 (Ashworth Underwood 1948, 891). Southwood Smith was also an active member of the health reform movement and set up the Health of Towns Association in 1839, and the Metropolitan Association for Improving the Dwelling of the Industrial Classes in 1842. He was the medical member of the General Board of Health when it was constituted in 1848 and remained in office until its dissolution in 1858. Southwood Smith worked closely with social reformer Edwin Chadwick and influenced the legislation that regulated London's burials. It was in this complex socio-cultural context that new and provocative ideas, such as Willson's proposal, started to visualise what was possible to do beyond London's existing urban fabric and colonise the countryside to expand the metropolis. Although there is limited historical material to understand more broadly the extent of Willson's vision, it is undeniable that his idea was both an opportunity to manifest a new kind of urban form that was informed by industrial and scientific knowledge. Projects like this one acted as a communication tool to rulers, developers and urban dwellers alike, to visualise possible futures (Vidler 2011, 17). They also addressed the tension between the need to find new fresh ideas yet practical solutions and the ambition to create something completely new in terms of aesthetics and functions. The untapped potential represented by the countryside was like a blank canvas on which to draw new spatial solutions that could decompress London's congested urban centre. The space available in the countryside around London, was available to test new burial typologies but how to proceed? Where to locate the new burials, as they had such a negative connotation at the time (overcrowding, unhealthy, unsafe)? They also needed to be accessible and connected to the city. How should they look? Who should build them? Who should manage them? Would their implementation ultimately resolve the issue of burial for once?

1.3 Ordering the dead

As we have seen earlier, the city was under constant pressure due to growing population numbers and consequently high density. As its growth was taking place organically, its expansion beyond the urban boundaries was patchy and dictated by a range of factors that were not only controlled at the government level but also by economic forces and private interests. By taking as a starting point the 1833 plan of London by John Shury, I will draw some observations on the conditions and characteristics of the urban and rural context around the fringes of the capital at the time. Shury's "Plan of London from Actual Survey" (see Figure 1.4) was published as a free supplement to the *United Kingdom* newspaper.

Observing the map clockwise, starting from the west, one can notice how the edges of London feature two distinctive typologies of the outline between urban and rural. Along the west and north-west borders, it looks like the northern boundaries of Kensington Gardens, Hyde Park and Regent Park are demarcating the urban border of the actual city, as little development is recorded beyond the parks by Shury. By contrast along the north-east and East End towards the Thames estuary, the boundaries of the capital were more fragmented and sprawling. However, in the south-east

Figure 1.4 Plan of London from Actual Survey 1833 – by John Shury. Crace Collection of Maps of London Port. 7.233 UIN: BLL01016128605. © The British Library.

part, the urban sprawl was less dense towards Rotherhithe and Greenwich. The urban development south of the river follows the sinuous contours of the river and stretches along it forming Southwark and Lambeth, as far as Vauxhall Bridge. When looking at Shury's map, it is possible to notice how different the character of London's urban fabric was. At first glance, one can spot how regimented (almost grid-like) West London is when compared to the East End and south parts of London. Here, the network of roads appears to be more organic, featuring narrow roads and a denser urban fabric. This tells us how diverse and not uniform the nature of urban development and growth in different parts of the capital was. According to Porter, Victorian London was "a scattered city" in terms of urban development, and unlike Paris or other large cities in continental Europe the metropolis "was not a coherent development, dictated by government, given form by a rational road grid". Porter commented on this by saying that London instead was likened to a "natural phenomenon" that was "evolving spontaneously". However, the "material transformations that were taking place in the city at the time" (2000, 252) forced high mobility and were responsible for the displacement and relocation of Londoners. He also said that in Victorian London: "Nothing ever stood still, nothing was constant except mobility itself, as Romantics rediscovered the country and sanitarians stressed the hazards of intercity miasmata" (252–3).

Indeed, a combination of factors such as high population density, poor living conditions, poverty and pollution was a threat to public health. For example, the inadequate network of narrow roads, particularly in the East End, not only posed the problems of accessibility and safety but precluded the circulation of fresh air. These, along with the lack of appropriate sewage systems, access to clean water and air pollution, were also closely connected with health concerns and high death rates in urban centres. These problems were not quickly resolved and afflicted London's poorer classes throughout the nineteenth century and beyond. A glimpse into these issues was given by Henry Mayhew in his book *London Labour & the London Poor*. Although the book was published in 1861 it gives us a sense of how the conditions in the poor parts of London were still unresolved beyond the mid-nineteenth century.

Mayhew, in one extract from an article published on the *Morning Chronicle* 24 September 1849 on the cholera outbreaks in London, describes the very narrow roads of Bermondsey; in one passage he says

> Continuing our course we reached "The Folly", another street so narrow that the names of the trades of the shopmen were painted on boards that stretched across the street, from the roof of their own house to that of their neighbour's.
>
> (2010, 434)

In another passage of the same article, Mayhew describes the peculiar dwelling arrangement in an area of Bermondsey named Jacob's Island, where some of the rooms of some houses are cantilevered out over the water. He explains: "across some parts of the stream whole rooms have been built so that house adjoins house". Mayhew carried on saying that

> on approaching the tidal ditch from the Neckinger-road, the shutters of the house at the corner were shut from top to bottom. Our intelligent and obliging guide, Dr. Martin, informed us that a girl was then lying dead there from cholera, and that but very recently another victim had fallen in the house adjoining it.
>
> (432–3)

Back in 1843, before Mayhew documented the hard reality of Londoners living in the East End, social reformer Edwin Chadwick commissioned a "Report on the Sanitary Condition of the Labouring Population of Great Britain – A Supplementary Report on the Results of a Special Inquiry into the Practice of Interments in Towns". As most of the working-class population lived on very low salaries, their dwellings were unhealthy, unhygienic and unsuitable for living. He believed that by improving the living conditions people would live longer. Looking at the statistics used by Chadwick in his report, the average lifespan of a working-class East-Ender in 1839 was 27 years. Indeed, Chadwick admitted that overcrowded graveyards affected Londoners' health by polluting water sources. Chadwick connected the problems of London's churchyards to the poor living conditions of the working classes in the East End, as it was the primary reason for the high death rate in that part of the capital. Ultimately for Chadwick, graveyards in the city were too public and too noisy, and he felt that burials needed to be in more private, secluded spaces, away from the tumultuous everyday life. In his view new cemeteries were the answer, providing seclusion, solemnity and respect (Hamlin 1998, 153). To support his point, Chadwick gathered material to prove that people were not happy with churchyard burials:

> The feeling of a large proportion of the population appears to be dissatisfaction with the intra-mural parochial interments, less on sanitary grounds than from an aversion to the profanation arising from interments amidst the scenes of the crowd and bustle of the every-day life.
>
> (84)

Undeniably the East End areas that Chadwick and Mayhew wrote about were the ones that desperately needed not only new provisions of burials but of other sanitary measures including new sewage and clean water supplies. The need and ambition of upgrading the capital into a more modern metropolis were challenged by the constraints of its pre-existing urban fabric that, like many other UK cities, was not able to cope with large population numbers. The consequences of overcrowding, particularly in the East End of London, were unhealthy conditions, as many individuals lived in the squalor of insalubrious homes and work environments (Porter 2000, 136). Up to the Industrial Revolution, the urban core of UK cities was still based on the Roman or otherwise medieval organic unplanned formation of the urban fabric. London historically resisted any form of cohesive planning, even when after the 1666 Great Fire of London, Wren was in line to implement his urban vision of the capital. Instead, London was rebuilt following mostly the contours of the pre-fire boundaries, so instead of implementing larger interconnecting roads and new buildings the reconstructed London resembled what it was before being defaced by the flames. This resulted in an incredible variety of building solutions and architectural styles and indeed experimentations that gave London its unique aesthetic character and quirkiness in terms of city views.

However, not upgrading to a more coherent road system as the one envisaged by Wren precluded London from improving and making movement of people and goods through the city more efficient. These new roads could have also been used to quickly remove waste to prevent the development of hotbeds that could harbour diseases and which represented health risks for the masses. Historian Harold James Dyos touches on the poor situation of the Victorian streets of London and in one passage he explains that:

> The truth of the matter is that the streets of London remained in 1854 roughly in the same condition they had been twenty or thirty years before. A more sobering truth is that the road system of London as a whole scarcely changes except at three of four crucial spots, over an ensuing period twice as long.
>
> (1982, 197)

Dyos also mentions the fact that despite the abolition of road tolls, all the gates and bars (needed to regulate the tolls) were indeed obstructing London's roads, and, in some ways, slowing down the urban traffic (196–7).

Connectivity and accessibility to the metropolis were key for commerce and trade. It was within this context that private initiatives, financial efforts and ideas flourished and shaped the making of nineteenth-century London. We can say that the sudden growth of London's population, combined with the presence of a high volume of casual workers, capital investors and inventive flare provided a unique opportunity to rethink how the urban space of the capital should be thought through in new and more efficient ways, including burial provision. Competitiveness was the driver to innovation and galvanised the modernisation of the capital where private entrepreneurs and investors were racing one another. Therefore most of the innovative ideas pioneered solutions that allowed the fastest movement of large quantities of goods – as well as people – by road, water and later by rail. The scale was key to the redesign of a new London, everything was impressively bigger, higher, deeper and indeed technically ambitious. This also applied to roads, buildings as well as bridges, floating vessels, ducts, sewages and indeed cemeteries.

The development of faster transport connections in and out of the city would have also provided the opportunity to decompress the congested urban core of London and move some services out of the city beyond the urban built environment of the capital. As we will see more in detail, the new London cemeteries at the time were among the first institutions to relocate to the outskirts of London, in areas that were already connected by road (or even by water, as in the case of Kensal Green Cemetery) to the city itself. Hospitals too were getting relocated to more rural settings. The combination of fresh air open spaces and the need to arrange hospitals in newly designed layouts to reduce the possibility of diseases spreading through the buildings, made the outskirts of London, particularly those locations higher up and with views and green areas nearby (as well as fresh air), suitable for hospitals and asylums, as they had a positive impact on the recovery of patients. In 1848 the Metropolitan Asylums Board opened the Highgate Smallpox and Vaccination Hospital to replace a smallpox hospital in St. Pancras, which had to be demolished as the Great Northern Railway needed the site for Kings Cross station. The Hospital – one of the two isolation hospitals in London at that time (the other was the London Fever Hospital in Liverpool Road) was intended to care for smallpox patients during the epidemic at that time. By 1867 it had 108 beds (as quoted in the Lost Hospitals of London website on 10 May 2021).

Although moving to the edge of the city was an opportunity to create new and safer burial spaces, as well as to build new and healthier hospitals, it was a different situation for London's industry. We have seen earlier how uniquely fragmented the nature of the London industry was but also how specialised it was in terms of craftsmanship and tailored to London's market and clientele. Historian Gareth Stedman Jones in his book *Outcast London: A Study in the Relationship between Classes in Victorian Society* (originally published in 1971) talking about the effects of the Industrial Revolution on London's industry explains that the rapid development of nineteenth-century London turned the metropolis into the centre of the world market and "at the heart of the transport and distribution network" (20). However, these conditions put pressure on the scarce availability of urban land and, as a consequence, pushed the rent in the central areas of London (20). With the improvement of the transport connections (new commercial waterway connections and later railways), some of the London-based industries that experienced the challenges caused by the rising rental costs of the Victorian metropolis moved to the provinces or elsewhere in the country. This was the case for the coffin furniture industry from London to Birmingham, in the early nineteenth century (Litten, 1991, 109). This however was not only due to availability of better suited and cheaper rent but also because Birmingham and London were better connected by commercial waterways networks such as the Grand Union Canal, as we will see later in Chapter 3. The implementation of new transport networks, as well as relocation of cemeteries and later (following the implementation of the County Asylums Act in 1845), hospitals and asylums, started an irreversible process of suburbanisation around the outskirts of London (see Figure 1.5).

The implementation of the new private cemeteries, in particular, brought mixed reactions. The positives were that the new cemeteries were seen as healthy, safe and solemn spaces, compared to the unhealthy and gloomy old churchyards. Indeed a more strategic approach to integrating burials – in the broader context of planning new areas of London – could have at least been experimented with in practice. Still, London, as we saw, was resilient to centralised urban planning strategies, and its growth was more organic and instead driven by private commercial interests. Along with the implementation of the first privately owned suburban cemeteries, some theoretical visions of urban futures that also integrated pioneering burial solutions started to be elaborated, published and discussed. At the time, however, there were concerns about the new private cemeteries. Chadwick, for example, felt that although overall the new cemeteries were an impressive improvement to London, the cemetery directors lacked management skills. He observed incompetence with regard to the choice of the sites, the

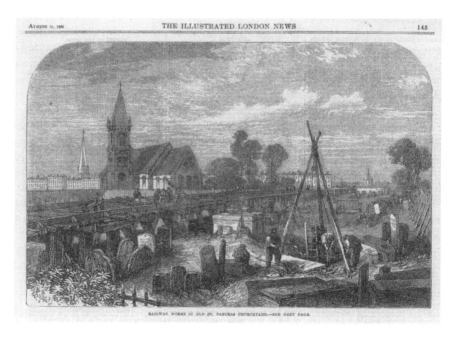

Figure 1.5 Railway work done near St. Pancras Old Churchyard. Illustration published in The *Illustrated London News*. 11 August 1866. Source: Author's Collection.

drainage system in place, preparation of the soil and mode of burial. The lack of managerial skills also extended to trees and shrubs that adorned the new cemeteries. In some cases, Chadwick observed that they did not thrive well and needed replacing, yet the cemetery directors were reluctant to invest money in the plantations which were part of the cemeteries, to cut maintenance costs (1842, 139).

Loudon's approach was not strictly concerned with the health issues addressed by Southwood Smith, Walker and Chadwick. Instead, he was interested primarily in the decorous order of cemeteries. This approach was outlined in his book *On the Laying Out of Cemeteries*, published in 1843. This practical manual on the ordering and maintenance of the cemetery is a comprehensive and unique text in which Loudon outlines his approach to cemetery design including such minutiae as how to organise and run a cemetery: from suitable planting to its everyday maintenance. Loudon's research on cemeteries expanded well beyond Britain, in his book he included research gathered from travel literature that specifically described and illustrated cemeteries in Turkey, Persia and China. Loudon noticed that in Eastern burial cultures, cemeteries were more integrated into the social life of cities. Particularly in Turkey, Loudon explains, burial grounds such as the one in Pera (now a district of Istanbul), were used by the locals as a promenade especially in the evening (70).

Loudon's extensive theoretical work on the laying out of cemeteries, their management and characteristics, had marginal influence in practical applications. The private entrepreneurs were already working to establish cemeteries that provided substantial financial returns, and undermined Loudon's moral sentiments and ideas. Loudon, however, used his book to air his personal opinions on cemeteries, without reserve; the author expressed his dissatisfaction with the quality of London's cemeteries in terms of planning and layout. In the chapter entitled "London Cemeteries and Gardens – The Present State of the London Cemeteries Considered Chiefly as Cemetery Gardens", the author writes:

> The planting of all the cemeteries is, in our opinion, highly objectionable ... It is too much in the style of a common pleasure-ground both regarding the disposition of the trees and shrubs, and the kinds planted ... the plantation in most of London's cemeteries appear to have been made without the guidance of any leading principle.
>
> (69)

His concerns about London's cemeteries went further:

> It will not be denied, we think, that in all London cemeteries there is an appearance of confusion in the placing of the graves and monuments;

there is no obvious principle of order or arrangement [...]. In our opinion, all the cemeteries require reformation in this particular area without delay.

(68)

There was no time for reformation, as things were well underway to get implemented. It was simply a matter of urgency and very short time to find quick solutions to large-scale problems. Things needed to be designed and built fast. That resulted often in poor quality materials this was not only to do with making things cheap but it was also to do with the fact that they needed to be produced fast and built fast. There was indeed a space to imagine the possible futures but there was also a challenging reality that required fast solutions to urban problems and simply there was no time to waste or to wait for theories to manifest in the long term; it needed to happen immediately.

Although centralised and structured plans were not suited to London, this did not deter thinkers from putting forward imaginary visions for the capital that included an integrated vision about burial to the new urban space of the city and not seen in isolation, as in the case of Willson with his pyramid cemetery proposal. Loudon too, besides writing on existing cemeteries, gardening and architecture, also explored possibilities and solutions to be adopted in future cemeteries and cities. In a short essay titled, "Hints for Breathing Places for the Metropolis and Country Towns and Villages, on Fixed Principles" (1829), Loudon imagined a long-term plan for a future London. His idea of urban space was attempting to integrate both urban and rural aspects and functions. Loudon foresaw a series of concentric circles that radiated outward from the centre of the city, alternating areas of green and built-up environment. In his plan, cemeteries were to be part of the green belt areas, where he also envisaged having slaughterhouses, museums and markets. However, Loudon's proposal for London was going to take over two centuries for its completion (1981, 86–90).

He did not give details of what architecture style to adopt, but it was more of a master plan idea, a system. Somehow, the poor and unhealthy conditions of graveyards in large cities such as London not only led to the establishment of new and healthier cemeteries, but also triggered a chain reaction about possible ideas for the future of the urban space in the city.

To conclude, we can say that the necessity to find a solution for the future of burial was a driving force behind the establishment of the new suburban cemeteries, but with that impetus also came a series of other ideas and proposals that not only stimulated people's imagination but also brought attention to urban issues and combined new technologies, ingenuity, creativity and commercial spirit to activate change and urban renewal. In the next chapter we will see more in detail how the private cemetery companies formulated a practical response to theoretical visions (such as Willson's pyramid) and took a gamble in fixing the problem of London's burials, and in the process formulated a new paradigm for death and disposal.

Bibliography

Arnold, Catharine. 2006. *Necropolis: London and Its Dead*. London: Simon & Schuster.

Ashworth Underwood, Edgar. 1948. "The Centenary of British Public Health: Rise of Health Legislation in England and in London." *The British Medical Journal* 1, no. 4557: 890–92. May 8. Accessed August 24, 2020. http://www.jstor.com/stable/25363490

Bates, Alan W. 2010. *The Anatomy of Robert Knox: Murder, Mad Science and Medical Regulation in Nineteenth-Century Edinburgh*. Brighton: Sussex Academic Press.

Bibby, Miriam. "Thomas Wilson's Mortuary Pyramid" – online article appeared on Historic UK. (n.d.). Accessed January 19, 2020. https://www.historic-uk.com/CultureUK/Thomas-Willsons-Pyramid-Mortuary/

Brandon, David, and Alan Brooke. 2008. *London: City of the Dead*. Strout: The History Press Ltd. Accessed May 24, 2021. https://archive.org/details/londoncityofdead0000bran/page/n267/mode/2up

Briggs, Asa. 1968. *Victorian Cities*. Harmondsworth: Penguin Books.

Brooks, Chris W. 1989. *Mortal Remains*. Exeter: Wheaton Publishers Ltd.

Broun, Richard B. 1851. *Extramural Sepulture – Synopsis of the London Necropolis Company and National Mausoleum at Woking in the County of Surrey*. London: Trelawney Saunders.

"Burial in Towns." 1847. *The Leicester Chronicle: or Commercial and Agricultural Advertiser* 37, no. 1916. Saturday August 21.

Buxton, Pamela. 2019. "Unrealised Designs Show a Strange London That Might Have Been." *RIBA Journal*, October 18. Accessed January 19, 2020. https://www.ribaj.com/culture/the-london-that-never-was-unbuilt-bridges-buildings

Chadwick, Edwin. 1843. "Report on the Sanitary Condition of the Labouring Population of Great Britain. A Supplementary Report on the Results of a Special Inquiry into the Practice of Interment in Towns." London: Clowes and Sons.

Collison, George. 1840. *Cemetery Interment: Containing a Concise History of the Modes of Interment Practices by the Ancients*. London: J.Masters. Accessed July 10, 2020. https://books.google.co.uk/books?id=ut4wAQAAMAAJ&printsec=frontcover&source=gbs_ge_summary_r&cad=0#v=onepage&q&f=false

Curl, James Stevens. 2004. *The Victorian Celebration of Death*. Thrupp: Sutton Publishing.

Curl, James Stevens. 2001. *Kensal Green Cemetery. The Origins and Development of the General Cemetery of All Souls, Kensal Green, London, 1824–2001*. Chichester: Phillimore & Co.

Curl, James Stevens. 1984. "The Design of Early British Cemeteries." *Journal of Garden History* 4, no. 3: 223–54.

Dennis, Richard. 2008. *Cities in Modernity. Representations and Productions of Metropolitan Space, 1840–1930*. Cambridge: Cambridge University Press.

Dickens, Charles. 1993. *Bleak House*. Ware: Wordsworth Editions.

Francis, Doris, Leonie Kellaher, and Georgina Neophytou. 2005. *The Secret Cemetery*. Oxford: Berg.

Dyos, Harold J., and Michael Wolff. 1973. *The Victorian City, Images and Realities*. London and Boston, MA: Routledge & Kegan Paul.

Dyos, Harold J. 1982. *Exploring The Urban Past. Essays in Urban History*. Cambridge: Cambridge University Press.

Etlin, Richard A. 1984. *The Architecture of Death, The Transformation of the Cemetery in Eighteenth-Century Paris*. Cambridge (Massachusetts), and London (England): MIT Press.

Foucault, Michel. ([1973] 2009). *The Birth of the Clinic: An Archeology of Medical Perception*. London: Routledge.

Gaskell, Peter. 1833. *The Manufacturing Population of England*. London: Baldwin and Cradock.

Hamlin, Christopher. 1998. *Public Health and Social Justice in the Age of Chadwick: Britain 1800-1854*. Cambridge. Cambridge University Press.

Houses of Parliament Archives – Anatomy Act – 1844. *Hansard Anatomy Act – HC Debate 11 June 1844, Vol. 75, CC. 523–34*. Accessed August 24, 2020. https://api.parliament.uk/historic-hansard/commons/1844/jun/11/anatomy-act

Houses of Parliament Archives – Public Health. 1833. *Public Health – HC Deb 21 February 1833 Vol. 15, CC. 1049–59*. Accessed August 24, 2020. https://api.parliament.uk/historic-hansard/commons/1833/feb/21/public-health

Howard, Ebenezer. 1898. *To-morrow: A Peaceful Path to Real Reform*. London: Swan Sonnenschein & Co. Ltd.

Hurren, Elizabeth T. 2012. *Dying for Victorian Medicine. English Anatomy and its Trade in the Dead Poor, c. 1834–1929*. Basingstoke: Palgrave Macmillan.

Litten, Julian. 1991. *The English Way of Death: The Common Funeral Since 1450*. London: Robert Hale Ltd.

"Report of the Medical Officer of Health for London County Council." 1900. Accessed May 31, 2021. https://wellcomelibrary.org/moh/report/b18252497/2#?c=0&m=0&s=0&cv=8&z=0.0979%2C0.1649%2C0.9928%2C0.3876

"Lost Hospitals of London." website. Accessed May 24, 2021. https://ezitis.myzen.co.uk/stmaryshighgate.html

Loudon, John Claudius. ([1843] 1981). *On the Layout, Planting and Managing of Cemeteries and on the Improvement of Churchyards*. Redhill: Ivelet Books Ltd.

Loudon, John Claudius. 1832. *The Gardener's Magazine*, March. London: Longman, Rees, Orme, Brown, Green, and Longman.

Loudon, John Claudius. 1829. *The Gardener's Magazine and Register of Rural and Domestic Improvement* 5 (February): 214. Accessed March 1, 2020. https://books.google.co.uk/books?id=h2JJAAAAMAAJ&pg=PA214&dq=%22Metropolitan+Sepulchre%22&hl=en&sa=X&ved=0ahUKEwif5qrpt6TeAhWOecAKHaKfBAsQ6AEILzAB#v=onepage&q=%22Metropolitan%20Sepulchre%22&f=false

Mayhew, Henry. ([1861-2] 2010). *London Labour & the London Poor*. Oxford: Oxford University Press.

McKellar, Elizabeth. 1999. *The Birth of Modern London. The Development and Design of the City 1660–1720*. Manchester: Manchester University Press.

Olsen, Donald J. 1976. *The Growth of Victorian London*. London: B.T. Batsford Ltd.

Parsons, Brian. 2018. *The Evolution of the British Funeral Industry in the 20th Century. From Undertaker to Funeral Director*. Bingley: Emerald Publishing Limited.

Paxman, Jeremy. 2011. *Empire: What Ruling the World did to the British*. London: Penguin Books Ltd.

Porter, Roy. 2000. *London, A Social History*. London: Penguin Books Ltd.

Reader, John. 2005. *Cities*. London: Vintage.
Richardson, Ruth. 1989. *Death, Dissection and the Destitute*. London: Pelican Books.
Richardson, Ruth. 2008. *The Making of Mr Gray's Anatomy: Bodies, Books, Fortune, Fame*. Oxford: Oxford University Press.
Rugg, Julie. 1992. *The Rise of Cemetery Companies in Britain*. University of Stirling. Accessed May 25, 2021. https://dspace.stir.ac.uk/handle/1893/2017#.YKz yOpEY
Russell, Bertrand. 2008. *History of Western Philosophy*. London, New York: Routledge.
Sheppard, Francis. 1971. *London 1808–1870: The Infernal Wen*. London: Martin Secker & Warburg Limited.
Southwood Smith, Thomas. 1827. *Use of the Dead to the Living*. Albany, New York: Websters and Skinners. Accessed May 25, 2021. https://www.gutenberg.org/files/58460/58460-h/58460-h.htm
Stedman Jones, Gareth. 1971. *Outcast London*. Oxford: Clarendon Press.
Strange, Julie-Marie. 2005. *Death, Grief and Poverty in Britain, 1870–1914*. Cambridge: Cambridge University Press.
The Lady's Newspaper. 1853. Saturday 19 March. No. 325. Accessed May 31, 2021. https://www.britishnewspaperarchive.co.uk/viewer/BL/0002254/18530319/128/0028
"The Pyramid Cemetery." 1834. *Penny Magazine of the Society for the Diffusion of Useful Knowledge* (October 4): 389–90. Accessed March 1, 2020. https://books.google.co.uk/books?id=DsVEAQAAIAAJ&pg=PA389#v=onepage&q&f=false
Vidler, Anthony. 2011. *The Scenes of the Street and Other Essays*. New York: The Monacelli Press.
Walker, George Alfred. 1839. *Gathering Graveyards: Particularly Those of London*. London: Longman.
Walker, George Alfred. 1849. *Practical Suggestions for the Establishment of National Cemeteries*. London: Longman, Brown, Green, and Longman. Accessed May 24, 2021. https://wellcomecollection.org/works/dy9emamf/items?canvas=3
Ward Richardson, Benjamin. 1876. *Hygeia, A City of Health*. London: MacMillan & Co.
Wohl, Anthony Stephen. 1983. *Endangered Lives: Public Health in Victorian Britain*. London: Methuen & Co. Ltd.
Wohl, Anthony Stephen. 2009. *The Eternal Slum: Housing and Social Policy in Victorian London*. New Brunswick, New Jersey: Transaction Publishers.
Wood, Claire. 2015. *Dickens and the Business of Death*. Cambridge: Cambridge University Press.

2 Identity

2.1 Landscapes of remembrance

Planting and landscaping were striking new features that distinguished London's early Victorian cemeteries. Along with architecture and funerary design they formulated a new visual language for burial that was both unprecedented and impressive in scale. In the context of the new cemeteries, nature had a double role: emotional and functional. The emotional role was to provide picturesque settings for the graves. By contrast, the functional role of nature was to provide a healthy setting for the burials. In his book, *The Space of Death* (1983), French historian Michel Ragon explains that, since ancient times, vegetal elements such as flowers, shrubs and trees were used to adorn burial spaces and graves. This could be seen in some ancient Greek and Roman burial grounds, which were decorated by funerary gardens that included flower beds of roses (among other flowers) as offerings to the dead. Evergreen conifers were also planted in graveyards as they symbolise immortality. With the advent of Christianity, the practice of using vegetation in burial grounds was dismissed for its association with pagan cultures. Eventually, plants were thought to be responsible for making graveyards unhealthy. For example, all planting was forbidden in cemeteries in seventeenth- and eighteenth-century France in the name of hygiene, as trees were thought to hinder the air circulation in graveyards, and, therefore, made them insalubrious (1983, 113–5).

These interpretations emphasise the equivocal and conflicting relationship man has had with nature. Historically, man has given nature a role, which is the antithesis of man's social power because it is understood as destructive and violent. French historian Ariès explores this in his book, *The Hour of Our Death*, and explains that for thousands of years the progress of humankind was possible because of the defence system that it developed against nature. For Ariès, this system was achieved by organising society along the main axes, which acted as control barriers, namely morality, religion and collective discipline (1980, 391–3). These two contrasting aspects of nature (one benevolent, contemplative and symbolically associated with immortality, the other, destructive, violent and incompatible with humankind)

DOI: 10.4324/9781003178934-3

Identity 31

constitute a useful platform from which to observe if, and how, they were present in the landscape of the Victorian cemeteries. To understand how this process evolved, we need to look into the origins of the garden cemetery in France. In his book, *The Architecture of Death*, Etlin explains the transformations of Parisian cemeteries from the mid-eighteenth century to the development of garden cemeteries, in particular those of Père Lachaise, the first of their kind, which opened for burial in 1804 (see Figure 2.1).

A key and innovative feature of this cemetery was its vegetation. In conducting his research, Etlin was interested in understanding how this shift in attitude towards vegetation in mid-eighteenth-century France coincided with the Enlightenment. For Etlin, this process of "dechristianisation" was able to take place as people started to discover scientific reasons that

Figure 2.1 Print showing Père Lachaise Cemetery in Paris featuring vegetation, funeral monuments and views of the capital in the distance. *The Mirror*. 1823. Author's Collection.

explained the positive effects of good air quality and urban hygiene (1984, 15). This rational approach to nature followed the 1773 scientific discovery by English natural philosopher and theologian Joseph Priestley, that vegetation regenerates the air.

> Plants wonderfully thrive in putrid air, and the vegetation of a plant could correct air fouled by the burning of a candle, and restore it to its former purity and fitness for supporting flame and for the respiration of animals.
>
> (Ingen-Housz 1779, XV)

According to John Ingen-Housz, Priestley's discovery was first made public during a speech delivered at the Royal Society in November 1773 by the Society's president John Pringle:

> [From Priestley's] discoveries we are assured, that no vegetable grows in vain, but that, from the oak of the forest to the grass in the field, every individual plant is serviceable to mankind; if not always distinguished by some private virtue, yet making a part of the whole, which cleanses and purifies our atmosphere.
>
> (1779, XVI)

Nature, however, was not just praised for its – scientifically proven – healthy connotations, but also because its aesthetic qualities contributed to the embellishment of the built environment and metropolitan spaces alike. On 21 February 1833, the House of Commons appointed a Select Committee, which was to secure "open places in the neighbourhood of great towns, for the healthful exercise of the population" (Houses of Parliament Archives, Public Health 1833). The committee was established because of panic following the cholera epidemic. Concern was expressed over the health of London's population and of other large industrial cities, such as Manchester. The fast and unregulated expansion of most British cities left few open spaces available to the working classes for recreation on Sundays or holidays. It is important to notice, however, that most factory workers or artisans were not located in the western part of London, and that those benefiting from public open spaces such as St. James's Park were the more local middle-class residents of West London. The Royal Parks were used as a tissue to connect the otherwise fragmented areas around Westminster, which was gradually being built up in the nineteenth century. (Arnold 1982, 159).

Although a British scientist discovered the healthy properties of vegetation, the first cemetery design to integrate these new findings was by the hand of French architect Jacques Denise Antoine. Etlin discussed one of his design proposals for a cemetery, where Antoine introduced trees in the style of a formal garden, with planting ordered along pathways and borders. His inspiration came from the engravings of English country houses, executed by Dutch draughtsman and engraver Johannes Kip. According to Etlin, Antoine also referenced the use of intersecting geometrical forms, such as the circle in the square, as seen in the Italian gardens at Villa Lante and Villa d'Este (1984, 93–5). Furthermore, Etlin argues that the idea of the landscaped cemetery originated from the early eighteenth-century English landscape garden, which then later influenced the landscape and cemetery design on the continent. To support his theory, Etlin provides two examples: Leasowes Gardens, designed and developed by English poet William Shenstone between 1743 and 1763, and Stowe, designed by William Kent and Charles Bridgeman between 1730 and 1738. For Etlin, Leasowes combined the dual aspects of "pastoral amusement" and "solemn meditation", two contrasting aspects that, in his view, were to become the "underlying feature of the English landscape garden" (163, 176). By contrast, the distinctive feature at Stowe was the Elysian Fields in which memorials to great thinkers (including Shakespeare, Milton, Bacon, Locke, and Newton), "popularised the idea of honouring public virtues". In Etlin's words:

> The Elysian Fields at Stowe, perhaps more than any other British landscape garden, was to profoundly affect the French idea of what a cemetery should be. The history of Stowe is inseparable from that of the evolution of the landscape garden.
>
> (184)

Building on Etlin's findings, it is possible to say that Priestley's discovery provided a scientific explanation to vegetation, that justified its presence in the space of the cemetery. The garden cemetery became therefore a healthy alternative to the otherwise unhygienic and deleterious churchyards. This passage also marked a step forward in the process of secularisation of burial culture in modernity. The writer also asserts that the contemplative approach to nature originated in the gardens at Leasowes and Stowe. This reinforces – or shows continuity in history – the use of flowers and vegetation in the cemetery space as we saw with Ragon. Nature is still an integral part of burials, but its benefits are now rationally explained by scientific discovery. Furthermore, Etlin clarifies that the broadly disseminated idea that Victorian cemeteries were inspired by Père Lachaise is not fully accurate, as it was inspired by the English landscape garden of the late seventeenth and early eighteenth century. Lastly, we saw how the landscape, especially in Stowe, anticipated the celebration of human achievements and knowledge in the form of memorials set within the landscape. This suggests the reconciliation between man and nature, in a kind of new cosmological order, which is not understood in terms of faith and religious belief (whether pagan or otherwise), but explained by human reason and its scientific advances. Whether they were an inspiration or not to London's companies, the Parisian cemeteries made use of the landscape in a very different way from the Kensal Green or Highgate cemeteries. Père Lachaise for example has a specific urban feel to it with vegetation contained in specific areas and cobbled stone avenues, which mimic Parisian avenues, unlike the more rural and picturesque looks of Kensal Green Cemetery.

To further understand the relationship between architectural language and landscape in London's Victorian cemeteries we will need to look into the idea of urban picturesque. In his essay "The Metropolitan Picturesque" published in 1994, Malcolm Andrews discusses the role of the picturesque in the context of nineteenth-century London. In particular, I will draw on one of his comments that helped to investigate the architecture and the role of the picturesque at the time. Andrews juxtaposes his critical statement on British nineteenth-century architecture with a remark on the picturesque, stating that:

> [The] picturesque connotes, then, variety, idiosyncrasy and individuality, cornerstones of the new political and economical philosophy of the age – laissez-faire, self-help, and entrepreneurial freedom.
> (1994, 285)

Andrews' statement can be taken as a good starting point to understand the Victorian cemetery and ascertain which picturesque elements were used as a metaphor to express individuality in Victorian times. In line with Andrews' claim, we could say that the architectural language of Victorian cemeteries was not particularly innovative per se, as they borrow their aesthetics from existing languages, (Kensal Green Cemetery in Greek Revival, Highgate Cemetery in Gothic Revival), however, these new cemeteries tested new combinations of architecture and landscape in an unprecedented way. The architecture of Victorian cemeteries with their chapels, monuments and mausoleums, is at one with the context of the natural landscape. This combination informed perception of the cemetery that has been defined as picturesque. In the context of privately owned Victorian cemeteries, this quality was used commercially for the sale of private burial plots. Although the idea of the picturesque is closely associated with the Regency architecture and landscape style of the late seventeenth and eighteenth centuries, it became relevant to the urban developments of nineteenth-century London.

Even if located in the outskirts of London, these spaces complied with the rules adopted for the supervision of other open spaces in the urban environment, such as squares, parks or leisure gardens, including a system to regulate the access of visitors by issuing specially designed tokens (see Figure 2.2).

In this respect, the new Victorian cemeteries encapsulated the idea of civic order and culture of a locality or even community. Town and city authorities were competing with one another to be seen to be carrying

Figure 2.2 Admission-ticket to Highgate Cemetery, issued by London Cemetery Company. Undated. © The Trustees of the British Museum.

improvements. If the collective meanings of the landscape were connected to civic order and decorum and cultural progress, for the individual purchasing a private burial plot, they had still to do with legacy and social status. The landscape, just like funerary architecture, was an instrument to create a benevolent façade to what was in reality, a business asset for a company.

Although the landscape of these cemeteries was laid out in such a way as to be perceived as one coherent piece of design, it was pragmatically subdivided into burial plots (of differing sizes) available for sale. Graves were therefore marketed on their size, prominence, features, accessibility and geological makeup. In the case of Kensal Green Cemetery, the more costly plots were in proximity to the graves of "liberal" royals such as Prince Augustus Frederick, Duke of Sussex, who died in 1843 (and his sister Princess Sophia in 1848) and that of Prince George, Duke of Cambridge (in 1904). They were all related to King George III, father of Prince Augustus Frederick and Princess Sophia, and the grandfather of Prince George (Curl 2001, 112–13, 122–23). Their presence contributed towards the reputation of this cemetery and the General Cemetery Company. This later also happened in Highgate Cemetery where famous thinkers, writers and artists chose to be buried. Similarly, on an undated map of Brookwood Cemetery, burial plots are ranked as 2nd and 3rd class. Thus we can say that the social hierarchy of the urban space is reproduced and imposed along the contours of the cemetery's landscape, according to the commercial laws that established the fee scale for burial plots.

These arrangements encapsulated what the middle classes ultimately aspired to and wanted to be associated with: social status and legacy. Therefore, buying a burial plot within these landscapes satisfied both needs. However, when observed on the small scale of a private burial plot, it is possible to notice how privacy was also important, as the landscape acted as a

36 Identity

Figure 2.3 Print showing graves at Kensal Green Cemetery. Undated. Author's Collection.

curtain that screened with a layer of privacy even over the most extravagant Victorian graves and monuments (see Figure 2.3).

To conclude, we can say that when the Victorian cemeteries first opened, their landscape was a prominent feature and was more legible and coherent. One could argue that the cemetery companies did not retain the same interest in the aesthetics of the landscape, over the long term. This is demonstrated by the tight filling of new graves, tombs and mausolea particularly in the case of Kensal Green Cemetery. Lastly, we can say that the landscape in the Victorian cemetery attempted to address two contrasting aspects of nature by utilising the scientific rational explanations of nature's healthy qualities as a point of mediation. As its benefits were scientifically explained, nature became neutral with regard to past associations with pagan, Christian or other religious beliefs and therefore could be integrated into the new paradigm of burial in a way that suited the cemetery companies irrespective of their motives.

2.2 The business of burying the dead

The new private cemeteries stimulated radical changes that rationalised burial to the extent of making it hygienically safe and morally decent, despite the growing scale of London. In this respect, the companies effectively established a new set of standards for burials. But what were the motives that pushed private companies and entrepreneurs to deal with such a complex issue as burial? Certainly, the business opportunity presented itself as an attractive prospect, though there must have been other reasons connected to other socio-cultural aspects that should be considered equally motivational. Although the new private cemeteries were initially accessible only to a restricted portion of society, they made death and the status of burials more visible on the agenda of the social issues debated at the time.

The private companies effectively reformed the way of burying the dead, rationalised the actual burial processes and developed a unique model of organisation and sophistication that addressed the diverse and complex issues associated with burials. These included religious and hygienic concerns, the viability of the new burial model through its management, administration as well as its aesthetic language through funerary architecture and landscape design. Drawing from historical and archival material, I will question what their meanings were, and how other researchers, scholars and writers have interpreted them. I will focus solely on those cemetery companies selected as case studies, as this is the purpose of this research.

To develop a competent and ethical working model, the cemetery companies had to take into consideration manifold aspects related to the disposal of human remains. Among others, the new paradigm of burial needed to address: health concerns, functionality, commercial viability, existing laws, decency, morality and most of all the satisfaction of the board of directors and partners involved in the joint-stock company. Although essentially the burial method still consisted primarily of earth burial, its perception, organisation and meanings became more sophisticated. The fact that such a diverse range of factors was taken into consideration by the cemetery companies shows how the burial of human remains became culturally complex and layered with meanings that ranged from practical issues connected to public health to those related to the personal feelings of mourners.

As well as addressing the above-mentioned conditions, each cemetery company had to be granted permission to operate a cemetery by an Act of Parliament, and after the 1850s also had to comply with the new laws set by the Burial Acts. However, they did not conform to any restrictions in terms of centralised planning strategies, as London did not have one at the time. When it came to the architectural styles or landscape arrangements, each cemetery company was free to choose what best suited their image and the interests of their board of directors. It is for this reason that London's private Victorian cemeteries, and indeed the ones in the rest of the country, varied so widely in styles from one another and differed so much from their continental counterparts.

Scholars researching this field of study have previously addressed these differences. Among them Julie Rugg conducted a comprehensive study on cemetery companies which culminated in her thesis "The Rise of Cemetery Companies in Britain: 1820–53" (1992). Rugg maps 113 companies in the UK and studies the motives of the companies' directors. The author categorises the companies in three types, starting from the early cemetery companies that emerged in the mid-1820s, which saw the burial problem mostly as a religious-political issue and used the cemeteries to provide a burial space which was independent of the Anglican Church. Moreover, Rugg demonstrates that within this typology there were different degrees of "dissenting militancy"; these companies had a degree of political significance as they were threatening to deprive the Church of England of its established income monopolies over burials (7, 191). The second type of company, in Rugg's view, emerged in the mid-1830s and saw burial primarily as a speculative business opportunity. These types of cemetery companies were a restricted phenomenon, contrary to what is often understood by historians, both in time (most formed between 1835–37 or 1845), scale, and geographical locations (London, Manchester, Glasgow and Edinburgh). These companies were primarily concerned to provide luxury burial services or by contrast offer burial provisions in the poorest areas of London.

Rugg reminds us that speculative companies interested in making profits by selling the right of burial as a luxury commodity were a very small minority and indeed an exception, that until now has received wide attention by historians and has led to the misleading conclusion that most companies were primarily speculating on burials when it was not the case. The author identifies that only four companies formed to sell status burials. Three of these companies were located in London, and they were: the London Cemetery Company, owners of Highgate Cemetery and Nunhead Cemetery; the South Metropolitan Cemetery Company, founders of Norwood Cemetery; and the London and Westminster Cemetery Company which initiated Brompton Cemetery. Strangely, the General Cemetery Company is not included, although as we saw earlier, status burials took place in Kensal Green Cemetery. Rugg also notes that speculative cemetery companies were successful mostly in large cities, because of the concentration of wealth there, and did not reach out to the provinces. Other reasons for this geographic restriction are grouped by the researcher under three factors: the existence in London of a long tradition of private burial grounds, the success of Kensal Green, the first large suburban cemetery opened by the General Cemetery Company in 1833 and the increase in the demand for elaborate graves and memorials (1992, 7, 93–4, 208, 225–6, 232). Rugg lastly states that the third type of company which emerged by the mid-1840s was primarily concerned with burial as a sanitary measure, and therefore defines them as public health enterprises. Although these were less successful than the speculative cemetery companies, they helped to disseminate the idea that this type of cemetery contributed to the civic pride of the town or city (7, 225, 250).

Overall Rugg's findings shed a completely new light on the nature of the cemetery companies, their motives and objectives. Her research demonstrates that it was not all to do with financial returns but a more complex issue that also included other aspects such as religion, local politics and civic pride. Although this seminal work answers some of the questions on the formation and nature of the cemetery companies, it does not explore in greater detail how the socio-cultural context of the time influenced these motivations. Historian David Thomson addressed this question in his research and identifies a direct connection between the motives of the Victorian entrepreneur and morality. In his 1955 book, *England in the Nineteenth Century (1815–1914)*, Thomson explains that, although on one side, Victorians were driven by morality as predominantly derived by their religious principles, on the other they took pride in material progress. In Thomson's view, the Victorian industrial and commercial classes had gained control over the economic life of the country in the mid-nineteenth century. This also allowed them to affect society and culture, resulting in a unique combination of contrasting elements that Thomson defines as "at once materialist and moral, aggressive and religious, self-satisfied and self-critical" (117). This social complexity helped to shape a form of moral liberalism that transcends all barriers of religious sects, and that was more interested in how people in society put their belief into "good" practice. It was a natural consequence of this freedom of religious worship and thinking to demand freedom of enterprise and trade.

For Thomson, the permanent motivating ideal of nineteenth-century England was "the greatest happiness of the greatest number" (1955, 107, 117, 225–6). This was, as seen earlier in Chapter 1, the leading philosophical principle of Bentham's radical Utilitarian thinking which promoted liberalism both in society and the economy. Thomson again explains how convenient it was, in a moment of expansion such as the middle of the nineteenth century, that Britain's central government adopted a laissez-faire attitude. This condition suited the growth of private initiatives, of commerce and the development of the city, including the creation of new cemeteries. Although this is not a full and accurate picture, Rugg and Thompson have identified some key aspects that could give us a better understanding of the philanthropic nature that moved and catalysed the Victorian entrepreneur (religion, morality and philosophy). In the next section, I will focus more specifically on the commercial aspects of the cemetery company and the role of the entrepreneur.

If for Thomson the philanthropic nature that moved and catalysed the Victorian entrepreneur was religion, morality, and philosophy, for German economist Werner Sombart, it was purely a matter of cold rationality. Sombart's explanation of capitalism is disconnected from any historical event, a kind of tabula rasa. In *Economic Life in the Modern Age*, one of Sombart's texts in English, the author, with a distinctive lucidity, explains that the spirit of the economic outlook of capitalism is dominated by three ideas: acquisition, competition and rationality, and that capitalism is formed by "three constituent elements – spirit, form, and technology". The "form" of the system, in a structural sense, is defined by Sombart as "aristocratic", as there is a disproportion between the small numbers of economic agents with the power of control and the rest of the population taking part in economic life (2001, 6, 10). Technology, as an aspect of the capitalist system, is one that allows for "improvement and perfection". The constant technological improvement is, for Sombart, the "weapon in the hands of the capitalist entrepreneur who seeks to eliminate his competitor and to extend his market by offering goods superior in quality or lower in price". Sombart explains this process of seeking perfection through "scientific, mechanistic technology" as a way of making use of natural science to overcome the limitation of nature and the "organic environment". This process of technological advancement brings with it the idea of commodity and impersonality of economic relationships. In Sombart's own words:

> The depersonalisation of commercial as well as technical management transforms them into satisfactory instrumentalities for the practice of a technology based on the depersonalisation of human labor.
>
> (2001, 12)

Sombart also defines the capitalist enterprise as an "economic organism", which is "independent from the individuals that constitute it". In short, it is an abstract entity in itself. The author also discusses the role and motivations of the capitalist entrepreneur in his view:

> The motives of capitalist entrepreneurs are by no means restricted to acquisitive drives; among them, the craving for acclaim, the impulsion to serve the common good, the urge to action.
>
> (13)

If we apply Sombart's theory to the specific case of the entrepreneurs behind the cemetery companies, we could suggest that they had a "calling" to form new cemeteries to "serve the common good" and possibly struck a chord with Bentham's "greatest good for the greatest number" principle. The economist also attempts to outline what he defines as the "Ideal Entrepreneur", a character that, in his view, should combine:

> The traits of the inventor, discoverer, conqueror, organizer, and merchant. He is an inventor, not so much of technical innovations as of new forms of organization for production, transportation, and marketing. Moreover, the entrepreneur as inventor does not terminate his activity

with the formulation of the invention; in utilizing it he improves and vitalizes it in countless ways.

(13)

Sombart's outline of the private entrepreneur is a good opportunity to draw together a few reflections on the cemetery companies and their directors. It is interesting, for example, to observe how, in some cases, one person could be not only business manager but also engineer, architect and surveyor. This was the case with Stephen Geary, the architect who designed Highgate Cemetery. He was the founder of the London Cemetery Company thanks to the support he received from Thomas Wakley, the medical reformer, and MP for Finsbury. Wakley was coroner for Middlesex and therefore directly involved in death matters. He also provided similar support for other cemetery companies set up in those years.

2.3 Architecture and legacy

The architectural styles adopted for each one of the new cemeteries, through their aesthetics also communicated the ethos and identities of their respective company. This was an attractive message for wealthy Londoners, interested in articulating their taste and social status to posterity well beyond their graves. There is, however, an initial clarification to be made as there is a substantial difference between the architecture that the companies adopted and the funerary architecture that the cemeteries contained. This section will discuss the two issues separately. Ultimately this part, through an analysis of the historical archival materials available, will attempt to conclude how the architectural language chosen by the cemetery companies was intentionally lavish to disguise its evident speculative inclinations. It also will demonstrate how the architecture styles adopted gradually changed from elaborate to minimal and were restrained by society's changes of taste in funerary culture. Despite differences in intentions, the cemetery companies had a common denominator in architecture, as it was an expressive element that allowed them to physically and aesthetically manifest their beliefs and motives. The range of new architectural styles developed by the cemetery companies was unprecedented and adapted in eclectic ways architectural elements borrowed from Neoclassicism to Gothic Revival and from Greek and Egyptian revivals. We will see this more in detail with the three selected case studies: Kensal Green Cemetery, Highgate Cemetery and Brookwood Cemetery, where each of their respective private owners adopted a distinct architectural style.

Being commercial ventures, the architectural aesthetics chosen by the cemetery companies were strongly driven by what was fashionable at the time with the Victorian middle classes, who represented their target customers. Following such a volatile point of reference, the architecture had therefore to adapt and change according to the pace of these trends. Despite these limitations, the architecture gave each company a public coherent visual image and translated their ethos and values into physical forms. However, the process of selecting a particular architectural style, or indeed creating a new one, wasn't simple and, at times, the final built project was the result of internal battles and compromises. In some cases – notably Kensal Green Cemetery and Highgate Cemetery – the built designs were completely different from the original proposals, as we will see next.

The original scheme for Kensal Green, designed by Edward Kendall, was in the Gothic Revival style. In his proposal, Kendall also included a water gate on the canal that marked the south-west boundary of the cemetery. This design solution envisaged the integration of the existing waterway to facilitate the transportation of coffins and mourners to the cemetery, and for the display of funerals. Despite its grand scale and attractive beauty, this scheme was never implemented. In his book, *The Origins & Development of the General Cemetery of All Souls, Kensal Green, London 1824–2001* (2001), Curl explains in detail the internal battles (among shareholders) that eventually resulted in the selection of the "official" architectural style of the cemetery. Although Kendall's proposal was the award-winning design, the final scheme which was then built was drafted by John Griffith, a protégé of Sir John Dean Paul, chairman to the board of the General Cemetery Company. The Greek Revival style adopted by Griffith was associated with antiquity and in favour at the time for its connection with pure classicism. By contrast, the Gothic Revival became associated with Christian worship and morality (75, 152–3). Irrespective of its direct association with Christianity, it was the Gothic Revival style that was adopted for both Anglicans and Dissenters for the West Cemetery in Highgate. The two equally sized chapels occupy the two halves of the entrance building and are connected through an archway that leads onto the main terrace (see Figure 2.4).

It is worth noting that this unique arrangement does not feature any architectural difference in style or scale that could lead the viewer to think of a hierarchical order between Anglicans and Dissenters, as these religious denominations were both formally and equally represented. There was, however, a distinction in the quality of burials between the two halves of the cemetery, as the left section of the West Cemetery was more expensive than the right one. Entering through the arch in the main gate flanked by the chapels and landing on the terrace, it is still possible to see today how the left avenue winding up to the higher part of the cemetery was grander in terms of layout, plantings, quality of burials and funerary architecture.

The original plan for Highgate Cemetery, however, was different from the one that was eventually implemented. Designed in the early 1830s by Geary, and featured by historian John Richardson in his book, *Highgate Past* (2004, 82), the proposal architecture featured two entrances to the cemetery, one on the south end of the cemetery (on Swain's Lane), and another at the north end (by St. Michael's Church). It also appears that Geary intended to annex the existing St. Michael's church to the cemetery

Figure 2.4 The entrance to Highgate West Cemetery. 1902. Author's Collection

and make it effectively the upper entrance to the cemetery. This is London's highest church building, which was rebuilt in 1832 in a Gothic Revival style by the design of Lewis Vulliamy. It was previously in the parish of St. Pancras and then moved to Highgate Parish. The West Cemetery at Highgate and St. Michael's Church were on the site of Ashurst House, built for Sir William Ashurst in 1694. Ashurst House was used by the Highgate Mansion House Academy for Young Gentlemen in 1816 and demolished in 1830. In the drawing, this part features a terrace that enhances Highgate's distinctive vista over London and the southern counties. Furthermore, the layout suggests that Geary was thinking of using the church for funerals, as he did not include an Anglican chapel in his scheme, but only the "non-conformist" one in Gothic Revival style, which in the drawing is positioned in the south part of the cemetery. This could be interpreted as a desire by Geary to allocate to Anglicans and Dissenters two distinct sections of the cemetery, with their separate entrances and chapels. Lastly in Geary's drawing, there is little sign of a high perimeter wall that enclosed the cemetery and restricted its access through specific gated entrances. The only entrance to be seen in the proposal was the one on Swain's Lane, which consisted of a rather modest building containing the dwelling of the cemetery superintendent and featuring an archway and very little ornamentation. Most strikingly though, and specifically for this building, it appears that Geary drew his inspiration from the Greek

Revival archway designed by Griffith for the entrance of Kensal Green Cemetery.

It is not possible to establish what the reasons were that made Geary and the London Cemetery Company abandon this scheme, as there isn't any specific historical document that could support it. As we will see in more detail later in Chapter 4 there are historical records related to a dispute that almost stopped the consecration of the cemetery before its official opening. The controversy was initiated and led by Harry Cester, an influential resident in Highgate village and was the founder of the local Literary and Scientific Institution in 1839. The complainants claimed that the public using that part of the cemetery could overlook their private properties and forced the company to abandon the proposal for a public access from the side of St. Michael's Church to Highgate Cemetery. This however did not affect the impressive composition and aesthetic arrangement between St. Michael's Church, the staircase entrances onto the cemetery and the catacombs in the Circle of Lebanon as can be seen in historical prints featuring the upper part of Highgate Cemetery (see Figure 2.5).

We need, however, to remind ourselves that architectural proposals such as the one for Highgate, despite their alluring aesthetics, were ultimately designed to suit the speculative nature of the company and attract new buyers. Granted that was the case, we can also see how the architect attempted to integrate existing architectural features, such as St. Michael's Church, with the existing topography of the site, to form a new visual and architectural continuum (more details on this in Chapter 4). This demonstrated sophistication and understanding in the modelling and planning of a cemetery, taking into consideration the immediate context in a rather extroverted way, and intending to blur the boundaries between the cemetery and its surroundings, rather than simply marking a physical separation between the two with a boundary wall. Furthermore, we can see that although Geary and the London Cemetery Company did not succeed in implementing this scheme, they challenged the cemetery design by proposing an alternative to the example set by Griffith with Kensal Green Cemetery a few years earlier. Geary's design was also challenging one of the key hygienic requirements for cemeteries, which was a boundary wall to physically mark the boundaries of the burial ground. To summarise this section, we can say that in the case of Kensal Green Cemetery as in that of Highgate Cemetery, the companies pursued new avenues in terms of cemetery design. Beyond the aspects discussed above, their design was also attempting to blend urban and rural elements, as after all these were both entirely new cemeteries at the edge of the city, where the city and countryside needed to be bound together.

However, this wasn't a trend that other companies necessarily followed, as in the case of the London Necropolis Company, founders and owners of Brookwood Cemetery in 1854 (see Figure 2.6). This was a rare example in which the offices of the company and the actual cemetery were physically connected by a railway line. The London Necropolis Company took up

Figure 2.5 Print showing the upper-end of Highgate West Cemetery at night time. Note St. Michael's Church spire in the distance. Undated. Author's Collection.

this challenge by adopting two different architectural styles that responded respectively to the urban context of the city and the rural setting of the cemetery. The city end had to deal with the spatial limitation of the urban setting, as space was a premium there, whereas the other end had to respond to the grand scale of a cemetery that allegedly had enough space to accommodate burial for 500 years.

The company offices and railway station near Waterloo Station marked a further shift in architecture terms as well as burial culture. In the space of 15 years (this is the time gap between the opening of Highgate Cemetery and Brookwood Cemetery), London's railway network expanded, and with it, the possibilities to open new cemeteries further away from the city, where the land was less expensive for purchase by cemetery companies.

46 *Identity*

Figure 2.6 Brookwood Cemetery bird's-eye view. *The Illustrated London News*. 26 April 1856. Author's Collection.

The architectural language used for the railway station was as utilitarian as most of the railway architecture seen at the time. The archway leading to the Necropolis Station effectively became a substitute for the main entrance to the cemetery, as this was the first point of contact for any mourner or client. As can be seen in a photograph, its style wasn't in any way as grand as Kensal Green or Highgate cemeteries, but instead combined a rather ordinary brick building to an archway entrance, adjacent to Waterloo's railway bridge, which was leading to the actual station (see Figure 2.7).

As well as burial services, the London Necropolis Company also provided funeral services that included preparing the corpse of the deceased for the funeral, designing and building their coffin and their gravestone or memorial. The company therefore must have integrated all of these activities and spaces for offices, mortuaries, workshops and a railway station in the very congested site we can see in the photograph in Figure 2.7. The interior of the Necropolis Station, as seen in an undated print published at the time in the press, was unadorned and utilitarian; its scale was modest as it accommodated only two rail tracks and one platform. By contrast, the architectural styles adopted for the chapels in Brookwood Cemetery were referencing a rustic country vernacular. Even the station's buildings here tried to blend in with the landscape along with graves and memorials (see Figure 2.8), just as the premises at the London end were blended in with the city's urban context.

Identity 47

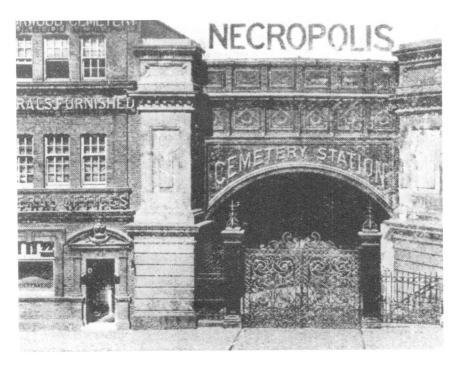

Figure 2.7 Façade of the Necropolis Station – London Necropolis Company. Undated. Author's Collection.

As the works for the expansion of Waterloo Station were undertaken around the turn of the nineteenth century, the London Necropolis Company had to relocate further down the Westminster Bridge Road. The scheme was designed by Cyril Bazett Tubbs in 1899 and completed in 1900. Tubbs' front façade is tall and narrow on the street front and features an archway entrance at street level. Horse-drawn carriages and later, motor hearses, would drive through this archway and turn left to the mortuaries where corpses were taken up to be prepared for their funeral, which would have taken place in the new chapel that Tubbs incorporated in the new scheme. The coffin and mourners would then board specially designed trains directed to Brookwood Cemetery for the actual burial. The spatial organisation devised by Tubbs for this scheme is admirable, given the modest scale of the site. The interiors are functional, yet well detailed and crafted, as we will see later. In one of the existing drawings for the station level it is possible to observe that two separate entrances existed for first-class and second-/third-class funerals. The length of the first-class platform is outlined with individual waiting rooms for the

48 Identity

Figure 2.8 One of the two cemetery stations at Brookwood Cemetery. Early 1900. Author's Collection.

different parties of mourners waiting to board the train to Brookwood Cemetery.

However, privacy also meant the separation of different social groups, as seen in the design of the new Necropolis Station. Here first-class mourners did not meet with the second- and third-class ones, as the spaces were designed specifically to avoid this direct contact. From a photograph featured in the promotional brochure of the new facilities, it is possible to see that the two platforms were separated along their length by a partition that would avoid any visual contact between the different social groups of mourners. Surely the intention was to give everyone a private space of his or her own in such a moment of sorrow. From this, we can assume that, by the turn of the century, the fashion for funerals had shifted considerably in tone from a lavish affair to a private and intimate phenomenon, which started to address the needs of the broader society and not only the wealthy classes.

To summarise, so far we have seen that stylistically the architecture of cemetery companies did adopt architectural styles that suited their identities. However, this was more relevant to early companies that saw architecture styles as a way to demonstrate their position and perhaps their reliability. Although the architectural language chosen by the speculative cemetery companies discussed in this section was intentionally lavish to disguise their lucrative intentions, we also saw how companies gradually moved away from elaborate architecture to embrace a more restrained and functional aesthetic language by society's changes in taste. This becomes more evident when observing how the notion of individuality, independence and self-expression advocated by cemetery companies was mirrored by the funerary architecture.

As seen earlier on in this chapter, the companies offering for sale the burial rights in perpetuity gave an assurance to the deceased and their families as an incentive to invest in the design and construction of elaborate funerary architecture. This lack of restrictions by the cemetery companies in regulating the scale or style of the memorials to be erected encouraged the flourishing of commercialised mourning. Although this has been identified as a phenomenon of national scale, it was in London that it reached its peak in terms of concentration and diversity of funeral architecture. The reason for this limited geographical setting was the concentration of wealth to be found in Victorian London, which was well complemented by the presence of speculative cemetery companies that offered their luxury burial services to a thriving market (Rugg 1992, 79, 232–4). The celebration of death was not however an occurrence restricted to British culture but it was experienced across the continent in mainland Europe, in the same vigorous and individualistic spirit of memorialisation of the individual through funerary architecture.

However, self-expression in funerary architecture wasn't granted to all. It was closely intertwined with the social status and wealth of individuals and coincided with the rise of the Victorian middle classes, allowing people to leave their mark on history. To some extent, it is possible to say that this wasn't dissimilar to what happened in the Renaissance period in Italy with families such as the Medici in Florence. The Medici family didn't belong to the aristocratic circle but ascended to it and, therefore, wanted to create an identity for themselves, a history that would disguise their recently assumed status. For this reason, such families adopted and adapted architectural styles drawn from the past. London's Victorian middle classes, in particular, emulated this process, as they wanted to establish a legacy for themselves. This was expressed in London's townhouses as it was in funerary architecture, however, this would later change and become more understated and subtle. About this transition, Andrews comments that:

> The Victorian bourgeoisie was promoting architectural idiosyncrasy and individualism in a period when the powerful members of that class were themselves becoming more uniform ... Just as in its architecture it repudiated the stucco facades of Nash's Regency terraces
>
> (1994, 286)

This gives us clues on how architecture and design were used by a restricted group within Victorian society as a vehicle to express their unique individual taste and personality, whether it was a house or a grave. We can see that as the middle classes became more visible in the space of the Victorian cemeteries, the graves of working-class individuals and poor became practically invisible. In most Victorian cemeteries the burial spaces allocated to the poor were in more secluded parts of the cemeteries, away from the main avenues and often along the boundary walls. We have seen though, how in cases such as the London Necropolis Company, burials and funerals started to become less exclusive, and basic standards started to be set in terms of affordability and decorum. Paradoxically people at the opposite end of the social spectrum experienced, in different ways, the same pressure with regard to carrying out their burial duties for their families and relatives, as they too were trying to give an affordable, decent and safe burial to their lost ones. Following up on how architecture was both used by the companies and individuals to express respectively their motives and legacy, the next section will research more specifically into which role and meaning landscaped vegetation had in the paradigm of the Victorian cemeteries and how it complemented architecture styles and funerary design.

2.4 Rational minds

The innovative identity of the companies was not only substantiated by their aesthetic appearance in the context of the actual cemeteries but also in the administrative structures that rationalised burial processes. The range of bureaucracy connected to the private cemetery companies included a wide range of administrative paperwork, which is indicative of the complexity within which the companies were operating. For this research, and to give a sense of the variety of the newly introduced administrative structures especially designed by the companies, a selection of this historical documentation retrieved in national and local archives will be used to illustrate this section.

To start, it is worth saying that due to the intrinsic nature of the type of companies this book is studying, they all needed their burial grounds to be consecrated. This implied that each company had to be granted permission by an Act of Parliament, which validated the company and established the principles and constraints within which each company operated. The Act covered the basic details of the company including its initial capital and stipulated in detail the restrictions imposed on the company with regard to the alienation of consecrated burial grounds. This particular point was to avoid the companies to speculate on the land sale. The administrative paperwork for the formation of the company was just the tip of the bureaucratic iceberg that a cemetery company had to deal with, for example in the case of consecration of the company's burial ground the enterprise also had to exchange deeds with the Church of England. In this case, together with the official request for the consecration, a company also had to submit to the attention of the Bishop of London a plan showing the boundaries of the consecrated ground. In the case of Highgate Cemetery and Kensal Green Cemetery, these documents are to be found in the London Metropolitan Archives. The existing consecration plan drawing for Kensal Green Cemetery, dated from 1832, shows the original boundaries of the whole cemetery, and marked in green is the area that needed to be consecrated by the Church which was the vast majority of the whole cemetery when compared to the Dissenters' ground the company had set aside.

Bishops agreed to consecrate ground only when there was evidence of permanency in the formation of a company, such as an Act of Parliament. Dissenter's companies, because of the nature of their motives, had a less convoluted administration system that did not involve any transaction with the Church (Rugg 1992, 74–6). As we saw earlier, cemetery companies were also a threat to the Church's burial incomes, and therefore the religious institution had to explore alternative ways to retain at least a stake in this business. Consecration was one of them as, at a local level at least, the opposition of the Church to the consecration of new ground had the power to determine the failure of a cemetery company. The threat however was contained in part by the bishop of London Charles James Blomfield, who managed to retain a secure position for the Church by enforcing clerical fees on the consecrated grounds of the newly formed private cemeteries (Johnson 2001, 58). This was essentially a form of compensation for the loss of earnings to the local parishes, as the deceased was to be buried elsewhere other than the parish churchyard where he or she came from. The payment was proportional to the burial expense the mourners sustained, therefore the more expensive the burial the higher the fee to pay to the Church (1992, 185–88).

As parish churchyards were running out of burial space, they were able to get allocated a dedicated new portion in one of the private cemeteries. This agreement was regulated by new acts especially drawn in these cases that added another layer of administrative paperwork to regulate the settlement between the cemetery company and the Church. Some of these documents still exist as in the case of the act drawn between the General Cemetery Company and the Church of England to stipulate a portion of the consecrated ground of Kensal Green to be set aside for the use of the parish of St. Luke in Chelsea. These transactions became more and more frequent following the introduction of the Burial Act 1 July 1852, which enforced a stop on burials taking place in existing intra-mural London's churchyards.

The paperwork that regulated the contracts between a cemetery company and the Church was just one side of the administrative coin. More complexity is to be found in the administrative documentation that recorded the legal aspects of the formation of a joint-stock cemetery company including its capital, structure of its shareholdings, and rights and obligations of the shareholders. The initial capital of a typical cemetery company was divided into shares of £25 each, as in the case of the London Cemetery Company, which owned Highgate and Nunhead cemeteries. With the financial transaction in the purchase of a share, the buyer entered an agreement of rules and regulations set for the Government of the Company, which subscribers had to observe and comply with. In a share issued by the General Cemetery Company, the rules were listed directly on the back of the actual document. These stated, among other points, that the responsibility of the proprietors was limited to the amount of the respective shares, and that new shareholders were not entitled to vote in the first six months. Also from here, we understand that voting rights were related to the number of shares owned: five shares one vote; ten shares two votes. Shares were not transferable until three-fifths were paid up, to prevent new shareholders from investing for pure speculation purposes. If the administration of shareholders had its degree of complexity, it was in dealing with the day-to-day maintenance of the cemetery that the administrative qualities of the companies were at their best (see Figure 2.9).

The detailed administrative recording systems that cemetery companies developed were impressive. For example, among the archival records for the London Cemetery Company, it is possible to find burial receipts issued by the company to settle a payment. Among the list of burial costs pre-printed on the side is also stated that "a monument or gravestone, whose design must be approved by the company, will need to be built within 12 months from the burial date". This stipulation must have added extra pressures on the mourners that were already facing expensive funeral costs. The London Cemetery Company also introduced a logbook to list the type of

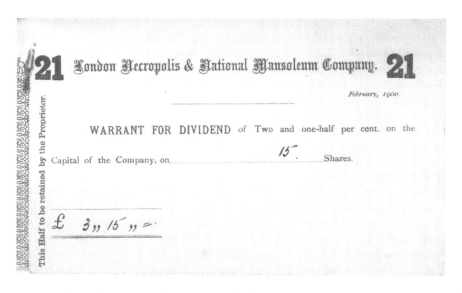

Figure 2.9 London Necropolis Company dividend token. 1900. Author's Collection.

preferred flowers or plants and the maintenance they needed. It is not possible to establish the exact date of when these records were first introduced, however, one surviving example includes entries between 1934 and 1940 and is specifically related to squares 1–62 which was the way Highgate Cemetery was subdivided for the administration of the graves. Things got more complex as cemeteries were gradually becoming filled. Detailed location records of each grave and its owners had to be kept along with the deeds of each one of the sales. The extent of this administration was new to burials, and it was mainly in place to guarantee a degree of governance within the companies, as well as the running of the actual cemeteries and control over the flow of money in and out. If on one side this could be seen as an empire of paper records, on the other the structured recording system led to a better organised way of keeping records of who was deceased, where they would have been buried, what the status of their grave was and who was responsible for it. This rationalised and organised system also helped to control the business of people tracing their ancestors or next of kin, in the degree that was allowed, as in the case of a letter sent to the secretary of the General Cemetery Company asking for help in identifying a grave.

To counterbalance the more internal administrative aspects of a cemetery company, it is important also to understand what the commercial strategies adopted by the cemetery companies to promote their business were, in particular how they made use of the media to advertise and gauge the interest of potential investors as well as new clients. The language they adopted in the advertisements that appeared in the press at the time was particularly captivating and designed to address all the key aspects that their prospective clients were looking for when buying a burial plot. When the London Cemetery Company opened Highgate Cemetery for business in 1839 it employed commercial strategies to attract potential customers to buy burial plots, part of this was to run a series of advertising campaigns in newspapers and magazines. In one particular extract that appeared in October 1839, in the weekly magazine *The Era*, Highgate Cemetery is described as "secure, elevated, and admirable grounds". It also describes its catacombs as "excellent" and states that "police attend all night". The advert even includes the omnibus fares from selected locations in London. They continued to advertise extensively in newspapers for many years after the cemetery opened.

The new cemeteries, however, were also criticised by Loudon, who described them as "inadequate", "unsafe", "overcrowded" and not well built as he found the foundation of the tombs to be "insufficient". Curl reports in his article "The Design of Early British Cemeteries", published in the *Journal of Garden History*, that Loudon's campaign of criticism on cemetery design had been raging since 1830 when some of the private cemeteries were already open for business (Liverpool Necropolis for example opened in 1825). Perhaps this was also one of the reasons why the private companies did not follow Loudon's published research on how to layout and maintain cemeteries. More criticism was raised later on in the nineteenth century by gardener and journalist William Robinson (1838–1935), an advocate of cremation and urn-burial.

Robinson was known primarily for promoting the "wild garden" (a movement that rejected the regimented Victorian formal gardening) and for designing the landscape for London's first crematorium in Golders Green (opened in 1902). In his book, *God's Acre Beautiful or The Cemeteries of the Future* published in 1880, Robinson expresses his concerns over the redundant Victorian funeral industry:

> What a gain it would be to get rid of much of this Monster Funeral, the most impudent of the ghouls that haunt the path of progress! Vulgar shows may, of course, be indulged in as much one way as the other; but it is pleasant to think of the ugly things and trades that may be abolished in cities when urn-burial became practicable.
>
> (19)

Robinson also warns that the commercial scope of the funeral industry may lead to overcrowding in suburban cemeteries:

> So large and so important a question as the burial of the dead should never be in the hands of those who merely regard it for money-making. It is well known that the profits from certain cemeteries in some of the pleasantest suburbs of London are very large; the temptation to continue burial in them, longer than decency or sanitary reasons would permit, will probably lead to danger in the future from the pollution of air and water. The present state of some of our cemeteries close to London is already dangerous and offensive.
>
> (59)

Yet, if the use of printed media to advertise the opening of a new cemetery in London was unprecedented, so too was the administrative complexity of the new suburban cemeteries as private enterprises. Sombart defined these as an "integrated system of relationships treated as an entity in the sciences of law and accounting". Indeed, it was through these two disciplines (law and accounting) that the cemetery companies institutionalised and regulated burials, just like any other private company.

It is relevant in this respect to also note that the abstract nature of the rules and regulations of an enterprise was, in Sombart's view, considered as an independent economic organism that was created over and above the individual(s) who constituted it. This brings us to critically assess the Victorian cemetery as an abstract institution and a bureaucratic machine, which was formally set up to serve the common good, but practically brought financial reward to its investors. As a consequence, burial was possibly reduced to a commodified and depersonalised financial transaction.

The physical appearance of the cemetery belies its commercial nature, with its distinctive architectural language and its natural landscape, yet everything was an orchestration of the cemetery's commercial nature. However, it is also true that the work of the cemetery companies had the effect of weakening the traditional Anglican control of burial provision in favour of other denominations, under a clause established by the Act of Parliament that permitted the private companies to operate a new cemetery.

To conclude this section we can say that a process of rationalisation of burials took place specifically with the introduction of a new administrative system that recorded and regulated the transactions between the cemetery companies, central government, the Church and the private parties, whether investors or third party buyers. Despite this systematised approach to order and governance, the commercial nature of the early Victorian cemeteries was still a problematic one on many levels, as it was criticised for their speculative nature as well as quality and standards. In particular, there were complaints about the lack of appropriate drainage systems in most of the new cemeteries (which was also a public health issue) and the lack of maintenance of the plantations and landscapes (Loudon and Robinson). This criticism must have been true, at least in part, as there was no specifically appointed authority to supervise the work of the companies in terms of quality and standards, even though most companies were granted permission to open a new cemetery by an Act of Parliament.

Lastly, this chapter attempted to deconstruct and analyse the main elements composing the paradigm of London's Victorian private cemeteries. From the existing literature and research material gathered there is strong evidence suggesting that the changes brought by cemetery companies to death culture in London were unprecedented and impressive in scale. We should remind ourselves how relatively quickly things changed over 20 years in terms of cemetery design, from the opening of Kensal Green Cemetery in 1833 to the integration of a railway link between London and Brookwood Cemetery in 1854. These companies contributed to a process of rationalisation of burial that eventually played a part in setting new standards in funerals, by making them available to the larger spectrum of society. The directors of the cemetery companies were stimulated to activate change in burials on many levels, from religious and political to hygienic and financial. The administrative structure set in place by these companies allowed for new registers and paperwork to be introduced to manage the large administration of the newly formed businesses.

Motives were matched by the architectural styles and landscape design the companies adopted, which shaped their public image and perception. Funerary architecture became a metaphor that expressed individualistic values and social status for the middle classes at the time. Paradoxically, as the middle classes became more visible in the space of the Victorian cemeteries, the graves of the lower classes became almost completely invisible. We also saw how the landscape in the Victorian cemeteries attempted to address the two contrasting aspects of nature (benevolent and destructive) through the medium of science and its findings of the healthy qualities of vegetation. The landscape in the Victorian cemeteries drew heavily from the eighteenth-century arrangements seen in aristocratic country estates and became a commercial version of the more traditional English landscaped garden. By observing the paradigm of the Victorian cemetery we can also identify what kind of social changes were taking place at the time. Firstly, we can say that it was a sign of the social changes that took place in the death culture in Victorian London. The speculative companies were after commercial success and needed to expand their market and meet the needs of the potential clients. However, leaving aside the commercial aspects of these companies, London's burial reform would not have happened without the intervention of private enterprises that initiated a process of dramatic transformation in the death culture and beyond that stimulated and influenced the character of their immediate local context, as we will see in the coming chapters.

Bibliography

"A Bill for Preventing the Unlawful Disinterment of Human Bodies and for regulating Schools of Anatomy." 1829. *The Lancet* 12, no. 298 (May 15): 205–09. Accessed June 30, 2021. https://doi.org/10.1016/S0140-6736(02)98743-X

Andrews, Malcolm. 1994. "The Metropolitan Picturesque." In *The Politics of the Picturesque. Literature, Landscape and Aesthetics since 1770*, edited by Stephen Copley and Peter Garside, 282–98. Cambridge: Cambridge University Press.

Ariès, Philippe. 2008. *The Hour of Our Death*. New York, Toronto: Vintage Books.

Arnold, Dana. 1982. *Rural Urbanism. London Landscapes in the Early Nineteenth Century*. Manchester, New York: Manchester University Press.

Blanchard, Samuel Laman. 1843. *The Cemetery at Kensal Green: the grounds & monuments. With a memoir of His Royal Highness the late Duke of Sussex*. London: Cunningham & Mortimer. Accessed April 8, 2020. http://access.bl.uk/item/viewer/ark:/81055/vdc_100023808732.0x000001#?c=0&m=0&s=0&cv=0&xywh=-1476%2C-147%2C4557%2C2906

Bland, Olivia. 1986. *The Royal Way of Death*. London: Constable & Company Ltd.

Briggs, Asa. 1968. *Victorian Cities*. Harmondsworth: Penguin Books.

Brooks, Chris W. 1989. *Mortal Remains*. Exeter: Wheaton Publishers Ltd.

Broun, Richard B. 1851. *Extramural Sepulture – Synopsis of the London Necropolis Company and National Mausoleum at Woking in the County of Surrey*. London: Trelawney Saunders.

Clarke, John M. 2004. *London's Necropolis. A Guide to Brookwood Cemetery*. Stroud: Sutton Publishing.

Curl, James Stevens. 1984. "The Design of Early British Cemeteries." *Journal of Garden History* 4, no. 3: 223–54.

Curl, James Stevens. 2001. *Kensal Green Cemetery. The Origins and Development of the General Cemetery of All Souls, Kensal Green, London, 1824–2001*. Chichester: Phillimore & Co.

Curl, James Stevens. 2004. *The Victorian Celebration of Death*. Thrupp: Sutton Publishing.
Dyos, Harold J., and Michael Wolff. 1973. *The Victorian City, Images and Realities*. London and Boston: Routledge & Kegan Paul.
Dyos, Harold J. 1982. *Exploring The Urban Past. Essays in Urban History*. Cambridge: Cambridge University Press.
Etlin, Richard A. 1984. *The Architecture of Death, The Transformation of the Cemetery in Eighteenth-Century Paris*. Cambridge (Massachusetts), and London (England): MIT Press.
Fyfe, Paul. ([2015] 2020). *By Accident or Design. Writing the Victorian Metropolis*. Oxford: Oxford University Press.
Gaskell, Peter. 1833. *The Manufacturing Population of England*. London: Baldwin and Cradock.
Houses of Parliament Archives – Anatomy Act – 1844. *Hansard Anatomy Act – HC Debate 11 June 1844. Vol. 75. CC. 523–34*. Accessed August 24, 2020. https://api.parliament.uk/historic-hansard/commons/1844/jun/11/anatomy-act
Houses of Parliament Archives – Public Health. 1833. *Public Health – HC Deb 21 February 1833. Vol 15 CC. 1049–59*. Accessed August 24, 2020. https://api.parliament.uk/historic-hansard/commons/1833/feb/21/public-health
Hurren, Elizabeth T. 2012. *Dying for Victorian Medicine. English Anatomy and its Trade in the Dead Poor, c. 1834–1929*. Basingstoke: Palgrave Macmillan.
Ingen-Housz, John. 1779. *Experiments Upon Vegetables. Experiments Upon Vegetables Discovering Their Great Power of Purifying the Common Air in the Sun-shine, and of Injuring it in the Shade and at Night. To which is joined, A new Method of Examining the Accurate Degree of Salubrity of the Atmosphere*. London: P. Elmsly and H. Payne.
Jackson, Kenneth T., and Camilo Jose Vergara. 1989. *Silent Cities: The Evolution of the American Cemetery*. New York: Princeton Architectural Press.
Jalland, Pat. 1999. *Death in the Victorian Family*. Oxford: Oxford University Press.
Johnson, Malcolm. 2001. *Bustling Intermeddler? The Life and Work of Charles James Blomfield*. Leominster: Gracewing. Accessed June 9, 2021. https://www.google.co.uk/books/edition/Bustling_Intermeddler/xLAX1Pb1bhwC?hl=en
Johnson, Peter. 2008. "The Modern Cemetery: A Design for Life." published in the journal, *Social & Cultural Geography* 9, no. 7 (November): 777–89. London: Routledge.
Justyne, William. 1865. *Guide to Highgate Cemetery*. London: J. Moore, Exeter Street.
Litten, Julian. 1991. *The English Way of Death: The Common Funeral Since 1450*. London: Robert Hale Ltd.
Loudon, John Claudius. ([1843] 1981). *On the Layout, Planting and Managing of Cemeteries and on the Improvement of Churchyards*. Redhill: Ivelet Books Ltd.
Loudon, John Claudius. 1832. *The Gardener's Magazine*, March. London: Longman, Rees, Orme, Brown, Green, and Longman.
Loudon, John Claudius. 1829. *The Gardener's Magazine and Register of Rural and Domestic Improvement*, Vol. 5 (February): 214. Accessed March 1, 2020. https://books.google.co.uk/books?id=h2JJAAAAMAAJ&pg=PA214&dq=%22Metropolitan+Sepulchre%22&hl=en&sa=X&ved=0ahUKEwif5qrpt6TeAhWOecAKHaKfBAsQ6AEILzAB#v=onepage&q=%22Metropolitan%20Sepulchre%22&f=false

Mayhew, Henry. ([1861–2] 2010). *London Labour & the London Poor*. Oxford: Oxford University Press.

Matless, David. 1998. *Landscape and Englishness*. London: Reaktion Books.

McKellar, Elizabeth. 1999. *The Birth of Modern London. The Development and Design of the City 1660–1720*. Manchester: Manchester University Press.

Olsen, Donald J. 1976. *The Growth of Victorian London*. London: B.T. Batsford Ltd.

Parsons, Brian. 2018. *The Evolution of the British Funeral Industry in the 20th Century. From Undertaker to Funeral Director*. Bingley: Emerald Publishing Limited.

Paxman, Jeremy. 2011. *Empire: What Ruling the World did to the British*. London: Penguin Books Ltd.

Ragon, Michel. 1983. *The Space of Death: A Study of Funerary Architecture, Decoration, and Urbanism*. Charlottesville: University Press of Virginia.

Richardson, John. 2004. *Highgate Past*. London: Historical Publications Ltd.

Robinson, David. 1995. *Saving Graces: Images of Women in European Cemeteries*. London: W. W. Norton.

Robinson, William. 1880. *God's Acre Beautiful or The Cemeteries of the Future* (3rd Edition with Illustrations ed.). London: The Garden Office.

Rugg, Julie. 1992. *The Rise of Cemetery Companies in Britain*. University of Stirling. Accessed May 25, 2021 https://dspace.stir.ac.uk/handle/1893/2017#.YKz yOpEY

Sheppard, F. H. W. 1973. *Survey of London: Volume 37: Northern Kensington*. British History Online. Accessed May 25, 2021. https://www.british-history.ac.uk/survey-london/vol37

Smiles, Sam. 2016. "The Fall of Anarchy: Politics and Anatomy in an Enigmatic Painting by J.M.W. Turner." *Tate Papers*. No. 25, Spring. Accessed May 25, 2021. https://www.tate.org.uk/research/publications/tate-papers/25/fall-of-anarchy-politics-anatomy-turner

Sombart, Werner. 2001. *Economic Life in the Modern Age*. New Brunswick, New Jersey: Transaction Publishers.

Suzuki, Akihito. 2007. "Lunacy and Labouring Men." In *Medicine, Madness and Social History. Essays in Honour of Roy Porter*, edited by R. Bivins and J. V. Pickstone, 118–28. Basingstoke, New York: Pelgrave Macmillan.

Taylor, Lou. 1983. *Mourning Dress. A Costume and Social History*. London: George Allen & Unwin Ltd.

Urban, Sylvanus [Edward Cave]. 1835. "Panorama of Pere-Lachaise." *The Gentleman's Magazine* (January): 74. Accessed May 26, 2021. https://babel.hathitrust.org/cgi/pt?id=uc1.l0071190250&view=1up&seq=88

3 Suburbs/Kensal Green

3.1 Metropolitan picturesque

The need to identify a quick solution to address London's lack of burials eventually led to the introduction of private cemeteries in the outskirts of London. Kensal Green, in 1833, was the first one of this new typology of burial spaces. For cemetery history scholar Richard Etlin, the introduction of new cemeteries in Victorian London marked an unprecedented evolution from the medieval graveyard to a modern system of burials. In his book *The Architecture of Death* (1984) Etlin discusses how the new designs of Victorian cemeteries became the preferred alternative to the small graveyards in use since the Middle Ages and notoriously associated with the macabre aspects of death. This however was not a seamless and fast transition, as graveyards still remained in use while the new cemeteries were getting established. Etlin also comments on how original Victorian cemeteries are for combining in a picturesque manner landscaped vegetation and architecture. Ultimately, in his view, the new picturesque landscape designs adopted in Victorian cemeteries originates from the garden arrangements seen in England in early eighteenth-century country estates (163).

The notion of picturesque in the urban context was also studied by Malcolm Andrews in his 1994 seminal essay "The Metropolitan Picturesque". There, the author argues that the picturesque was effectively an architectural principle in the development of Victorian London. In this respect, Victorian cemeteries were the manifestation of a local jurisdiction beyond the urban setting of the city, and therefore connected, in an unprecedented way, the urban and the rural aspects of a city (285). Undoubtedly the opening of the new cemeteries outside the urban centre of London contributed to an irreversible character-change of the surrounding areas, and activated a process of transformation from rural to urban. Locations such as Kensal Green became one of the early incubators for London's metropolitan expansion, where urbanisation took place organically and without a structured plan. Somehow the new private cemeteries highlighted the hybrid nature of the liminal space where they came to exist: in between the urban and the rural.

DOI: 10.4324/9781003178934-4

As a new typology of burial they embodied an "urban rurality" that combined elements of both, such as the picturesque and the functional. In this respect we could say that they shared the same genetic make-up of what became known as the typology of the municipal park that Dyos defined as:

> A Victorian transmutation of the English landscaped part of the eighteenth century and of the botanical garden which developed with such force in the late-Georgian and Regency period. [...] It provided a blend of the exotic and the indigenous in a way which no other English art could excel and contributed more subtly than we tend to think to the quality of urban life both and since.
>
> (1982, 61)

Dyos also points out that:

> Collectively, the parks, commons, walks, burial grounds, made a decent difference to the places that had them. They gave a place a style.
>
> (61)

Two character-defining moments for the Kensal Green area came with the cutting of the Paddington Arm of the Grand Union Canal in 1800 and the arrival of the cemetery in 1833. These two major changes in the landscape delineated the future trajectory for the development of the area and integration in the metropolis via transport routes. To get a visual sense of how those changes took place in particular around the Kensal Green area, we can look at the 1847 "New Topographical Map of the Country in the Vicinity of London" drawn by James Wyld (see Figure 3.1). From the section featuring North Kensington, Kensal Green and part of Paddington, we can see how, at a relatively short distance from the northwest boundaries of Kensington Gardens and Paddington, along the Harrow Road, the urban density of the built environment did drop dramatically, and the character of these areas were predominantly rural. In the top centre part of the map, it is possible to see the site where Kensal Green Cemetery was established – wedged between the Regent Canal (marking its south boundary), and the Harrow Road (marking the North part of the cemetery).

In the first few years after its completion, the waterway connection was a commercial success, however, it was eventually superseded by the arrival of the railway, which provided faster connections across the country. However, as the commercial traffic of the canal system diminished these were still used by Londoners for out of town pleasure trips. There were passenger boats that connected Paddington to Uxbridge. In 1818 in his book *Single Day Excursions from the Metropolis* (Vol. 2), water-colour artist and engraver John Hassell, recommended the journey by water (on the Union Canal)

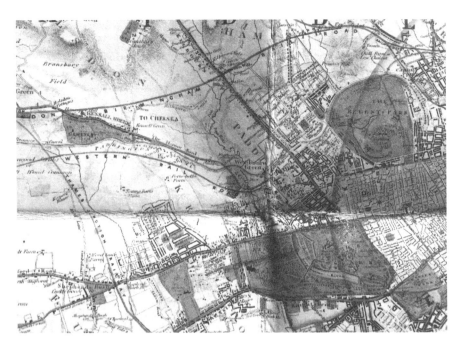

Figure 3.1 Detail of "The Vicinity of London" historical map by James Wyld, showing the location of Kensal Green Cemetery in relation to the urban core of London. 1847. Author's Collection.

to Harrow-on-the-Hill, and he describes the scenery along the way. From Hassell's book, we get a sense of the charming rural qualities the vicinity of the cemetery still retained at the time (243–50). Hassell reminds the readers that Harrow-on-the-Hill (only ten miles from London at the time) is the highest hill in the county of Middlesex and that its hilltop commands views over the metropolis (looking east) and the Surrey Hills (towards south) and Windsor Castle (243). Hassell provides details for road and water routes to reach Harrow, which include Kensal Green in the journeys. The unobstructed views over Wormwood Scrubs (from the Union Canal near Kensal Green) are mentioned as picturesque at any time of the day. Most of the properties along the way were complemented by landscaped gardens and well-kept fields. Considering also that the passenger's boats described by the author had on-board facilities to provide refreshments to the passengers along the journey, one gets a sense of the leisurely type of experience the day-trippers had, venturing on those out-of-the-city excursions. From Hassell's description, we gather that Kensal Green was already a known location among the genteel classes of London (or at least West London). It was known that Harrow Road, along Kensal Green Cemetery, was one of the Royal Family's favourites, and they often stopped in the area to admire its rural settings and views (*Morning Advertiser* 1846, 4). Victorian editor and writer Edward Watford in his 1878 publication titled *Old and New London: Volume 5* reported that "beyond the cemetery there is but little of interest to note in this part of Paddington. An old tavern once stood here, called The Plough" (222). Watford is referring to the part of Harrow Road on the west end of Kensal Green Cemetery, leading out of London (see Figure 3.2).

Undeniably the arrival of the cemetery in 1833 did contribute, with its landscaped plantation, to picturesque qualities of this part of London. Not only this but it also provided architectural interest both with its chapels and funeral architecture, all of which was visible from the Union Canal to the day-trippers following the routes drawn by Hassell in his excursion books. In an article that appeared in *The Gentleman's Magazine* in January 1835 (only two years after the opening of Kensal Green Cemetery), the journalist sang his praises of the new London cemetery for its ornamental qualities:

Figure 3.2 Print showing the Plough Tavern in Kensal Green set against rural surroundings near the Harrow Road in 1820. Author's Collection.

> We are glad to see a partial adoption in this country of the ornamental cemeteries of our neighbours, particularly as it is likely to put a stop to the baneful practice of burial in crowded towns, and as it is calculated to encourage the arts of architecture and sculpture.
>
> (Urban 1835, 74)

British author and journalist Samuel Laman Blanchard, in his guide book *The Cemetery at Kensal Green: the grounds & monuments*, published in 1843, praised the cemetery as an escape from the gloomy graveyards of the metropolis. In a passage, Blanchard states:

> What an escape from the atmosphere of London burial-places to the air of Kensal Green – from the choker charnel-house to that wide verdant expanse, studded with white tombs and infinite shapes and stone-marked graves covered with flowers of every brilliant dye.
>
> (2)

In another part of the guide book Blanchard describes the novelty of the cemetery natural landscape:

> The surrounding landscape, so rich in cultivation, in character so diversified, in extent so sweeping. ... It is scarcely ten years since the sheep were driven from their pasture, and already there have been about six thousand interments within that noble and spacious enclosure.
>
> (4)

Although Blanchard's writing style may come across as bias to the new cemetery, it is, however, undeniable that the establishment of new suburban cemeteries, such as Kensal Green, provided an unprecedented opportunity at the time to pioneer new funerary architecture and art that manifested itself in a broad range of forms and materials. The combination of an especially designed and planted natural landscape, complemented by the architecture of the tombs and mausolea, was modern and hygienically safe. This was a major departure from the congested urban churchyards and a very modern statement at the time about how death culture was undergoing a unique change. With regard to this Blanchard noted that:

> There is no late step in the progress of opinion or the habits of society so broad as the distinction between the city Churchyards and the suburban cemetery.
>
> (1)

Echoing Blanchard, one can say that the way death and burial were changing in early Victorian London was seen as a sign of social, civic and cultural progress but also as a generator of early integration and urbanisation in otherwise rural areas. Indeed the access to the picturesque rural settings of that part of outer London, and day trips away from the busy city, was, in early Victorian London, limited to those with disposable incomes who could afford the time off work to explore the countryside beyond London's urban boundaries. We have seen earlier with Hassell and Blanchard a positive appreciation of developments such as new commercial transport routes or the large scale of Kensal Green Cemetery. Along with activating a character-change of the area's rural settings, these also unleashed further developments and fast urbanisation of that part of London. Curl touches briefly on the spatial consequences that manifested following the implementation of the cemetery. The historian points out that within a decade of the cemetery's consecration, changes took place which "irreversibly altered the genius of Kensal Green" (2001, 303–5).

The apathy of local landowners overlaid with the bureaucracy of both Church and later local authorities, and a small local community with no sense of collective agency, are some of the elements that made it difficult to visualise a plan for the development of the area from the start. This however was not atypical for London, as the capital resisted centralised planning and instead preferred organic and scattered growth that was somehow unpredictable (Sheppard 1973, 333–39). The readability of the built environment in the Victorian metropolis was addressed by American historian Steven Marcus in his essay "Reading the Illegible" which is part of the publication *The Victorian City: Images and Realities*. There Marcus states that:

> The discontinuities and obscurities, the apparent absence of large, visibly related structures, the disorganisation, and disarticulations, seem to compose the structure of chaos, a landscape whose human, social and natural parts may be related simply by accidents, a random agglomeration of mere appearances.
>
> (1973, 257)

Although at first sight, the formation of nineteenth-century London may have appeared as incoherent and even accidental, its visual appearance was the outcome of a new and complex reality. Partly due to land ownership but also because of the speculative opportunities of private investors, buildings happened for specific reasons. Sometimes those reasons may not be apparent or visible to us today, but there is always the motivation behind a capital investment that manifests in a building. A critique of the formation of the urban space in relation to capitalism has been widely studied and theorised by Michel Foucault. In his lecture series book *Security, Territory, Population. Lectures at the Collège de France, 1977–78* the author explains that since the eighteenth century, the urban space of the city had undergone dramatic changes. These included cutting new routes through the existing fabric of the city, widening roads to improve ventilation and preventing the nesting of diseases. Although these interventions were primarily done for hygienic reasons, they were also implemented to improve the economy of the city, its trade networks of exchange, and the circulation of goods in and out of the city. For Foucault, this process was also related to that of security and surveillance over the circulation of goods and people (2009, 18). To summarise, for Foucault, trade networks and commercial aspects generated improvements of the built environment of a city, yet the urban space was primarily tailored to fit the purpose of production and consumption. Also, the urban space of the city started to become a clockwork-like structure that promoted efficiency and functionality, through spatial and social order in the name of commerce, governance and hygiene. It is worth remembering, however, that although Foucault's theories provide a critical and valid platform for discussion, they are only partly applicable to the specific context of nineteenth-century London.

Among other scholars, Dyos specifically studied the urban expansion of London and its population movement and formulated an original theory that identified two contrasting yet complementary processes of centripetal and centrifugal forces taking place, almost simultaneously, in Victorian London. In his view, "the centripetal forces helped to release the powerful centrifugal ones" (1982, 39). Dyos posits that the "metropolitanisation" process occurred in London during the nineteenth and twentieth-century. For Dyos, London's dominating influence over the national economy and political scene was already emerging, even before new technological progress released the industries from the dependence on coal supplies in the early twentieth century. In this respect, London acted as a magnet not just at a provincial or regional scale, but on a national one as well. In this first centripetal shift, people moved to the city or within its metropolitan radius, attracted by the possibilities that London represented at the time. In an extract from his essay Dyos explains:

> [This] meant packing London with people from the country, with country ways, with provincial attitudes perhaps, foreign customs certainly, which produced in the capital a concentration of wealth or control over it and therefore a disproportionate share per head of benefits (and conceivably, the penalties) of a relatively rich society.
>
> (39)

Dyos defines the second and contrasting process as a "centrifugal deployment" of the population into the metropolitan (suburban) areas. The author directly claims that this process was a way to "homogenise" the provincial behaviour and attitudes of a very diverse population of London into a "metropolitan culture" (39). Although Dyos proposed a plausible theory of the formation of London's social fabric, it needed to be tested in the context of specific areas, to be validated. London's unique organic growth and resilience to centralised and structured urban plans is something we have already encountered in Chapter 1 when discussing the public health and sanitary reasons that triggered the formation of the new Victorian cemeteries. In his book *By Accident or Design* historian and academic Paul Fyfe tries to understand the emergence of the modern metropolis as "a unique phenomenon in the history of human settlement" (2020, 1). Fyfe takes as a starting point a curated selection of Victorian writing about "accidents" in the metropolis. His approach provides an original reading of nineteenth-century London, which is not about the incoherence or illegibility of the city but it is about change and "the new enfranchisement of chance" that started to emerge in Victorian England. Fyfe is concerned with what he calls "design failures" when accidents take place in a metropolis where the urban and industrial life are blurring into one another (1). Although the aim of this research is not to explore the consequences of design failures, it echoes Fyfe's reminders that the emergence of the modern metropolis was a unique event in human history. In this respect this book celebrates the Victorian spirit in testing, through design, technology and science, to innovate and improve the city and urban life.

3.2 Testing ground

On 29 September 1849, *The Illustrated London News* published an article titled "Picturesque Sketches of London Past and Present". Penned by the Victorian poet and novelist Thomas Miller, the article praises the healthy qualities of out-of-town burials, and dismisses the inner-city churchyards as a threat to public health. Miller had a love for the countryside, and in his piece also made a point about how important it was, in his view, that the dead were away from the hustle and bustle of everyday urban life. In one passage he says that:

> Their business with the world has ended, they have finished their long day's work [...]. The price of corn, the state of the money-market, or the rising and falling of the funds, are matters which ought to be discussed far away from these we followed, and wept over, and consigned to their silent chambers, there to sleep till the last trumpet sounds.
>
> (221–22)

Miller was not alone in believing that the living and the dead should be separated and spatially distant. As we saw in Chapter 1, Chadwick also shared the same views, and not only for sanitary reasons, but also for respect towards the dead. However, new developments started to materialise in the vicinity of the cemetery over ten years after its opening. Looking back at Wyld's 1847 map it is possible to see that new development took place along the waterways with Kensal New Town, where laundries and workshops were established. Workers and communities that could not afford to live in London lived close to where they worked and started to populate the area. The development of Kensal New Town was initiated in the early 1840s along Harrow Road, immediately at the east end of Kensal Green Cemetery (in the direction of Central London). A railway station on the London to Birmingham line was opened in 1842; it was named Willesden Junction and was an exchange station between the London to Birmingham line and the Thames Junction Railway which in turn linked the Kensington Canal to the Thames (as stated by Nick Catford in the Disused Stations website on 26 May 2017). It was used for both passengers and goods, particularly. This tidal creek flowed from Kensal Green, by North Kensington; the lower part was developed into the Kensington Canal between 1824–8 and ran along the west boundary of Brompton Cemetery, giving a picturesque quality to the site. There is a watercolour showing a view from what is now the West Brompton Station entrance by Victorian painter William Cowen (Hobhouse 1986, 322–38).

As mentioned at the start of the chapter, when the cemetery was first open Kensal Green was a small rural village of few houses. However, among the local community, there were some characters relevance to London's social and cultural life, such as the famous nineteenth-century gothic romance novelist William Harrison Ainsworth, who took up residence at Kensal Lodge in 1835. The small countryside property overlooked Kensal Green cemetery and Surrey Hills in the distance. In 1841 Ainsworth moved to an adjacent property called Kensal Manor House, which is marked in an 1888 map of the area, on the stretch of Harrow Road running towards the west end of Kensal Green Cemetery. There, together with the Kensal Lodge, Tavistock Villa and St. Mary's Terrace (the only one still existing today), a small cluster of buildings and private gardens were formed, overlooking Kensal Green Cemetery and Wormwood Scrubs (see Figure 3.3).

For 14 years, these two buildings, although located out of the city centre, became hubs of West London literary and social life thanks to Ainsworth being a lavish entertainer. Many famous Victorian literary figures came to dine at the two buildings, including novelist William Makepeace Thackeray (also known for his satirical works such as his 1848 novel *Vanity Fair*, and the 1844 novel *The Luck of Barry Lyndon*), George Cruikshank (the artist and illustrator of Dickens's work as well as some of Ainsworth's), politician Benjamin Disraeli and Charles Dickens (Ellis 1911, 270–71). Ainsworth was possibly the only record of local residents in the Kensal Green area, who was also a recognised public figure in the literature and publishing circles of London, and it was not clear if he had a personal connection with the cemetery. However, Dickens was emotionally attached to Kensal Green Cemetery as it was the resting place of his sister-in-law Mary Scott Hogarth (who died in 1837) and was buried there (Slater 2009, 100).

Following the arrival of the cemetery as well as the laundries and workshops in Kensal New Town, the community of local residents started to grow and by 1842 it had reached 2,000 individuals. As reported in a short article published on 19 May 1842 in *The St. James's Chronicle*, this saw a

68 Suburbs/Kensal Green

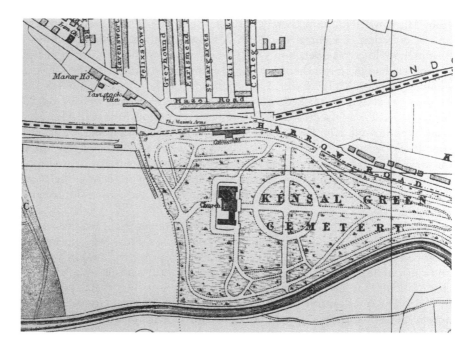

Figure 3.3 Detail of the 1888 map of the Kensal Green area showing the location of Kensal Lodge, Kensal Manor House, Tavistock Villa and St. Mary's Terrace. Author's Collection.

critical point that triggered the need for a place of worship for local residents (1). St. John's the Evangelist Church was the first building of significance to be built in the area after the completion of the cemetery and gave presence and agency to the community, as well as a physical focal point through belief. In a short notice published on Tuesday 14 November 1843 (No. 65 Vol. 6) by the *Ecclesiastical Gazette* (101), it was stated that the first stone for a new church in Kensal Green had been laid. The article mentioned that the land where the church was to be erected was donated by the All Soul College Oxford. It also pointed out that Kensal Green "comprises portions of the parishes of Chelsea, Paddington, Kensington, Willesden, and Hammersmith" (101). This gives us a sense of the strategic position of the new church, literally standing at the junction of so many parishes. St. John's Church stands on the busy crossroads of Harrow Road, Kilburn Lane and Ladbroke Grove and on the boundaries of the London boroughs of Brent, Kensington and the City of Westminster, in which it stands. It is effectively the first church of the City of Westminster when coming into London via the Harrow Road (see Figure 3.4).

Suburbs/Kensal Green 69

Figure 3.4 Print showing St. John the Evangelist Church. 1844. Author's Collection.

70 Suburbs/Kensal Green

Designed by Henry Edward Kendall Junior, St. John's is an early example of Victorian ecclesiastic architecture that combines, in an eclectic way, the Romanesque architectural features with a Gothic style chancel. Even in the actual materials, Kendall combines the typical yellow London brick with flintstone features (Baker 1989, 252–59). Although there are no apparent connections between St. John's and Kensal Green Cemetery, it is worth noticing that Kendall Junior's father was Henry Edward Kendall. His original Gothic style design for Kensal Green Cemetery (as we have seen in Chapter 2), was awarded first prize following a competition, but was never built. So it is an interesting coincidence to see that Kendall Junior was appointed to design the church in the first place. After its completion in 1844, St. John's facade became a prominent visual landmark in the area. Ainsworth was one of the first churchwardens at St. John's. The novelist had a deep appreciation for Gothic architecture and the history of London (Minott-Ahl, 2006). In an etching executed at the time of its completion, featuring a view of the church's twin towers from the Kensal Green entrance gate, the church contributed to the picturesque quality of the cemetery view towards Paddington (see Figure 3.5).

Figure 3.5 Etching showing the view from Kensal Green Cemetery over to St. John's Church (on the right-hand side). Undated. Author's Collection.

Both the new cemetery and the new church embody the technological advances in architecture and engineering that in the nineteenth century allowed them to be built in a very eclectic way by combining architectural styles: the Greek Revival adopted for Kensal Green Cemetery and the Romanesque-Gothic of St. John's. So even if there wasn't any apparent connection between the two, they started to create a visual dialogue together that contributed to the character of the area. For its strategic position, the new church also became a gateway to Kensal New Town. In the year St. John's was finally open for services, the Western Gas Company started the construction of their gas works, strategically positioned between both the canal and the railway (Curl 2001, 303–4). The plant was also located on the fringes of the wealthy part of West London; the company could supply gas to the southern districts of London, including Notting Hill, Ladbroke Grove and Kensington (Pedroche 2013, 114–6). The Western Gas Light Company produced cannel gas at the Kensal Green plant; this was a variety of coal-extracted gas that was more expensive to produce but produced a brighter quality of light. When gas was initially introduced it was mainly used for commercial purposes and street lighting, eventually it was also adopted for domestic use.

> There are in the aggregate upwards of a million and a half tons of coal used every year in the manufacture of gas in the metropolis, and the quantity of gas consumed amounted in the past year to about 13 millions of thousands of cubic feet.
>
> (Chubb 1876, 350)

From an 1865 map of Kensal Green & West Kilburn (see Figure 3.6) it is possible to see that the Gas Works occupied the area west of Kensal New Town, where laundries, small factories and workshops needed gas supply for their activity. What is evident at a glance from the map is that the arrangement of the new developments had no intention to isolate the cemetery but rather build in its proximity, which is a sign that it was seen as an asset to the area, rather than detrimental. Kensal Green Cemetery, the older buildings (pre-arrival of the cemetery), Kensal New Town and the new addition of the Gas Works formed the core of the new district of which the cemetery was at its heart.

Although there are very tenuous connections between the pre-existing cemetery and the development of the Gas Works in Kensal Green, the two became visually interconnected (as in the case of St. John the Evangelist Church), with the large scale of the new plant dramatically changing the landscape of the area. The picturesque views of Surrey Hills that were once a feature and pride of the cemetery were tainted by the pollution and disagreeable odour due to the nature of the gas production. With the coming of the Gas Works, the day excursions to Harrow-on-the-Hill, by water on the Union Canal as described so romantically by Hassell in 1818, were gone.

72 Suburbs/Kensal Green

Figure 3.6 Historical map of the Kensal Green built environment up to 1865. Author's Collection.

The coming of the Gas Works to the area was seen as both a nuisance that had effects on the "tone" of the area (see Figure 3.7). The General Cemetery Company (owners of the Kensal Green Cemetery) attempted to lobby with other local owners to act together against the Gas Light Company, to contain the smell emanating from the plant. Eventually, in 1872, the Western Gas Light Company was amalgamated to the Gas Light & Coke Company and eventually expanded on the land formerly owned by the General Cemetery Company (Curl 2001, 140). The plant was eventually converted to produce coal gas. In 1872 and later in 1886 and in 1889 the company updated all the machinery on the Kensal Green site (Pedroche 2013, 114–6).

Lewis Mumford in his book *The City in History*, explained that manufacturing plants for the production of illuminating gas became a feature in the edge of towns and cities. According to the American historian:

> Such structures were not necessarily evil; indeed with sufficient care in their segregation they may have been comely. What was atrocious was the fact that, like every other building in the new towns, they were dumped almost at random; the leakage of escaping gas scented the

Figure 3.7 View of Grand Union Canal (towards Paddington) with Kensal Green Cemetery on the left and Gas Works on the right, the railway line and telegraph poles. 1884. Author's Collection.

so-called gas-house districts, and not surprisingly these districts frequently became among the most degraded sections of the city. Towering above the town, polluting the air, the gas tanks symbolised the dominance of "practical" interests over life-needs.

(1991, 536)

Although, as Mumford mentioned, the gas works looked as though they were "dumped almost at random" along the edges of London; in the case of Kensal Green, their coming provided an opportunity for the local community to come together and challenge the Western Gas Company. An article published in the *Morning Advertiser* on 5 November 1846 reports that about 100 people, between workers from Kensal New Town and landowners such as All Souls College Oxford, signed a petition and expressed their concerns to the Western Gas Company directors about the consequence of the gas works on the environment of the area. In return the directors organised a public meeting to explain their intention to test a new method of production of gas that was less harmful to the environment and by consequence detrimental to the value of properties in the area (1). The explanations given by the company engineer at the meeting, about the new process, satisfied the community of locals, and eventually the construction of the gas holders could go ahead as planned. From the article it is also possible to gather that the opening of the establishment in

Kensal Green would bring more job opportunities and improve the local economy (1). Inevitably though, the gas works had negative consequences on the environment and social respectability of the area. However, the coming of the new industry in the area established a synergy within Kensal New Town in terms of local provision of workforce and economy. Both laundry and gas works fluctuated with the seasonal needs of West End residents. The laundry high season of work was between June and August, this coincided with the low season of gasworks, when the demand was lower in the hottest time of the year. This cycle between the two industries was an attractive opportunity for the domestic economies of families, as women were able to work in those periods when their husbands had less work or were out of work completely (Malcolmson 1981, 446).

In the early 1830s, the public health concerns focused on the dead and the question of suitable burial spaces; however by the early 1870s started to address the spaces for the living. On 3 April 1872, Prime Minister Benjamin Disraeli delivered his "Sanitas Sanitatum, Omnia Sanitas" (Health Cures All Health) speech, at the Free Trade Hall in Manchester. In a key passage Disraeli stressed the importance of public health, and he states:

> I think public attention regarding these matters ought to be concentrated upon sanitary legislation. That is a wide subject, and, if properly treated, comprises almost every consideration which has a just claim upon legislative interference. Pure air, pure water, the inspection of unhealthy habitations, the adulteration of food – these and many kindred matters may be legitimately dealt with by the legislature.

Disraeli's speech started a race to obtain a standard of habitability in all houses in London. The complex and individual bureaucratic system each local administration had in place made it almost impossible to achieve a standard across the metropolitan area. In a report on the situation of London dwellings published in 1874 it is possible to sense both the aspiration to achieve such a unified approach but also the frustration with the bureaucratic system. In a passage the writer states:

> The other point is one which can be attended to at once, and that is to obtain a "standard of habitability" of dwelling-houses for all London. This can be done by an Act of Parliament only; as, although it might perhaps be worked out from the different Acts now in force in the metropolis, yet, as each magistrate has his own opinion as to the interpretation of the Acts, and each local authority has issued different regulations under the Sanitary Act, no standard can possibly be arranged. It is much to his regret that the regulations were not made uniform for every district, which could readily have been done, as they were not in force until the signature of the Secretary of State had been affixed

thereto. This opportunity of uniformity having been lost, we now wait for further legislation.

(*Metropolitan Dwellings* 1874, 20)

Capitalist philanthropist Sidney Waterlow (involved in providing housing for London's lower classes) pointed out that the demolition of unhealthy houses would have reduced mortality and disease. These improvements, in his view, would have benefited the economy of the capital: "Waterlow claimed that for every person who died there were two more unfit for work through disease" (Heffer 2013, 800). The issue of rebuilding London housing stock was just as urgent as building new houses. In this respect the suburban areas, with more affordable space available, were the right places where to test new housing typologies. Kensal Green was in a favourable position for this, as a large portion or land, north-east of the cemetery, was still relatively rural and solely owned by All Souls College Oxford. An article which appeared in the *Kilburn Times and Western Post* on 24 September 1874 reports on how the Artizans' Company secured 80 acres of land in the area with the intention to establish the Queen's Park Estate in Kensal Green. In the article the new development was addressed as a new town, modelled on the Shaftesbury Park Estate the company had already initiated in Battersea. The housing typology of Queen's Park Estate was also adopted for the Hornsey Estate in North London (see Figure 3.8).

Effectively it was the size of a small town as, on the estate, they accommodated houses for about 16,000 people (5). The Artizans' Company believed that by giving the tenants a decent local environment they would have formed

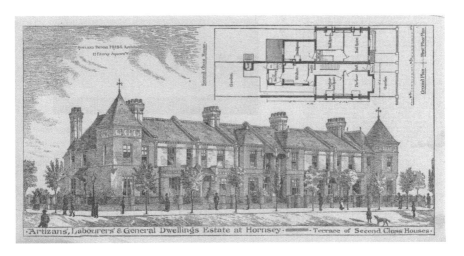

Figure 3.8 Artisans, Labourers & General Dwellings Estate at Hornsey by architect Rowald Plumbe. Print showing a typology of housing and the typical floor plans of the interiors. 1884. Author's Collection.

communities. The organisation promoted sobriety, frugality and temperance. Beyond the dwellings the Artizans' Company also built mission halls, institutes, shops and later a public library (see Figures 3.9, 3.10 and 3.11).

The Company provided all the houses with a front and back garden; however, the area was very densely built to maximise the number of houses on the site. The roads were wide and planted with lime trees, which gave the roads a more genteel and picturesque quality as the trees got established, as well as providing fresh air, since there wasn't any public garden in the estate. Queen's Park, like other developments initiated by the Artizans' Company, was also defined as an urban village or cottage estate. The secretary of the Artizans' Company, William Swindlehurst, promoted flower shows in Queen's Park as well as the company's other development in Battersea: "The flowers were judged where they grew in the gardens and yards, or on windowsills, by professional gardeners from Kew and Battersea Park – a tradition that continued into the twentieth century in council cottage estates" (Willes 2014, 234).

The Queen's Park Estate featured model dwellings arranged by typologies, designed for differently sized family incomes. For example, the Type 3 mid-range house would be a three-bedroom dwelling with a toilet as well as front and back garden (Whitehead, n.d.). Some of the Queen's Park Estate roads were also provided with gas mains, in case the lodges wanted to make

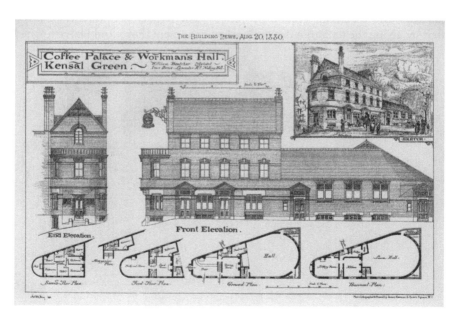

Figure 3.9 Coffee Palace and Worksman Hall Kensal Green. *The Building News*. 20 August 1880. Author's Collection.

Suburbs/Kensal Green 77

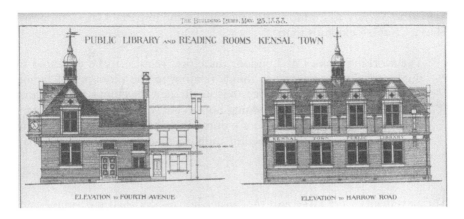

Figure 3.10 Public Library and Reading Rooms in Kensal Town London by Karslake and Mortimer Architects. *The Building News*. 25 May 1880. Author's Collection.

Figure 3.11 Postcard showing the reading room interiors of the public library in Kensal Town. 1905. Author's Collection.

use of the service. In an article published in 1876 in the *Journal of the Statistical Society of London*, the secretary of the Imperial Gas Company – Harry Chubb – explains that:

> The working classes of London, therefore, require to be educated in this particular among other things relating to the economy of living, and it is satisfactory to notice that in the new dwellings for artisans, and in some of the model lodging houses lately erected, the promoters of those excellent institutions are doing their best to this end by fitting the several rooms with the needful appliances, so that the occupiers may avail themselves.
>
> (365)

The pavements were large and the corner houses, by road junctions, were treated differently aesthetically and featured more distinctive architectural details. The layout of the roads and avenues also included planted trees, grass areas and large pavements. This arrangement created a greater distance between the actual road traffic and the houses. The presence of trees more green areas and gave more privacy to the houses and provided better air circulation on the roads and between buildings. This arrangement anticipated the work of Ebenezer Howard and Raymond Unwin with the Hampstead Garden Suburb in North London, in the early twentieth century, where the integration of housing design, circulation and landscaping (see Figure 3.12), were carefully considered through planning (Miller and Gray 1992, 51–67).

It is possible to get a sense of the scale of the project by looking at the figures of the 1881 annual report that stated that the number of houses completed in Shaftesbury Park Estate was 1,199; while on Queen's Park, where building was going on by then on an extensive scale, the number of houses completed reached a total of 1,248 (478). Most people living in the Queen's Park Estate commuted to work. This situation pushed the Artizans Company to get the railway companies to offer special rates for working class commuters, to make sure that people would stay in the suburb and not relocate elsewhere. Other means of transport, such as trams, served the area and the Kensal Green Cemetery, such as Line 60 that connected Kensal Green to Cricklewood via Paddington and Edgware Road (see Figure 3.13).

As much as living in the suburbs had an appeal for workers at the time, it also had its drawbacks like the daily commutes and the limitation of the hours of work. Therefore living in the suburbs was not an option after all for most of the London working classes (*Metropolitan Dwellings* 1874, 20). However, there is evidence of exchanges the Artizans' Company were having over time with the local railway service providers in their 1885 company's reports (4), to secure cheap train tickets to be used at particular times of the day by commuting workers.

Suburbs/Kensal Green 79

Figure 3.12 Hampstead Way part of the Hampstead Garden Suburb. Undated postcard showing the planned road layout and housing design. Author's collection.

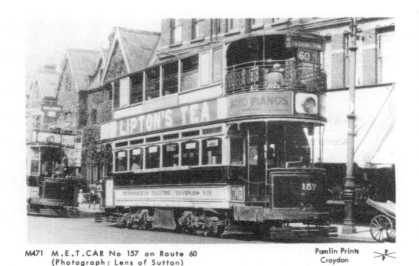

Figure 3.13 The Metropolitan Electric Tramways Limited operated electric tram services in the suburbs of London. Here is Line 60 servicing the Kensal Green area: Paddington – Edgware Road – Maida Hill – Kensal Green – Harlesden – Willesden – Willesden Green Station – Cricklewood. Early 1920s. Author's Collection.

80 Suburbs/Kensal Green

3.3 A new suburb

The essence of Kensal Green as a suburb was captured in a 1938 aerial view of Kensal Green, which shows the development of the area at its peak (see Figure 3.14). Here the gasometers of the former Western Gas Light Company and the plant of the motor manufacturers Sunbeam Talbot cling to the railway lines, as in the past warehouses did to wharves and rivers. The dense rows of terraced housing in Kilburn and Maida Vale can be seen in the distance and, in the foreground, Kensal Green Cemetery also densely filled with graves. This suburb was one of London's industrial inner districts, which shows how the relationship between the industry and the urban space of the city changed from the early Victorian period when the two were strictly intertwined, and the boundaries between urban and industrial life were more blurred (Fyfe 2020, 1–3).

Although, as we know, the suburb was not planned as a whole prior to the arrival of the cemetery, by the end of the nineteenth century it had its own spatial order that combined some key functions of urban life: dwelling, work, education, belief, social life and death. Each element contributes

Figure 3.14 [EPW058335] The Kensal Green Gas Works alongside the Kensal Green Cemetery and the surrounding residential area, Kensal Town, 1938. © Historic England

simultaneously to the suburb and to the functioning of the growing metropolis. For example the gas works in Kensal Green produced gas to light and heated the residences and streets of West London. The laundries in Kensal New Town were also providing services for residents located elsewhere in the city. The cemetery was serving the capital and not necessarily the local community. From an 1894 Ordnance Survey map of Kensal Green (see Figure 3.15), we can see that the cemetery was extended westward. The Gas Works were expanded and doubled in size from the original 1846 site. We can also notice that the junction where St. John's Church and the entrance to Kensal Green Cemetery are located is the fulcrum of the suburb. The crossing of the main roads features shops and other outlets to service the local communities. The crossing also marks the division in four quadrants between Harrow Road (east-west), Kilburn Lane (north) and Ladbroke Grove (south). Each quadrant has a function. Starting from the north west, this quadrant was where residences such as Hainsworth's Kensal Lodge and Kensal Manor House were located before the arrival of the cemetery. Maybe we would call this today the historical heritage area or cultural quarter. Going clockwise, the north-east quadrant was solely formed by the Queen's Park development and St. John's Church, so mainly residential.

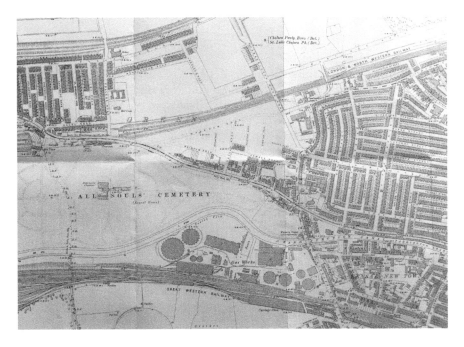

Figure 3.15 Historical map showing the development of the built environment in Kensal Green up to 1894. Author's Collection.

The south-east quadrant constituted by Kensal New Town features a mix of houses and light industry: laundries and furniture workshops and warehouses by the Union Canal. Finally the south-west quadrant is constituted by Kensal Green Cemetery (north of the Union Canal) and the Gas Works (north of the Union Canal).

Olsen theorised on how the process of the spatial reorganisation that took place in nineteenth-century London, by extension, produced what he defined as "single-purpose, homogeneous, specialised neighborhoods" (Olsen 1974, 267). In his view this process had started already in the seventeenth century "when Covent Garden, St. James's, and Bloomsbury were first developed, and the distinction between the City and the West End began to be made" (267) and reached its peak in Victorian times. Olsen also speculated that the spatial reordering of London was driven by specific motivations. He explained that:

> The Victorians were, in part consciously, transforming the metropolis into an environment designed to reinforce certain specific values, notably privacy for the individual and his family; specialisation and segregation were important means to that end. They gave London order and system, not – like the Paris of Baron Haussmann – essentially visual and spatial in nature; but rather functional, moral, and social. The virtues of today's London exist not in spite of, but as a result of, their approach.
>
> (267)

Reading the spatial arrangement of Kensal Green as a suburb, through Olsen's theory, we can say that the spatial organisation of the suburb started with the arrival of the cemetery. The new typology of burial, as seen in more detail in Chapter 2, prototyped a new system of ordering the dead in a space, that eventually, was also applied to the living, as in the case of the Queen's Park Estate. The presence of the industry in the suburb was mainly to do with services such as production of gas, laundries and small workshops, partly connected with the funeral industry (masonry, coffin making, undertakers or furniture). In this respect Kensal Green was not strictly "single-purpose" as theorised by Olsen; however, if we consider it from its social makeup, the suburb was most likely "homogenous", as its community of local residents was mostly formed by workers.

When looking at the aesthetics of the suburb we can see that the visual dialogue between the cemetery, St. John's Church, Gas Works and the Queen's Park Estate is one of juxtapositions. For example, the horizontal vast extension of the cemetery and housing contrasts and complements the vertical presence of the gasometers with their new aesthetic language that was both solid and ethereal at the same time, due to their distinctive, lace-like structures made of steel. Their presence, still to this day, is a distinctive visual landmark of Kensal Green as they "represent a valued local landmark, with intrinsic aesthetic appeal and associations with the industrial origins of the area" (Franklin 2015, 21).

Earlier in this chapter we looked at theories on the formation of new urban space. French philosopher Henri Lefebvre theorised on the notion of simultaneity concerning the formation of space and identified three key defining elements: the physical, social and mental space (2009, 12–3). For Lefebvre, it is not only about how urban space looks (aesthetics) but also its functions, social context and indeed individual experience and perception of the urban space people live in. Each one of the buildings that collectively form an urban built environment has a function that can be traced back to the social, and – in Lefebvre's words – they "serve to distinguish, but not to isolate, particular spaces" (16). For example, the Gas Works, the cemetery, the church and residential area are also spaces that beyond their spatial presence have a social function, and indeed also exist in the mental space of people that experience them, in their everyday life. As a whole, each element contributes to the distinctive identity and character of a place. In this respect, through its unique range of diverse and contradictory visual and spatial elements, Kensal Green provides a template for a new notion of built environment that challenged previous ideas of spatial harmony between buildings and functions.

For Lefebvre, civic and religious buildings historically acted as a guide or reference for the arrangement and harmonisation of the new built environment. In a passage he explains that:

> Facades were harmonised to create perspectives; entrances and exits, doors and windows were subordinates to facades – and hence also to perspectives; streets and squares were arranged in concord with the public buildings and palaces of political leaders and institutions. At all levels, from family dwellings to monumental edifices, from "private" areas to the territory as a whole, the elements of this space were disposed and composed in a manner at once familiar and surprising which even in the late twentieth century has not lost its charm.
>
> (2009, 47)

However, in the case of Kensal Green there weren't any of those guides or hierarchies in place to follow as references, to create harmonised perspectives, across the whole suburb. We can say though that a sense of harmonised perspectives was attempted within the context of each development, such as the cemetery, or Queen's Park Estate, where the Artizans' Company considered the street view and its social role as a shared space, and as a space of representation of civic life. Each one was a fully formed self-contained fully functioning system. But at the same time they were atomised, individualised, not necessarily explored or considered beyond the boundaries of each individual development. However, some developments had more visual impact than others.

For example the visual impact of Queen's Park Estate was very low key in scale, as it did not interrupt existing views across the suburb. The same was for the cemetery, the waterway and the railway. In their cases the visual impact was minimal as they were horizontal. But from 1845 the verticality of St. John's and the Gas Works redefined the landscape of the area, and they established themselves as the landmarks of Kensal Green and they spoke about private enterprise, industry and religion. They also spoke about capital, labour and social change through policies, but not of culture or governmental and civic presence as one would see in the historical part of London. The fragmentation and demarcation of the private spaces also spoke of separation, possibly segregation as well as control and order, but without an overarching civic authority that represented in some way the state or the government authority. Everything was in the hands of private landowners or entrepreneurs. Space was rationalised and ordered to their needs and means but not to those of local dwellers or workers. The work of capitalist philanthropists in the local area of Kensal Green mitigated and mediated the uncontrolled spread of private interests across the whole area. The results of the work started to manifest in the second half of the nineteenth and well into the twentieth century, particularly with regard to new housing and public open spaces such as Queen's Park Estate. With the new housing, schools and later a library also came to the area and started to provide the areas not only with new spaces for social interaction but also access to knowledge and culture. In the rural settings of pre-industrialised societies, one can say that the paradigm was not dissimilar, but in the context of Kensal Green, despite the rural setting, labour in the cultivated fields or pastures was replaced by labour in the factory. The railway connections that run through Kensal gave the area its very unique identity creating a series of separations and barriers, starting from the walls of the cemetery marking its boundaries to the railway tracks separating communities as well as the waterways, or the gas works segregating other areas. Slicing and dividing separate. Markers, walls, railways and waterways – they all act as dividers. For these reasons, bridges played a crucial role in connecting Kensal Green to other areas. For example, the main crossing points over the Grand Union Canal were at Ladbroke Grove, Carlton Bridge and Westbourne Park. There was also the Wedlake Street footbridge, but people until 1885 had to pay a toll to use it (McDonald and David 1990, 17–8).

To conclude, it is possible to say that Kensal Green, at least at the time, conformed to Harvey's theory on the fragmentation and institutionalisation of space, as at a glance here we can distinctively see areas rationally shaped by secular forces such as trade and industry. It is also possible to see the force of Foucault's argument on the rational improvements of the urban environment for hygienic reasons, hence the separation between residential areas and burial spaces. These also facilitated the growth of the city's economy and trade, as Kensal Green was certainly one of those industrial hubs that contributed to it. Although it is not possible to identify one place as the civic heart or centre of Kensal Green, it is also true that each development was a centre of its own: from the cemetery to the library, housing development and the workplaces. The combined presence of a new cemetery, industry, housing, transport links and other services for the communities that settled in the area provided a framework for a new spatial model of urban space, for the living and the dead. In the case of Kensal Green it is interesting to note that the area was initially identified as being the location of the first new typology of cemetery that served West London, and by the late nineteenth century was a suburb that accommodated one of the first large-scale housing projects for the working classes. So from a place (initially) associated with the burial of the dead, it became a place associated with industry and pioneering housing for the living. However, by contrast, for the poor and the destitute, the sick and the convicts, the insane and the elderly, the suburb was a place with gloomier prospects, a liminal space. For the maligned groups in society at the time, it was a place of segregation, as Masterman observes, "the places of all forgotten things" (1905, 155), yet it was an essential cog in the clockwork of London. Ultimately we can assert that the presence of the cemetery in a local context in Kensal Green contributed to stimulating a process of change, experimentation and development in terms of spatial arrangement and functions. The combination of all of those changes produces a new prototype of suburban space that simultaneously contributes to the decentralisation and formation of London's metropolitan areas.

Lastly we can speculate that Kensal Green Cemetery acted as a point of reference, a physical spatial anchor, in the otherwise open spaces of rural Kensal Green in the first part of the nineteenth century. Its cemetery along the transport routes into and out of London defined the orientation of navigation of this otherwise semi-rural area. Through its architectural aesthetics, the new cemetery acted as a beacon of new order, in the otherwise isolated and architecturally non-descriptive area. Its scale set the bar for the level of ambition and challenge necessary to innovate and invent new typologies of buildings and institutions that were unprecedented and unknown. Along these lines, two observations can be highlighted: first, that there was an obvious need for new concepts of urbanisation that were driven by economic development and structural transformation. Second, Kensal Green Cemetery and the suburb that eventually emerged in its surroundings are the manifestation of the policies of transition that at the time governed the urban growth of London. These spatially indifferent development policies have determined urban spaces of the everyday lives of urban citizens for better or – too often – worse. Although this was a top-down approach driven by capital investors, we can say that the private forces set up a directional path for both problem definition and problem-solving with regard to issues such as burial, housing, transport and industry.

Bibliography

Andrews, Malcolm. 1994. "The Metropolitan Picturesque." In *The Politics of the Picturesque. Literature, Landscape and Aesthetics since 1770*, edited by Stephen Copley and Peter Garside, 282–98. Cambridge: Cambridge University Press.

"Artizans' Dwellings Acts: Report of Delegates from the Metropolitan Vestries and District Boards." 1880. London: Harrison and Sons. Accessed June 30, 2020. https://www.jstor.org/stable/60202243

Artizans', Labourers' and General Dwellings Company. "Report of the Eighteenth Annual Meeting of the Shareholders." 1885. Artizans', Labourers' and General Dwellings Company (March 11). Accessed June 30 2020. https://www.jstor.org/stable/60226610

Blanchard, Samuel Laman. 1843. *The Cemetery at Kensal Green: The Grounds & Monuments. With a Memoir of His Royal Highness the Late Duke of Sussex*. London: Cunningham & Mortimer. Accessed April 8, 2020. http://access.bl.uk/item/viewer/ark:/81055/vdc_100023808732.0x000001#?c=0&m=0&s=0&cv=0&xywh=-1476%2C-147%2C4557%2C2906

Baker, T. F. T., Diane K. Bolton and Patricia E. C. Croot. 1989. "Paddington: Churches." In *A History of the County of Middlesex: Volume 9, Hampstead, Paddington*, edited by C. R. Elrington, 252–259. London: Victoria County History. *British History Online*. Accessed May 26, 2021. http://www.british-history.ac.uk/vch/middx/vol9/pp252-259

Briggs, Asa. 1968. *Victorian Cities*. Harmondsworth: Penguin Books.

Brooks, Chris W. 1989. *Mortal Remains*. Exeter: Wheaton Publishers Ltd.

Broun, Richard B. 1851. *Extramural Sepulture – Synopsis of the London Necropolis Company and National Mausoleum at Woking in the County of Surrey*. London: Trelawney Saunders.

Chubb, Harry. 1876. "The Supply of Gas to the Metropolis." *Journal of the Statistical Society of London* 39, no. 2 (June): 350–80. Accessed July 1, 2020. http://www.jstor.com/stable/2339120

Clarke, John M. 2004. *London's Necropolis. A Guide to Brookwood Cemetery*. Stroud: Sutton Publishing.

Clarke, William Spencer. 1881. *The Suburban Homes of London: A Residential Guide to Favourite London Localities, Their Society, Celebrities, and Associations, with Notes on Their Rental, Rates and House Accommodation*. London: Chatto and Windus. Accessed June 5, 2021. https://www.google.co.uk/books/edition/The_Suburban_Homes_of_London/xKYHAAAAQAAJ?hl=en

Corton, Christine L. 2015. *London Fog: The Biography*. Harvard: Harvard University Press. Accessed July 17, 2020. http://www.jstor.com/stable/j.ctvjnrshm.3

Curl, James Stevens. 1984. "The Design of Early British Cemeteries." *Journal of Garden History* 4, no. 3: 223–54.

Curl, James Stevens. 2001. *Kensal Green Cemetery. The Origins and Development of the General Cemetery of All Souls, Kensal Green, London, 1824–2001*. Chichester: Phillimore & Co.

Curl, James Stevens. 2004. *The Victorian Celebration of Death*. Thrupp: Sutton Publishing.

Dennis, Richard. 2008. *Cities in Modernity. Representations and Productions of Metropolitan Space, 1840–1930*. Cambridge: Cambridge University Press.

Dickens, Charles. 1843. *A Christmas Carol. In Prose. Being a Ghost Story of Christmas*. London: Chapman & Hall. Accessed February 8, 2021. https://www.christies.com/lot/lot-dickens-charles-a-christmas-carol-in-prose-5280682/?
Disraeli, Benjamin. 1872. *Sanitas Sanitatum, Omnia Sanitas* speech, delivered at the Free Trade Hall in Manchester, England (April 3). Accessed July 1, 2020. http://www.emersonkent.com/speeches/sanitas_sanitatum_omnia_sanitas.htm
Dyos, Harold J. and Michael Wolff. 1973. *The Victorian City, Images and Realities*. London and Boston: Routledge & Kegan Paul.
Dyos, Harold J. 1982. *Exploring The Urban Past. Essays in Urban History*. Cambridge: Cambridge University Press.
Ellis, Stewart Marsh. 1911. *William Harrison Ainsworth and His Friends*, Vol. 1. London: John Late The Bodley Head. Accessed June 11, 2021. https://archive.org/details/williamharrisona01ellirich
Etlin, Richard A. 1984. *The Architecture of Death, The Transformation of the Cemetery in Eighteenth-Century Paris*. Cambridge (Massachusetts), and London (England): MIT Press.
Fletcher, Joseph. 1846. "A Statistical Account of the Municipal Provisions for Paving, Lighting, and Cleansing the Streets and Public Places of the Metropolis, and for Protecting them from Nuisances." *Journal of the Statistical Society of London* 9, no. 3 (October): 204–22. Accessed July 2, 2020 http://www.jstor.com/stable/2337860
Franklin, Geraint. 2015. "Old Oak Outline Historic Area Assessment." Research Report Series No. 8. English Heritage. Accessed May 26, 2021. https://www.london.gov.uk/sites/default/files/33._old_oak_outline_historic_area_assessment.pdf
Foucault, Michel. 2009. *Security, Territory, Population*. Basingstoke: Palgrave Macmillan.
Foucault, Michel. ([1973] 2009). *The Birth of the Clinic: An Archeology of Medical Perception*. London: Routledge.
Fyfe, Paul. ([2015] 2020). *By Accident or Design. Writing the Victorian Metropolis*. Oxford: Oxford University Press.
Gaskell, Peter. 1833. *The Manufacturing Population of England*. London: Baldwin and Cradock.
Harvey, David. 1992. *The Urban Experience*. Oxford: Blackwell Publishing.
Hassell, John. 1818. *Picturesque Rides and Walks, with Excursions by Water, Thirty Miles Round the British Metropolis*. Vol. 2: 243–50. London: Printed for John Hassell.
Heffer, Simon. 2013. *High Minds: The Victorians and the Birth of Modern Britain*. London: Random House Books.
Hobhouse, Hermione. 1986. "The Kensington Canal, Railways and Related Developments." In *Survey of London: Volume 42, Kensington Square to Earl's Court*, 322–38. British History Online. Accessed May 26, 2021. https://www.british-history.ac.uk/survey-london/vol42/pp322-338
Kilburn Times and Western Post. 1874. "The Queens Park Estate." Vol. 13, no. 341. September 26. Accessed June 22, 2021. https://www.britishnewspaperarchive.co.uk/viewer/BL/0001813/18740926/044/0005
Johnson, Malcolm. 2001. *Bustling Intermeddler? The Life and Work of Charles James Blomfield*. Leominster: Gracewing. Accessed June 9, 2021. https://www.google.co.uk/books/edition/Bustling_Intermeddler/xLAX1Pb1bhwC?hl=en
Latour, Bruno. 2020. *Critical Zones*. Accessed June 30, 2021. https://www.zkm.de/en/zkm.de/en/ausstellung/2020/05/critical-zones/bruno-latour-on-critical-zones

Lefebvre, Henri. 2006. *Writings on Cities*. Translated and Edited by Eleonore Kofman and Elizabeth Lebas. Malden: Blackwell Publishing.
Lefebvre, Henri. 2009. *The Production of Space*. Malden: Blackwell Publishing.
Lipman, Vivian D. 1962–67. "The Rise of Jewish Suburbia." *Jewish Historical Society of England* 21: 78–103. Accessed July 2, 2020. https://www.jstor.org/stable/29777992?seq=1
Malcolmson, Patricia E. 1981. "Laundresses and the Laundry Trade in Victorian England." *Victorian Studies* 24, no. 4 (Summer): 439–462. Accessed July 2, 2020. http://www.jstor.com/stable/3827224
Mayhew, Henry. ([1861²] 2010). *London Labour & the London Poor*. Oxford: Oxford University Press.
Marcus, Steven. 1973. "Reading the Illegible." In *The Victorian City*, edited by Harold J. Dyos and Michael Wolff, Vol. 1, 257–76. London: Routledge and Kegan Paul.
Masterman, Charles F. G. 1905. *In Peril of Change: Essays Written in Time of Tranquillity*. New York: Huebsch.
Masterman, Charles Frederick Gurney. ([1902] 1980). *From the Abyss: Of its Inhabitants, by One of Them*. London: Garland.
Matless, David. 1998. *Landscape and Englishness*. London: Reaktion Books.
McDonald, Erica, and David J. Smith. 1990. *Artizans & Avenues: A History of the Queen's Park Estate*. London: City of Westminster Libraries.
McKellar, Elizabeth. 1999. *The Birth of Modern London. The Development and Design of the City 1660–1720*. Manchester: Manchester University Press.
"Metropolitan Dwellings." 1874. *British Medical Journal* 1, no. 679 (January 3): 20–2. Accessed June 30, 2020. https://www.jstor.org/stable/25236219
Miller, Thomas. 1852. *Picturesque Sketches of London, Past and Present*. London: Office of the National Illustrated Library. Accessed May 26, 2021. https://www.gutenberg.org/files/46565/46565-h/46565-h.htm#CHAPTER_XX
Minott-Ahl, Nicola. 2006. "Building Consensus: London, the Thames, and Collective Memory in the Novels of William Harrison Ainsworth." *Literary London: Interdisciplinary Studies in the Representation of London* 4, no. 2 (September). Accessed June 10, 2021. http://www.literarylondon.org/london-journal/september2006/ahl.html
Morning Advertiser. 1846a. "Western Gas-Light Company Works." No. 17290 (October 10). Accessed June 21, 2021. https://www.britishnewspaperarchive.co.uk/viewer/BL/0001427/18461010/042/0004?browse=False
Morning Advertiser. 1846b. "Kensal Green. The Western Gas-Light Company." No. 17310 (November 5). Accessed June 21, 2021. https://www.britishnewspaperarchive.co.uk/viewer/BL/0001427/18461105/045/0001?browse=False
Mumford, Lewis. 1947. *Technics and Civilization*. London: George Routledge & Sons Ltd.
Mumford, Lewis. 1967. *The Myth of the Machine. Technics and Human Development*. London: Secker & Warburg Limited.
Mumford, Lewis. 1974. "The Garden City Idea and Modern Planning." In *Garden Cities of To-Morrow*, edited by E. Howard, 29–40. London: Faber and Faber.
Mumford, Lewis. 1991. *The City in History*. London: Penguin Books.
Mumford, Lewis. 1996. *The Culture of Cities*. San Diego: Harcourt Brace & Company.
Murray, Lisa Marie. 2001 "Cemeteries in Nineteenth-Century New South Wales: Landscapes of Memory and Identity." Doctoral Thesis, The University of Sydney. Accessed June 27, 2021. http://hdl.handle.net/2123/16784
Olsen, Donald J. 1976. *The Growth of Victorian London*. London: B.T. Batsford Ltd.

Olsen, Donald J. 1974. "Victorian London: Specialization, Segregation, and Privacy." *Victorian Studies* 17, no. 3 (March): 265–78. Accessed June 19 2021. https://www.jstor.org/stable/3826665

Parsons, Brian. 2018. *The Evolution of the British Funeral Industry in the 20th Century. From Undertaker to Funeral Director.* Bingley: Emerald Publishing Limited.

Paxman, Jeremy. 2011. *Empire: What Ruling the World did to the British.* London: Penguin Books Ltd.

Pedroche, Ben. 2013. *London's Lost Power Stations and Gasworks.* Strout: The History Press.

Rugg, Julie. 1992. *The Rise of Cemetery Companies in Britain.* University of Stirling. Accessed May 25, 2021 https://dspace.stir.ac.uk/handle/1893/2017#.YKz yOpEY

Simmel, Georg. ([1903] 2006). "The Metropolis and Mental Life." In Neil Leach, *Rethinking Architecture*, 69–79. London, New York: Routledge.

Slater, Michael. 2009. *Charles Dickens.* Yale: Yale University Press.

Sheppard, F. H. W. 1973. *Survey of London: Volume 37: Northern Kensington.* British History Online: 333–39. Accessed May 25 2021. https://www.british-history.ac.uk/survey-london/vol37/pp333–339

"Sun Life Properties Ltd". n.d. *The National Archives.* Ref. IV/122. Accessed July 4, 2020. https://discovery.nationalarchives.gov.uk/details/r/a3a1dae2-836a-4e4d-8db1-fd67396620b6#0

Miller, Thomas. 1849. "Picturesque Sketches of London Past and Present." *The Illustrated London News* 15, no. 392 (September 29): 221. Accessed June 23, 2021. https://www.britishnewspaperarchive.co.uk/viewer/bl/0001578/18490929/058/0013

"The Artisans', Labourers', And General Dwellings Company." 1881. *The British Medical Journal* 1, no. 1056 (March 26): 478. Accessed June 30, 2020. https://www.jstor.org/stable/25256568

The St. James's Chronicle. 1842. No. 13197. Accessed June 21, 2021. https://www.britishnewspaperarchive.co.uk/viewer/BL/0002193/18420519/008/0001?browse=true

Urban, Sylvanus [Edward Cave]. 1835. "Panorama of Pere-Lachaise." *The Gentleman's Magazine* (January): 74. Accessed May 26, 2021. https://babel.hathitrust.org/cgi/pt?id=uc1.l0071190250&view=1up&seq=88

Walker, Dave. 2017. "On the border 6.1: Canal." Accessed May 26, 2021. https://rbkclocalstudies.wordpress.com/2017/12/07/on-the-border-6-1-canal/

Walker, George Alfred. 1839. *Gathering Graveyards: Particularly Those of London.* London: Longman.

Walker, George Alfred 1849. *Practical Suggestions for the Establishment of National Cemeteries.* London: Longman, Brown, Green, and Longman. Accessed May 24, 2021. https://wellcomecollection.org/works/dy9emamf/items?canvas=3

Walford, Edward and Walter Thombury. 1878. "Paddington." In *Old and New London: Volume 5*, 204–24. London: Cassell, Petter & Galpin. British History Online. Accessed June 12, 2021. https://www.british-history.ac.uk/old-new-london/vol5/pp204–224

Willes, Margaret. 2014. *Gardens of the British Working Class.* Yale: Yale University Press. Accessed June 30, 2020. http://www.jstor.com/stable/j.ctt5vkwrf.13

Whitehead, Jack. n.d. "The Building of Queen's Park." Accessed June 11, 2021. https://www.locallocalhistory.co.uk/mp/p050/page078.htm

4 Suburbs/Highgate

4.1 The village at the edge of the metropolis

The opening of a new private commercial cemetery in Highgate in 1839 was not so positively received as the one of Kensal Green six years before. Why was this so? What had shifted in public opinion in such a short period of time? Before the consecration of Highgate cemetery, the London press expressed concerns about the new private commercial cemeteries taking up London's most beautiful and healthy spots. One of the articles that captured these concerns was published in *John Bull* on 21 April 1839. In some passages, the journalist denounced that private commercial enterprise was given too much freedom by Parliament to initiate new cemeteries in London and voiced the opposition of the local residents in Highgate to the opening of the new cemetery in their village:

> The Highgate Cemetery is not yet consecrated – the inhabitants of that healthy and beautiful hamlet oppose it as a terrible nuisance – while the fact of establishing a vast receptacle for dead bodies on the side of a hill whence issue the springs with wich the principal portion of the north London is supplied with water, is one so perfectly disgusting as to be met with no palliative; except indeed, that if were a part of the great scheme for furthering the interests of the Company, to increase the number of burials.
>
> (186)

> A great deal has been done – or rather said – in Parliament about securing open spaces in the neighbourhood of great towns, wherein the People on their holidays, or in their leisure hours, might enjoy the blessings of air and exercise, but as no joint-stock company has yet started to carry the plan into effect, little progress has been made in that project. Under a jobbing mercantile operation, all the open spaces in the vicinity of all our large towns are being converted into these cemeteries. Why not let the people of this once happy island enjoy their comforts; and in well-arranged gardens, like those of the Zoological or the Horticultural

DOI: 10.4324/9781003178934-5

Societies, and where climate and view would really be essential, look up with cheerful hearts to GOD, through his wonderful and beautiful works, instead of traversing burial grounds, seeing at almost every step they take, the sad memorial of some departed friend or brother. The occasional visits to such scenes of sorrow and solemnity are salutary and serviceable, who shall deny? What we deny are the decency and propriety of mingling the grave the gay, of making our burial place "sights to go and see", walks to frequent, or scenes of amusement. The objection cuts both ways; if the sight of tombs and the presence of death have their proper effect, the localities where they exist are not calculated to afford recreation to well-regulated minds; if they have not that effect – and the localities where they exist have been studiously contrived to counteract it – then the opening them as pleasurable promenades is shameful and disgraceful.

(187)

This article provides us with an insight into how the press reception of the new Victorian cemeteries started to criticise their fast multiplication across the suburban areas of London. However, not all press was negative and in opposition to the implementation of the new cemeteries. Highgate Cemetery, for example, was praised for the quality of its architecture and landscape, as mentioned in the article published on 21 December 1839 by *The Penny Magazine*:

The beauties of the place, indeed, appear to be fully appreciated, for the gardens, as we may not inappropriately call the grounds, are daily filled with persons, evidently enjoying the quiet, the pure air, and the splendid landscape.

(489–90)

In the same article the journalist also highlighted how the cemetery appeared to complement and integrate its surroundings:

From the entrance broad gravel paths wind to the right and to the left, whilst a carriage-road conducts visitors up the steep face of the hill towards the new and handsome church of Highgate, dedicated to St. Michael, which crowns the summit, appearing from different parts of the grounds to great advantage, and which even seems, as a hasty glance, to appertain to the cemetery.

(489)

Indeed the combination of the Gothic architectural style of St. Michael's church and the Egyptian revival style of the Circle of Lebanon in Highgate West Cemetery created an eclectic, if not unique, dialogue between the two. These architectural features, combined with the topography and the presence of the landscape, constituted a picturesque setting for a promenade among the funerary monuments (see Figure 4.1).

Highgate Cemetery is formed of two halves: the West Cemetery (or Old Ground), which opened for burial in 1839, and the East Cemetery (New Ground), in 1857. Although they are two halves of the same cemetery, they have different identities. The West Cemetery benefited from striking views over the city (see Figure 4.2) and the physical proximity with the village historical centre. This part also benefited from the great number of funerary monuments and mausolea. The new East Cemetery, by contrast, is more regular in its layout, and due to its topography and location is more secluded and therefore visually disconnected from both the village and the city. Even its entrance on Swain's Lane does not complement the architectural statement of the Tudor-inspired West Cemetery entrance just opposite, giving the impression that they are two separate entities.

The views from Highgate village have been an attraction for centuries due to its unique location. Situated 400 feet (about 120 m) above sea level, it was because of its height and location that travellers leaving London did the first change of horse there. Sheep and cattle were driven into London via Highgate. It was also here, in the local butchers' shops of Highgate, that livestock was prepared for the city's markets. This trade attracted travellers to stay overnight in local accommodations (Webber and Burrows 2016, 3141–3). The good transport connections to the city, clean air and fresh water, not only attracted day-trippers from the metropolis, but also wealthy residents of liberal ideologies and intellectual temperament (see Figure 4.3). The cultural context of Highgate village was shaped by numerous organisations (including a theatre and museum) and charitable institutions during the nineteenth century. For example the Philanthropic Society for Highgate was established in 1833. The same year Highgate Cemetery opened for burials (in 1839), the Highgate Literary and Scientific Institution was founded at No. 1 Southwood Terrace and initiated its programme of public lectures. Private schools were also present in the area as early as 1710, where local wealthy families sent their children (Richardson 2004, 93). A working men's association, with its own library, was founded in 1861 in the old British school in Southwood Lane by Congregationalists. In 1893, even a Sanitary Museum opened its doors to visitors in North Hill (Baggs, Bolton, et al. 1980, 157–62). From the article "The Highgate Sanitary Museum" which appeared in the *Hampstead & Highgate Express* on 12 August 1893, we gather that during the first seven months from its opening in December 1883, the Highgate Museum of Sanitary Appliances had almost 13,000 visitors. The article states that this is the first museum of this kind in the country (7).

The presence of this unique museum in Highgate enhanced the connections of the village with health, hygiene and sanitation. All of these cultural and charitable organisations were embedded in the social fabric of the village, especially among the educated and well-to-do residents that actively

Figure 4.1 Entrance to the catacombs with St Michael's Church in the background. *The Penny Magazine*. Issue 495. 1835. Author's collection.

Figure 4.2 Print showing view from Highgate Cemetery over London. Note in the distance the dome of St. Paul's Cathedral. Undated. Author's collection.

Figure 4.3 View of Highgate from Parliament Hill. Postcard. 1903. Author's collection.

intervened in local matters. This was the case of Highgate cemetery's consecration, when a cohort of affluent and influential locals, led by Harry Chester (the founder of the Highgate Literary and Scientific Institution), delayed the opening of the cemetery. Chester's garden backed onto Highgate cemetery, and by law the private company needed to secure the consent of the owner of any house within three hundred yards from the cemetery before going ahead with its establishment (Dungavell, 2014).

This gives us a flavour of what a very different kind of social setting Highgate was when compared to the semi-rural context of Kensal Green in the early 1830s, where there wasn't an existing community that had the agency to intervene or influence the built environment of their local area. By contrast, local residents such as Chester were actively invested in preserving the distinctive identity of Highgate village. Chester's influence, however, was very limited and not able to stop the rampant expansion of London, or the scale of urban development or indeed the quality of its architecture. The identity of Highgate village was not only dependent on the development taking place in the actual village but also how the growth of North London (particularly Camden and Kings Cross) were affecting the quality of the views from Highgate. The two were intrinsically interconnected and affect one another. So what was changing in that visual dialogue between the village and the fast expanding city? What were those key changes? What were the functions of those buildings? Why was the coming of a new cemetery resisted by the locals, and the coming of other institutions (such as hospitals), as we will see, welcome?

4.2 Gravestones and vistas

As we have seen in the previous section, the press at the time of the establishment of Highgate cemetery denounced that new private enterprises were taking away the best viewpoints in the surroundings of London. However, the fast urbanisation of London was also affecting the views from Highgate over the metropolis. Indeed the scale of the new cemeteries, hospitals, prisons and asylums, as well as railway stations and other large-scale projects such as gas works, abattoirs and other services were redefining the cityscape of nineteenth-century London. Through their architectural forms they embodied the quest to improve the services of a fast growing metropolis; however, their large scale was also a new visual contribution to the city. Between the 1840s and 1850s the fast growing developments in the nearby areas of Kings Cross and Islington started to put pressure on Highgate and threatened the distinctive views of that part of the city as well as the air quality. Due to its location and morphology, London's prevailing winds travel from west to east. For this reason, the better-off resided in the west part of the city, and the east was where the poorer classes but also the docks and industry were historically located. Hampstead, Highgate and Blackheath were among those few locations in the eastern part of the city that due to the high elevation were exempt from the smokes, fumes and stinks travelling from the western part of the city to the east (Corton 2015, 20).

The scale of these developments was affecting the unique views that residents and day-trippers enjoyed from Highgate village. The new Cattle Market alone covered an area of 75 acres of land and, along with the new cemeteries as well as other services, was part of the upscaling and modernisation processes taking place in London (see Figure 4.4). Just like the old graveyards and the new suburban cemeteries, there was a stark contrast between the orderly site of the new market (also connected to railways and waterways) arranged according to type of animal and specifically designed with sites for slaughter when compared to the old chaotic market in Smithfield (Otter 2004, 51). What is interesting to notice here, is that although the planning of the actual city was very organic and uncoordinated, the new typologies of buildings and institutions that emerged in the Victorian era were carefully planned as self-sufficient entities. They often had their own water reservoirs or produced their own energy to light and heat their premises.

The Metropolitan Cattle Market (later known as Caledonian Cattle Market) was opened on Caledonian Road in 1855, designed by James Bunstone Bunning (1802–63), the city architect and surveyor of Highgate West Cemetery. In a short article published in *The Morning Chronicle* on 23 August 1852, the journalist anticipated the developments flourishing around the suburban cemeteries and the new cattle market, lamenting that the brick walls of the new houses would spoil the picturesque view over Highgate, Kentish Town and Fortess Terrace (3). This is the result of speculation, as the Metropolitan Cattle Market was in fact located on the edge of the urban development and acted as a threshold to the city. It confirms, however, that much like cemeteries and the dead, slaughterhouses and cattle needed more space away from the city centre, as we have also seen in Chapter 3 with Kensal New Town and the Gas Works near the Kensal Green Cemetery. This was also the case of new prisons. As well as the Metropolitan Cattle Market, Bunning also designed the City Prison on the north side of Camden Road (based on Warwick Castle), built between 1849 and 1852. City Prison was for convicts of all classes and was formed from six wings radiating out from a central tower (four for men, one for women and one for young offenders). Eventually, in 1878, the prison was taken over by the government and used only for women from 1903 (see Figure 4.5).

The northern part of this area, which leads to Upper Holloway, was still mostly free from buildings. It was here that in 1832, the Corporation of London bought ten acres to use as a cemetery during the cholera epidemic of 1832 and another 27 acres in 1848, on the north side of Camden Road, near the City Prison (Baggs, Bolton and Croot 1985, 29–37). Along the south of Caledonian Road (next to the Metropolitan Cattle Market) was Pentonville, a model prison. Built in 1840–42 with alterations by Charles Barry, it was based on plans by Lieutenant-Colonel Joshua Jebb and featured a reformed

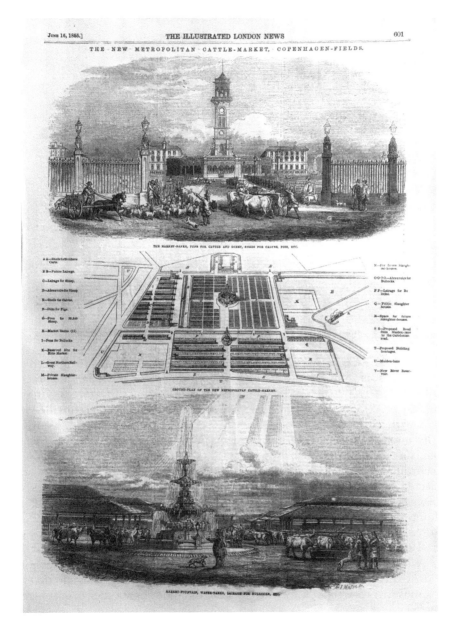

Figure 4.4 London Metropolitan Cattle Market at Copenhagen Fields. *The Illustrated London News*. 1855. Author's Collection.

Figure 4.5 City Prison (now Holloway Prison). Print. 1896. Author's collection.

and experimental system of separate confinement. This prison opened in 1842 and was unlike previous prisons that were less obvious and practically hidden away (such as the Female Convict Prison at Brixton, originally built in 1819). Similar to the prison designed by Bunning, Pentonville was built with five radiating blocks with 520 cells. This penitentiary was originally intended for short-term prisoners, but from 1848 was also used for long-stay mentally insane prisoners (Baggs, Bolton and Croot 1985, 29–37). According to Byrne, it was in Pentonville Prison that British convicts (mostly selected from the Millbank prison) were prepared for eviction to the British colonies (1989, 138). He also reports an extract from Sir James Graham, Home Secretary in 1841:

> I propose, therefore, that no prisoner shall be admitted into Pentonville without the knowledge that it is the portal to the penal colony and without the certainty that he bids adieu to his connections in England, and that he must henceforth look forward to a life of labour in another hemisphere.
>
> (138)

Byrne points out that this metaphorical portal was indeed Barry's grand entrance to the prison. The prison's entrance like that of the Victorian necropolis was celebrated as a ritual passage. Indeed, there is an uncanny parallel between the two (cemetery and prison) as they both mark the movement into another condition, in death or life. Despite Graham's statement, this form of punishment largely stopped in the 1840s.

On the northside of Pentonville Prison was the Royal Caledonian Asylum. This was built in 1827–28 on the east side of Copenhagen Fields (by 1855, this was the Metropolitan Cattle Market), and was a replacement for the original premises in Hatton Garden. The asylum – completed in 1828 by George Tappen in Greek Revival style – supported and educated the children of Scottish servicemen killed or wounded in war, and of poor Scots living in London. Most of the new institutions, just as it happened for the cemeteries, became an attraction for visitors near and far. In his 1860 *Guide du Voyageur à Londres et aux Environs*, French geographer and writer Élisée Reclus gives a comprehensive overview of London that is both historical and contemporary. Reclus covers aspects of the metropolis that beyond its attractions and amenities also touches on its mortality rates and an analysis of the healthier districts of the capital. Along the long list of the buildings suggested by Reclus to French visitors, he included the suburban cemeteries of Highgate and Kensal Green, among others. He also listed hospitals, workhouses, asylums and prisons. For all of them he provided details of what to do to gain access to them as well as opening times to the visiting public. Indeed for Reclus the identity and wealth of London was not only represented by its shopping districts and culture but also by its extended civic infrastructure, beyond parks and museums.

Architectural historian Annmarie Adams in the 2008 book, *Medicine by Design: The Architect and the Modern Hospital, 1893–1943*, explains that the new hospital buildings were "civic monuments" and were included in popular guidebooks as they were a touristic attraction to cities (4). These new typologies of buildings and reform institutions at the time made a statement on the progress of medicine and public health, as part of the modernisation process of London. Their presence in an area reinforced its healthy ethos (as in the case of Highgate), and reassured locals that those distinctive qualities were intact and preserved (air, open spaces, natural landscapes). Unlike cemeteries (which were often surrounded by high walls), the new hospitals and asylums were often more visible from the streets, and the scale of the elevation of their facades in particular contributed to the experience of the built environment.

In his book *The Birth of the Clinic: An Archaeology of Medical Perception*, Foucault argues that the birth of modern medical practice coincided with the application of the pathological method to medical observation and analysis of the human body. This pathological method found application through what Foucault calls the "medical gaze", explaining how at the time "The eye becomes the depositary and source of clarity" (2009, xiii). The gaze of the physician/surgeon was a way of understanding, by observation and examination, the human body and its diseases. The gaze brought into the realm of knowledge the otherwise unknown content of the body. The pathological method through the gaze became the only trusted instrument able to reveal the anatomy of the human body: "The residence of truth in the dark centre of things is linked paradoxically, to this sovereign power of the empirical gaze that turns their darkness into light" (xiii). Although Foucault does not address specifically the context of London, he provides the historical context by explaining how the methods of scientific and medical research in the late eighteenth and nineteenth centuries were adopted to identify solutions to public health issues. By reading Foucault we also understand how the development of the pathological method by medical science at the time was supported by a positive attitude, as the rational observation from the real (dissecting the human body) could lessen the probability of error (50–1). The scientific method became something that could be trusted, something true as based on observation, experiment and comparison. This is also explained in the work of Auguste Comte and his Law of Three Stages, in which he identifies the 3rd stage as the Positivity one. This Positivist attitude freed, and gave further powers to the medical gaze, becoming what Foucault calls "the unimpeded empire of the gaze". The unimpeded gaze exposes to the light of knowledge and space everything from the inner parts of the human body to the cosmos. Foucault focuses particularly on the effects of the trustworthy gaze of the doctor that polices everything from the body to disease, turning the invisible into visible, locating by observation the disease and eradicating it.

In the first part of the nineteenth century the pathological method applied to the body to isolate the seat of disease wasn't enough in itself to prevent death and improve life. The trustworthy scientific gaze in order to understand disease had also to understand the space in which the human body dwelled, worked, socialised, died and was buried; simply put, medical gaze entered the urban space of the nineteenth-century city. So it is possible to say that the medical gaze and the scientific method helped shape the planning of a large metropolis such as Paris or London, before the architect or the planner, along the canons of health and hygiene. As in the case of Highgate, the introduction of new hospitals was often in existing contexts where other buildings, and indeed communities, were already living and working. We have seen earlier how complex the coexistence of new institutions such as the small-pox hospital in Highgate was, due to the risks it presented to local residents in its proximity. As we have seen in section 4.1 of this chapter, London's overcrowded churchyards were seen as a hazard to the public health of Londoners, and new larger cemeteries started to be established in the suburban areas of the city. Hospitals too followed the same path; however, old hospitals did not face closure (as in the case of graveyards) but it was debated if it was worth it to expand in the vicinity of their original sites or build new ones elsewhere. The availability and affordability of land were important aspects that contributed to the identification of suitable sites, however fresh air and the proximity of open spaces were also crucial factors. Alongside the question of preferred locations, for the cemeteries there were questions about the accessibility of transport links to the hospitals, but also their distribution across the metropolitan area. North London had a high density population and Highgate and the nearby area of Holloway provided a good location for new hospitals.

In the 1882 article "Proposed Hospital For North London" published in *The British Medical Journal* (29 April) the writer explains the rationale behind the need for the new establishment in that part of London. From Highbury station on the North London Railway, the two nearest general hospitals, not including the small Great Northern Hospital, were University College and the Royal Free Hospitals, some two miles from Islington, a mile from the nearest part of North London, and consequently between five and six miles from Highgate, Tottenham and Hornsey, being further away still from some parts of the district:

> Putting the population of the North London District at 1,000,000 these made but one bed for every 33,000 of the inhabitants, and Mr. Burdett asked whether one hospital bed could be considered adequate to meet the requirements of a population of 33,000 human beings resident in one of the largest districts in a vast centre like London. The situation of the workhouse infirmaries might be fairly taken as evidence of the localities where hospital accommodation for the poor was likely to be most needed. In North London there were two large Poor-law infirmaries, viz., the Halborn and Islington Infirmaries, which collectively contained 1,157 beds, both of which were situated in the district, and within a radius of a mile and a half of Islington station. If the Poor-law authorities found the poor population so numerous as to require one bed for every 900 of the population, Mr. Burdett inquired how it had come to pass that there was only one bed provided in the general hospitals for every 33,000 of the population of the district.
>
> (635)

However, there were consequences in local areas due to the presence of certain hospitals. For example, in an 1886 article titled "The Metropolitan Small-Pox Hospitals" and published in *The British Medical Journal* (20 February 1886), the writer states that in a recent report on the health of St. Pancras hospitals, the public medical officer Shirley Foster Murphy discussed the effects on the neighbouring areas of the small-pox hospitals in Hampstead and Highgate (see Figure 4.6).

Murphy identified a pattern of the dissemination for the small-pox that apparently spread across the neighbouring residential areas in the proximity of the hospitals.

> That in the four years when the Hampstead Hospital was closed, the houses in the special area of one mile round the hospitals were attacked

Figure 4.6 The New Smallpox Hospital Highgate. Print. 1851. Author's collection.

less [by small-pox] than those in the rest of the parish, but that in the year 1884, when the hospital was reopened, the special area suffered three times as much as the rest of the parish.[...] Similarly, at Highgate Hospitals in the years 1881, 1883, and 1884, the distribution of small-pox in the special area, as related to the rest of the parish, and also in the different rings of the special area, resemble in its incidence the distribution of small-pox around the Hampstead Hospital during the year 1884. [...] Mr. Murphy regards, therefore, the St. Pancras evidence on the subject as tending to show that these small-pox hospitals, as at present constructed and managed, are a source of disease to the neighbourhood in which they are placed.

(361)

The 1894 article "New Hospitals Versus The Extension Of Old Hospitals For London" published in *The British Medical Journal* gives an insight into London hospitals at the time and the dilemma the institutions were facing between providing additional beds to the existing hospitals, or establishing new ones:

A reference to the fourth volume of Mr. Burdett's Hospitals and Asylums of the World, where plans of the sites of all the chief metropolitan hospitals are given, shows that unless further land be acquired it will not be possible to provide additional beds in new buildings at

Guy's, St. Bartholomew's, St. Thomas's, St. George's, King's College, Westminster, the Royal Free, Middlesex, and Charing Cross Hospitals.

(314)

This proves how prohibitive it was for those hospitals located in the urban centre of London to expand in their original sites by acquiring nearby properties and land, therefore they had to relocate in places where more hospital beds were most needed. The designs developed for the new hospitals (in London and other parts of the country) were not only innovative for their layout, circulation and architecture, but they were also more holistic in terms of hygienic innovation and services. There were effectively complex machines, unlike the Victorian cemeteries, that by comparison were very basic in their structure yet made an important contribution to the area as a receptacle of culture and architecture. In the next section we will see how the combination of the new cemetery and the new hospitals and asylums enhanced the character of Highgate as a healthy area.

4.3 New hospitals and clean air

In the 30-year period between its opening in 1839 and 1869, Highgate Cemetery remained isolated from the rest of the village and was mostly surrounded by open spaces which were privately owned. From an 1869 map of the area (see Figure 4.7) it is possible to see that the only building of relevance

Figure 4.7 Historical map showing the development of the built environment in Highgate up to 1869. Author's collection.

is St. Michael's Church which is crowning the highest point of Highgate, along the north boundary of the cemetery. The east boundary is marked by Swain's Lane and beyond that Lauderdale House and grounds purchased in 1865 by Sydney Waterlow (Richardson, 2004, 13), of which we will see more later in this section). Along the west boundary of the cemetery (starting from St. Michael's Church) were the William Cutbush & Son Nurseries. These date from 1822, prior to the arrival of the cemetery. From the map it is possible to see the long and narrow strip of land facing Highgate West Hill, where William Cutbush had his residence, shop, green and hot houses. Cutbush specialised in hyacinth and tulip bulbs as well as topiary design (Lovell and Marcham 1936, 67–8). In 1854 James Cutbush took over from his father after his death. According to census returns in 1881 the nurseries employed 58 men and 10 boys (The Williams Family Tree, n.d.).

It was only over the following 25 years (between 1869 and 1894) that new residential roads, new hospitals and workhouses were constructed in Highgate. As seen earlier in this chapter, the unique topography of Highgate made the village a healthy location and a desirable destination. This was also partly due to its rich cultural and social history and improved transport infrastructure that connected the area to Kings Cross. In this section we will look more closely at what kind of development started to manifest in the vicinity of the cemetery over the mid and second half of the nineteenth century.

The first development of significance took place along the south end of the East Cemetery. Completed in 1865, the Holly Village consists of a series of prototype dwellings and landscaped gardens. The project was commissioned by Baroness Angela Georgina Burdett-Coutts and designed in Gothic Revival style by architect Henry Astley Darbishire. It consisted of a small group of eight residential buildings arranged around a central green area, which revived the ideal village as a template for town planning. Considering the details of its features and quality of its materials and design, it is credible that the project aimed to attract middle-class residents to the area (Richardson 2004, 47). The Burdett-Coutts family were local residents and their country villa was on Highgate West Hill. The Holly Village was strategically positioned so as to be visible from the Burdett-Coutts' villa. In an undated print of the Village it is possible to see the visual dialogue between both St. Michael's Church and Highgate Cemetery. Burdett-Coutts, over the long period of her residence in Highgate, acquired land along the north and south boundaries of her property. According to Highgate local historian Jonathan Richardson, by the time Burdett-Coutts' estate went up for sale in the early 1920s "it was one of the largest open spaces in private hands in London" (47).

In 1869 the construction of the St. Pancras (North) Infirmary started. Also known as Highgate Infirmary (today Highgate Mental Health Centre), the institution was located along the eastern border of Highgate East Cemetery. At the time of its opening in 1871 *The St. Pancras and Holborn Journal* explained that "This infirmary is in connection with the Central London Sick Asylum District, consisting of the parishes of St. Pancras, St. Giles', Bloomsbury, Strand, and St. James's, Westminster" (3). The coming of the St. Pancras (North) Infirmary to Highgate, received extensive press coverage at the time of its planning and completion, particularly in the pages of *The British Medical Journal*. In an article titled "The Highgate Infirmary" published on Saturday 12 February 1870, we gather that:

> The institution will receive, when complete, five hundred inmates; and will, according to present appearances, be managed with a liberality much superior to what has, as a rule, hitherto prevailed in similar establishments. It is well situated and well built; and, whilst there has been no extravagance, all the arrangements as yet brought to completion have been made, we believe, without parsimony. [...] One important question which occurs at the outset is, should the principal part of the staff be resident, or visiting? and, if the latter, should those engaged in practice in the immediate neighbourhood of the hospital be employed? Much might be said in favour of the latter proposal, and many able men might be easily found for the posts. [...] There is an ophthalmic ward, and will probably be many eye-cases, a knowledge of this speciality should be essential to the consulting-surgeon; whilst that of skin-diseases should be required either of him or of his medical colleague. We have ventured to make the above suggestions in some detail because we think it a subject to which the attention of the profession should be directed. Other large Infirmaries of a similar kind will follow, and it is really a matter of great importance that the medical arrangements in respect to them should be made with forethought and judgment.
>
> (160)

The building's main facade overlooked Waterlow's private residence and grounds (from 1889 Waterlow Park) and its gardens covered a site of almost four acres of land. The plan drawings published in 1869 in *The Builder* (see Figure 4.8), showed that the infirmary's male wards overlooked the east part of the cemetery and the female wards were looking over Dartmouth Park Hill (27). The operating-theatres were located in the south end of the site. The dead-house is also located in the south-east end, and a separate building was where the mortuary and the post-mortem rooms were located. The building had a separate access for the removal of the dead without going near the main buildings. In a bird's-eye view of the proposal, also published in *The Builder*, the new complex is completely isolated, and it is not possible to get a sense of the immediate surroundings. The structure was erected for the St. Pancras Board of Guardians and designed by John Giles & Biven architects (also designers of other asylums). From the etching it is also possible to see the intention of the architects to include a landscaped garden with paths and shrubs (see Figure 4.9). From a postcard dated 1904, it is also possible to

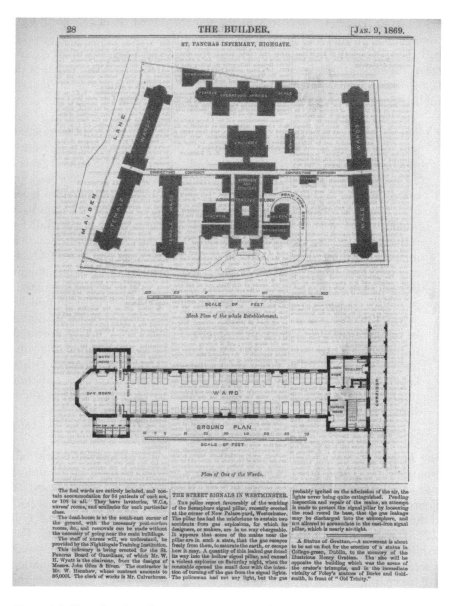

Figure 4.8 Plan drawing showing St. Pancras Infirmary published in *The Builder*. January 1869. Author's collection.

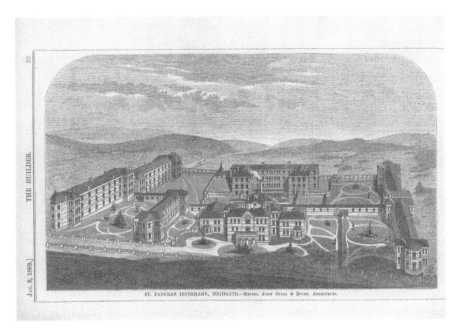

Figure 4.9 Bird's-eye view illustration of St. Pancras Infirmary published in *The Builder*. January 1869. Author's collection.

see that the infirmary's main facade benefited from the views over Waterlow Park, and in particular over its main landscaped pond (see Figure 4.10).

Major changes also took place in the vicinity of the West Cemetery in 1889 with the opening of Waterlow Park. These were once the grounds of Lauderdale House, which Waterlow initially made available to St. Bartholomew's Hospital in Smithfield. The house was converted into wards for convalescent patients with the hope that they would have a better recovery in Highgate, surrounded by green areas and clear air. The Victorian philanthropist and politician presented the land to London County Council, which designated the area as "a garden for the gardenless" (see Figure 4.11). By doing so, the combination of Highgate West and East Cemeteries and the new park formed an extensive open area of almost 70 acres of land in one of the most beautiful parts of London. The event was covered extensively by the London press which praised Waterlow's gesture as well the gratitude of local residents for the gift of a new open public space (*The Illustrated London News* 1889, 693–6).

With his gift to Highgate, Waterlow not only secured one of the most beautiful spots in the vicinity of London from possible building developers but also from any possible future expansion of the cemetery. The opening of Waterlow Park emphasised the importance of open spaces as assets to both

Figure 4.10 Postcard showing view of Highgate Infirmary from Waterlow Park. 1904. Author's collection.

the local character of Highgate and the metropolitan area of London. Just like the coming of the cemetery or the St. Pancras infirmary, the park had a civic function that away from the historical centre of London, contributed to the new metropolitan identity of the capital. Waterlow was a public figure actively involved within the debate of good quality housing at affordable prices. In 1863 he founded the Improved Industrial Dwelling Company which provided housing for the working classes in the areas of central and East London. The company was also active in Highgate and pioneered new healthier spatial arrangements for their housing. In plan drawings dated 1870 it is possible to see that each flat had its own toilet facilities, kitchen and coal storage. From the records it is also possible to see accounts of the mortality rates in the buildings and estates that the company owned and managed. This was to demonstrate that the better quality dwellings had an impact on the health and longevity of the tenants. As we saw in Chapter 3, Waterlow was also involved in the Artisans' and Labourers' Dwellings in Queen's Park Estate.

The opening of Waterloo Park not only consolidated the open spaces in Highgate but was also an opportunity to galvanise public opinion over the need to preserve open spaces across London and in general across large urban developments. The new park was in a very strategic location that allowed it to act as a binding element between High Street and Swain's Lane, as it made it possible to walk from High Street through the park to reach Swain's Lane and the East and West Highgate Cemeteries. For this it made the cemeteries less isolated, at least during the park opening hours.

Suburbs/Highgate 109

Figure 4.11 Print showing a collage of images about the opening of Waterlow Park. *The Illustrated London News*. 24 October 1891. Author's collection.

As we also saw from the 1904 postcard earlier (see Figure 4.10), the park established a visual dialogue with the St. Pancras Infirmary, therefore the two established a symbiotic relationship of mutual exchange and a constant reminder of those elements that made Highgate a unique place (for the sick and the healthy): its open spaces and air quality.

The sense of urgency, at the time, in preserving and maintaining open spaces around Highgate was visible even in relatively small areas around the village, such as Pond Square and the landscaped area opposite St. Michael's Church (*Hampstead and Highgate Express* 1885, 4)

In an article published in the Globe on 20 August 1896 titled "Open Spaces in St. Pancras", it is mentioned that

> St. Pancras, taken as a whole, seems happily endowed with open spaces. In the Kentish Town sub-district, where the density of person per acre is 59, there are Parliament Fields with its 267 acres 2 roods; Waterlow Park, 29 acres; Highgate Cemetery, 36 acres; Pond Square, Highgate, 3 roods 20 poles; and several smaller spaces.
>
> (3)

The article also reports that, in comparison, districts such as Somers Town had a density of population to acreage of 181. In some other districts of London the only open spaces available to the public were disused graveyards. It states:

> Tottenham-Court sub-district claims for its own Whitfield Burial Ground. This division of St. Pancras has relatively to each acre 183 inhabitants. Finally, the Gray's-inn-lane sub-district, with a density per persons per acre of 178 possesses two burial grounds laid out as recreation places, which combined are not 4 acres in extent.
>
> (3)

From a historical map of the area dated 1894 (see Figure 4.12), we can see how Highgate became more densely populated by residential streets. There we can see what buildings and open spaces started to cluster in the proximity of the cemetery, particularly at the east end of the cemetery.

By the mid-1890s, the only open spaces were the grounds of the institutions, two sports grounds and the gardens of a few large houses, especially along Hornsey Lane. Most of it became crowded with terraces between the 1870s and early 1880s. Houses in the area between Highgate and Holloway were still villas, although the demand for them was not as high as for lower middle-class terraces, which, by the 1860s, dominated the typology of houses in the area (Baggs, Bolton and Croot 1985, 29–37). By the beginning of the twentieth century, the development of Highgate as one of London's inner suburbs was complete. In a historical map dated 1936 (see Figure 4.13), it is possible to see how the open spaces were drastically reduced, and how, by then, a cluster of open space in this relatively dense area was formed by Highgate Cemetery with Waterlow Park, along the West Hill park of the village.

As we have seen earlier on in this chapter, because of its topographical configuration on top of a hill with striking views over London, Highgate

Suburbs/Highgate 111

Figure 4.12 Historical map showing the development of the built environment in Highgate up to 1894. Author's collection.

was considered a desirable place for living, particularly for its improved air quality, which as seen, made it also attractive for hospitals and other institutions. Unlike Kensal Green Cemetery, Highgate was only accessible by road and later by railway, but because of its height, its landscape remained only partially scarred by train lines and access roads. Both visually and in terms of development, Highgate has a more cohesive and intimate appearance. Even a number of institutions (which are still partially visible today) are less exposed, as in the case of the Kensal Green area. Highgate, despite its extensive development in the nineteenth century, had a pre-existing village and an active local community (unlike Kensal Green). This allowed the area to be more carefully planned in accordance with the existing buildings. Today, the cemetery is considered a key feature of Highgate, which did not detract from its status as a desirable suburb of London. The above-mentioned large-scale developments directly impacted Highgate's views over that part of the city, along with smaller scale new buildings such as stations and of course residential developments. Luckily Highgate still retained some of its open spaces and views.

In an article published on Saturday 12 August 1893 in the *Hampstead & Highgate Express* it was reported that:

112 *Suburbs/Highgate*

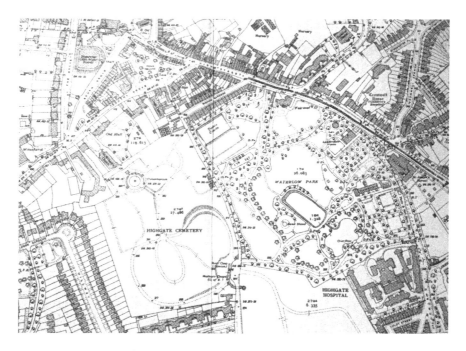

Figure 4.13 Historical map showing the development of the built environment in Highgate up to 1936. Author's collection.

Some thousands of holiday-makers visited Parliament-hill fields, lying between Highgate and Hampstead. From the summit of Parliament-hill the Crystal Palace, the Royal Albert Hall, St. Paul's, and a far-stretching panoramic view of the metropolis and the Surrey hills were plainly visible owing to the beautiful weather and the absence of London smoke.

(7)

The commanding views over the metropolis, as well as the good air quality and green spaces (Parliament Hill and Hampstead Heath) have been the key assets of the area for centuries and were still intact at the end of the nineteenth century despite the large-scale developments that altered the views over that part of London. In 1897 "The Movements for the Inclosure and Preservation of Open Lands" was researched by Robert Hunter (one of the founders of the National Trust). Hunter reported on the efforts made since 1865 to secure public open spaces across London, under the Metropolitan Common Acts (Hunter 1897, 400).

Along the west boundaries of Highgate West Cemetery between 1845 and the early twentieth century was the private property of philanthropist Angela

Burdett-Coutts, the grand-daughter of banker Thomas Coutts (Richardson 2004, 44–7). After her death the "sixty acres private estate without right of ways" (*The Tablet* 1907, 499), was put up for sale. Locals voiced their concerns in the local papers about the destiny of the estate and feared that it would attract wealthy developers who would build flats and houses, rather than being preserved as an open space and retaining all its existing natural landscape. The estate was purchased by Alderman Davis in 1923, and the plan to accommodate 500 homes on the estate was prepared (Richardson 2004, 47–51). Most of the west part of the estate accommodated detached and semi-detached houses that featured elements of Arts & Crafts architecture seen in the Hampstead Garden Suburb. However, the planning of Holly Lodge Estate maximised the number of houses and did not prioritise open spaces. The result was a leafy, yet gated suburb of private roads. The portion of the estate overlooking Swain's Lane featured Tutor-style blocks of flats, of which a section was dedicated to the Ladies Workers' Homes. (Richardson 2004, 48–9). Founded in 1914 by Davis, these were "affordable, well managed conveniently situated flats" for professional women working in London, including teachers, policewomen, businesswomen as well as actors, florists and hairdressers (Downing 2009, 6–13). These flats were frequently advertised in newspapers such as the *Daily Mirror* which stated their features and rent prices (see Figure 4.14 and Figure 4.15).

By 1936 another large-scale development along the west boundary of Highgate West Cemetery took place as the William Cutbush & Son Nurseries site was then replaced by South Grove House, a block of 50 flats stretching along the narrow site between the Holly Lodge Estate and St. Michael's Church. A small number of flats overlook the Circle of Lebanon and Egyptian Avenue, two of the cemetery's main architectural features (Highgate Conservation Area Appraisal and Management Proposals n.d., 24). We can say that the combination of the new South Grove House and Holly Lodge Estate marked a new era of commercial speculative development that although inspired by the new Garden City Movement, did not retain, or indeed provide, new open spaces for Highgate. There is a stark contrast when compared to the establishment of Waterlow Park in the late Victorian period, but this also tells us about how the sense of agency changed in the local community when it came to expressing their judgment, or support, for the new developments.

Reviewing the findings gathered on Highgate so far, we can say that the presence of an established community prior to the opening of the cemetery had an impact on the formation of the area. The active and influential role they had in the decision-making of new local developments taking place in the area was evident with the consecration of the cemetery in 1839. Having as local residents philanthropists such as Waterlow – and later capitalist investors (as in the case of the Holly Lodge Estate development) – also had a major impact in the shaping of the area. This confirms Harvey's theory that outlined how rational thinking and secular forces, such as the political and

114 Suburbs/Highgate

Figure 4.14 Holly Lodge Estate advert showing the overall building. 1935. Author's Collection.

capitalist power, contributed to the fragmentation and institutionalisation of urban space.

To conclude we can say that the coming of Highgate Cemetery initiated the development of the west hill on Highgate and preservation of open spaces. This part was more disconnected and secluded. The coming of Waterlow Park consolidated the open spaces and views over the metropolis from Highgate. Although development was slow to start with, by the end of the nineteenth century, new institutions and new open spaces started to

Figure 4.15 Holly Lodge Estate advert showing the interior of one of the flats within the estate. 1935. Author's collection.

cluster in the proximity of Highgate West and East Cemeteries. As we can see from an aerial photograph of the area dated 1939 (see Figure 4.16), they occupied the flank of the hill, along Swain's Lane, and connected the historical civic and residential heart in the higher part of the village with the new developments in the lower part of Swain's Lane, towards Kentish Town.

Unlike the large-scale developments seen in the vicinity of Kensal Green Cemetery, in Highgate, the very close proximity of the new built environment created a unique architectural and spatial dialogue between them, almost

116   *Suburbs/Highgate*

Figure 4.16 [EPW061151] Lady Workers' Homes Ltd flats at the Holly Lodge Estate, Highgate Cemetery and environs, Highgate. 1939. © Historic England.

an intimacy that complemented the knitted urban fabric of the old part of the village. Together, St. Michael's Church, the two halves of Highgate cemetery, Waterlow Park, the infirmary and the Holly Village provided an aesthetic continuum through the Gothic Revival architectural style. This is contrasted by the regimented and repetitive arrangement of the Holly Lodge Estate, in the south part of Swain's Lane. Although none of the new institutions effectively became a new civic focus for the village, together they were the physical manifestation of governmental policies that advocated the reformation of public health in London. Together, they also produced a new form of picturesque that was not urban or rural, it was a hybrid between the two. Each one of the institutions enhanced both the character of Highgate village and the new civic identity of the metropolis as a whole, which was emerging beyond the actual historical boundaries of London. Also, they not only contributed to the built environment of the village, but enhanced its character as a healthy place to dwell, heal and be buried.

When compared to the monumental scale of the gasometers in Kensal Green, the new development around Highgate Cemetery was segregated behind natural landscapes, and high boundary walls. So nature, in the context of Highgate, was the mediator, which at times discretely screened off and made more private places such as hospitals or the cemetery. Still to this day, Highgate retains its hybrid nature of "urban" village, where the elements of the city are experienced on a smaller scale and where the built environment, its architecture and urban fabric are mediated by the presence of nature and its unique topography that create an ongoing dialogue between Highgate and London, which is a constant reminder about their interdependent relationship.

Bibliography

Adams, Annemarie. 2008. *Medicine by Design: The Architect and the Modern Hospital, 1893–1943*. Minneapolis: University of Minnesota Press. Accessed July 17, 2020. http://www.jstor.com/stable/10.5749/j.ctttv5mt.6

Andrews, Malcolm. 1994. "The Metropolitan Picturesque." In *The Politics of the Picturesque. Literature, Landscape and Aesthetics since 1770*, edited by Stephen Copley and Peter Garside, 282–98. Cambridge: Cambridge University Press.

Ariès, Philippe. 2008. *The Hour of Our Death*. New York, Toronto: Vintage Books.

Arnold, Catharine. 2006. *Necropolis: London and Its Dead*. London: Simon & Schuster.

Arnold, Dana. 1982. *Rural Urbanism. London Landscapes in the Early Nineteenth Century*. Manchester, New York: Manchester University Press.

Baggs, A. P., Diane K. Bolton, and Patricia E. C. Croot. 1985. "Islington: Growth, Holloway and Tollington." In *A History of the County of Middlesex: Volume 8, Islington and Stoke Newington Parishes*, edited by T. F. T. Baker and C. R. Elrington, 29–37. British History Online. Accessed July 18, 2020. https://www.british-history.ac.uk/vch/middx/vol8/pp29–37

Baggs, A. P., Diane K. Bolton, M. A. Hicks, and R. B. Pugh. 1980. "Hornsey, Including Highgate: Social and Cultural Activities." In *A History of the County of Middlesex: Volume 6, Friern Barnet, Finchley, Hornsey with Highgate*, edited by T. F. T. Baker and C. R. Elrington, 157–162. British History Online. Accessed July 18, 2020. https://www.british-history.ac.uk/vch/middx/vol6/pp157–162

Baker Whelan, Lara. 2010. *Class, Culture and Suburban Anxieties in the Victorian Era*. New York, London: Routledge.

Barker, Felix. 1984. *Highgate Cemetery: Victorian Valhalla*. London: Murray.

Bates, Alan W. 2010. *The Anatomy of Robert Knox: Murder, Mad Science and Medical Regulation in Nineteenth-Century Edinburgh*. Brighton: Sussex Academic Press.

Bland, Olivia. 1986. *The Royal Way of Death*. London: Constable & Company Ltd.

Bradshaw, George. ([1862] 2013). *Bradshaw's Handbook to London*. London: Bloomsbury Publishing Plc.

Byrne, Richard. 1989. *Prisons and Punishments of London*. London: Harrap.

Bull, John. 1839. *The British Newspaper Archive*. 19. No. 958: 186. Accessed September 19, 2021. https://www.britishnewspaperarchive.co.uk/viewer/BL/0001945/18390421/009/0006

"Cemeteries". 1839. *The Penny Magazine*. No. 494. (December 21): 489–90.

Clarke, William Spencer. 1881. *The Suburban Homes of London: A Residential Guide to Favourite London Localities, Their Society, Celebrities, and Associations, with Notes on Their Rental, Rates and House Accommodation*. London: Chatto and Windus. Accessed June 5, 2021. https://www.google.co.uk/books/edition/The_Suburban_Homes_of_London/xKYHAAAAQAAJ?hl=en

Clement, Paul. 2017. "Highgate Cemetery Heterotopia: A Creative Counterpublic Space." *Space and Culture* 20, no. 4: 470–84. Accessed June 27, 2021. https://doi.org/10.1177/1206331217724976

Corton, Christine L. 2015. *London Fog: The Biography*. Harvard: Harvard University Press. Accessed July 17, 2020. http://www.jstor.com/stable/j.ctvjnrshm.3

Dennis, Richard. 2008. *Cities in Modernity. Representations and Productions of Metropolitan Space, 1840–1930*. Cambridge: Cambridge University Press.

Downing, Margaret. 2009. "The Story of Holly Lodge". Unpublished manuscript. Accessed June 9, 2021. https://myhlra.files.wordpress.com/2018/08/story-of-holly-lodge34141.pdf

Dungavell, Ian. "The Unseemly Events Surrounding the Consecration Of Highgate Cemetery." Friends of Highgate Cemetery Trust (FOHCT) Newsletter Vol. 2. N. 9 (April). Accessed June 6, 2020. https://highgatecemetery.org/uploads/Consecration_article.pdf

Foucault, Michel. ([1977] 1991). *Discipline and Punish: The Birth of the Prison*. London: Penguin Books Ltd.

Foucault, Michel. ([1972] 1995). *The Archaeology of Knowledge*. London: Routledge.

Foucault, Michel. 1997. "Of Other Spaces: Utopias and Heterotopias." In Neil Leach *Rethinking Architecture*, 350–6. London: Routledge.

Foucault, Michel. 2009. *Security, Territory, Population*. Basingstoke: Palgrave Macmillan.

Foucault, Michel. ([1973] 2009). *The Birth of the Clinic: An Archeology of Medical Perception*. London: Routledge.

"Inauguration of the New Cattle Market." 1855. *The Examiner*. No. 2472 (June 16): 377. Accessed June 30, 2021. https://www.britishnewspaperarchive.co.uk/viewer/BL/0000054/18550616/011/0009?browse=False

"Highgate Conservation Area Appraisal and Management Proposals." N.d. Accessed July 1, 2021. https://www.camden.gov.uk/documents/20142/7610500/Highgate.pdf/6995d361-b1c5-5650-4414-9669232073e1

Hunter, Robert. 1897. "The Movements for the Inclosure and Preservation of Open Lands." *Journal of the Royal Statistical Society*. 60. No. 2: 360–431. Accessed July 16, 2020. http://www.jstor.com/stable/2979801

Lovell, Percy and William McB. Marcham. 1936. "Nos 45 and 46 West Hill." In *Survey of London: Volume 17, the Parish of St Pancras Part 1: the Village of Highgate*. British History Online, 67–8. Accessed July 1, 2021. http://www.british-history.ac.uk/survey-london/vol17/pt1/pp67-68

"New Hospitals Versus the Extension of Old Hospitals for London." 1894. *The British Medical Journal* 1, no. 1728 (February 10): 314. Accessed July 27, 2020. https://www.jstor.org/stable/20227408

"New Public Park for North London: The Gift of Sir Sydney Waterlow, Bart." 1889. *The Illustrated London News*. 2641 (November 30):

693–96. Accessed July 1, 2021. https://www.britishnewspaperarchive.co.uk/viewer/BL/0001578/18891130/034/0017

Olsen, Donald J. 1976. *The Growth of Victorian London*. London: B.T. Batsford Ltd.

"Open Spaces at Highgate." 1885. *Hampstead and Highgate Express*. No. 1293 (August 22): 4. Accessed July 1, 2021. https://www.britishnewspaperarchive.co.uk/viewer/BL/0001981/18850822/050/0004

Otter, Christopher. 2004. "Cleansing and Clarifying: Technology and Perception in Nineteenth-Century London." *Journal of British Studies*. Cambridge: Cambridge University Press. 43, no. 1 (January): 40–64. Accessed May 27, 2021. https://www.jstor.org/stable/10.1086/jbs.2004.43.issue-1

Parsons, Brian. 2018. *The Evolution of the British Funeral Industry in the 20th Century. From Undertaker to Funeral Director*. Bingley: Emerald Publishing Limited.

"Proposed Hospital For North London." 1882. *The British Medical Journal* 1, no. 1113 (April 29): 635–36. Accessed July 27, 2020. https://www.jstor.org/stable/25259570

Reclus, Élisée. 1860. *Guide du Voyageur à Londres et aux Environs*. Paris: Librairie de L. Hachette et C.ie. Accessed July 30 2020. https://books.google.fr/books?id=W3IOAAAAQAAJ&pg=PA251&hl=fr&source=gbs_selected_pages&cad=2#v=onepage&q&f=false

Rockey, John. 1983. "From Vision to Reality: Victorian Ideal Cities and Model Towns in the Genesis of Ebenezer Howard's Garden City." *The Town Planning Review* 54, no. 1: 83–105. Accessed June 8, 2021. http://www.jstor.org/stable/40111935

Richardson, John. 2004. *Highgate Past*. London: Historical Publications Ltd.

Tafuri, Manfredo. 1976. *Architecture and Utopia. Design and Capitalist Development*. Cambridge, London: The MIT Press.

"The Williams Family Tree." N.d. Accessed July 1, 2021. https://williamsfamilytree.co.uk/tree/getperson.php?personID=I40209&tree=wft

"The Highgate Infirmary." *The British Medical Journal* 1, no. 476 (February 12): 160. Accessed July 17, 2020. https://www.jstor.org/stable/25218284

"The New Cattle Market and Highgate Cemetery." 1852. *The Morning Chronicle*. No. 26727 (August 23): 3. Accessed June 30, 2021. https://www.britishnewspaperarchive.co.uk/viewer/BL/0000082/18520823/008/0003

"The Metropolitan Small-Pox Hospitals." 1886. *The British Medical Journal* 1, no. 1312 (February 20): 361–62. Accessed July 27 2020. https://www.jstor.org/stable/25275088

The Tablet. A Weekly Newspaper and Reviews. 1907. Vol. 110. No. 3516 (28 September). Accessed June 9, 2021. https://www.britishnewspaperarchive.co.uk/viewer/BL/0002447/19070928/115/0023

"St. Pancras Infirmary." 1869. *The Builder* 28, no. 1353 (January 9): 27–9. Accessed August 6 2020. https://archive.org/details/gri_33125006201939/page/n29/mode/2up

Strange, Julie-Marie. 2005. *Death, Grief and Poverty in Britain, 1870–1914*. Cambridge: Cambridge University Press.

Udall, Lindsay. 2019. "Arnos Vale South Bristol: The Life of a Cemetery." Doctoral Thesis, The University of Bristol.

Ward Richardson, Benjamin. 1876. *Hygeia, A City of Health*. London: MacMillan & Co.

Webber, Richard, and Roger Burrows. 2016. "Life in an Alpha Territory." *Urban Studies* 53, no. 15 (November): 3139–54. Accessed July 16, 2020. https://www.jstor.org/stable/10.2307/26151273

5 Suburbs/Brookwood and Woking

5.1 Waterways and brick yards

In a short article published on Saturday 4 June 1796, the *Hampshire Chronicle: And Portsmouth and Chichester Journal* announced that the Basingstoke Canal was open for navigation and that "barges go now regularly every week from to and from Basingstoke to London". As well as listing the particulars of the rates for freights of goods to be transported in barges, the article explains that "The quantity of goods carrying on the canal far exceed what were expected at this early period" and based on these first results, it anticipated the prospect of a fast growing trade (Basingstoke Canal Navigation 1796, 1). The canal was an agricultural waterway that stretched 37 miles, and in the Woking area featured 14 locks and ten bridges that were built using bricks that were locally made, in brick yards that had easy road access to the new waterway (Wakeford, 1995, 6). Their designs were simple and functional, yet their aesthetics complemented the rural setting of its surroundings. In a period postcard dated 1906 (Figure 5.1), featuring the Victoria Cottage Hospital (on the right hand side of the bridge), it is possible to see the style of the brick arch bridges. However, partly to do with the poor quality of the building materials and techniques, most of them fell into disrepair and were replaced by concrete ones by 1914 (Wakeford 1995, 7).

Along with the brick kilns that already existed in the area, prior to the construction of the Basingstoke Canal, new ones were opened in the 1780–90s, mostly along Robin Hood Road, which connected the kilns and the canal. On a historical map dated 1897 the brick works are marked as "brick yard". In his book *A History of Woking*, local historian Alan Crosby records that the brick industry was still strong in the Woking area until the kilns were forced to close in 1942 due to the suspension of all building work during the Second World War. The construction of the railway connections between London to Southampton and Portsmouth also made use of the brick industry present in the area, for the construction of bridges and stations and service buildings, as this reduced the transport costs of building materials (2003, 133–4). With new trade opportunities, workers settled

DOI: 10.4324/9781003178934-6

Figure 5.1 The Chobham Bridge (also known as Victoria Bridge and Weathshaft Bridge) and the Victoria Cottage Hospital that served Woking and surrounding areas. Postcard. 1906. Author's collection.

in the area between Goldsworth and Woking. A new chapel, designed by architect George Gilbert Scott (St. Pancras Station and Albert Memorial in London), was commissioned to serve the new community. St. John the Baptist's (see Figure 5.2) was completed in 1842 in Early English (thirteenth century) architectural style. The stone building featured a series of narrow windows (named lancet) topped by pointed arches (100). St. John's eventually, in 1888, became a parish church (137).

The flat landscape and the sandy soil allowed for the establishment of nurseries and market gardens in locations between Knaphill, Brookwood and Woking. When establishing their cemetery in Brookwood, the London Necropolis Company made use of the local nurseries and workforce for planting and maintenance. According to Brookwood Cemetery historian John Clarke, the London Necropolis Company contracted Robert Donald, a local specialist supplier of exotic plants based in Goldsworth (Woking) for the cemetery planting. Already by 1861 – less than ten years since the opening of the cemetery – Donald's nurseries employed 40 and occupied 200 acres of land in the area (2004, 11). Although some of the local nurseries were not directly connected to the London Necropolis Company and Brookwood Cemetery as Donald was, they still were very large in scale and had an extensive trade. One can gather this from the adverts published by some of the local nursery owners. For example in an advert published

Figure 5.2 St. John the Baptist Church in Woking. Postcard. 1906.

on Saturday 9 December 1871 in *The Field – The Country Gentlemen Newspaper*, the George Jackman & Son nurseries of Woking, alongside mentioning the fact that they sell directly to the public through their catalogue at wholesale prices, also mention that their nurseries are 180 acres in extent (32). Anthony Waterer Nurseries based in Knaphill for example, made their name in rhododendrons and azaleas, and supplied some of the London Royal Parks for their planting, such Regent Park (*The Globe* 1880, 8) and Hyde Park in the 1880s and early 1900s (*Morning Post* 1906, 1). From a 1936 newspaper advertisement (see Figure 5.3) featuring Anthony Waterer Nurseries, we can also gather that along with planting they also specialised in golf courses. The area west of Brookwood Cemetery featured two golf courses (West Hill and Woking golf clubs) built on the land owned by the London Necropolis Company that for many years was the "cemetery reserve". Also West Hill golf club had strong connections with the company as one of its general directors, John Baker Walker, was president of the club (Clarke 2004, 31–65).

From a 1938 map of the area, it is possible to see how brickyards were still very present in the area between Brookwood, Knaphill, Goldsworth and Woking, up to the beginning of the Second War World, particularly north west of the Inkerman Barracks and west of the Brookwood Asylum (of which we will see more later). Large nurseries were located north of St. John's and along the north boundary of the Basingstoke Canal as well

124 Suburbs/Brookwood and Woking

Figure 5.3 Newspaper advertisement of the (late) Anthony Waterer Nurseries in Knaphill. 1936. Author's collection.

as south of Hook Heath, and along the railway tracks of the London to Portsmouth direct line.

Along with the cutting of the Basingstoke Canal and arrival of the railway lines, there were also other factors that contributed to radical changes that took place in the area, such as the implementation of the Enclosure Acts. These legislations activated the reclamation of waste land across England between 1780 and 1860. Although their objective was to raise the productivity of low-valued land, their implementation resulted in the displacement of rural communities that eventually ended up relocating into the nearest town or city to find work and shelter. Mechanisation and technological developments applied to agriculture also started to be implemented to scale up quantitative and qualitative productions of vegetables as well as meat and dairies. Ultimately the coming of the railway in the late 1830s made possible faster transport of goods, produce and even livestock between the places of production and those of processing, preparation and consumption (Williams 1970, 55).

The Enclosure Acts had a key role in defining the inception of Brookwood Cemetery and the influence of the London Necropolis Company over the development of the local area. Clarke covered in detail how the Enclosure Acts impacted the establishment of the London Necropolis Company by initially imposing the compulsory purchase of so-called "waste land" from local landowner, Lord Onslow. As a result of the transaction, the London Necropolis Company became the sole owner of 2,200 acres of common land, of which 500 were dedicated to Brookwood Cemetery (Clarke 2004, 4–8, 15). What was defined as "waste land" was actually common or heath, and represented most of the land that was enclosed in Surrey in the nineteenth century. This process brought a new perception of value to these typologies of land that ranged from speculative building development opportunities to conservation of open spaces for leisure purposes (Parton 1985, 58). The establishment of the London Necropolis Company and Brookwood Cemetery was a historically significant moment that marked the transfer of administrative powers from landed gentry to capitalist speculators, which opened up a series of opportunities and possibilities for land developments.

5.2 Cemetery and town

Upon the opening of their cemetery in Brookwood in 1854, the London Necropolis Company was on the verge of bankruptcy and it needed to make quick profits, possibly by selling part of the surplus land and acting as a landlord by collecting rents and other fees from locals. Brookwood Cemetery was a completely different model of private cemetery when compared to the ones in Kensal Green and Highgate. The company was not only selling burial plots to private individuals but was reserving land for London's parishes, to be used once they ran out of burial spaces in their own churchyards. Therefore its layout became almost a mirror of London with its various parishes. Over the years the company directors regularly reported on the progress of land reservations by the London parishes within the cemetery. There were also charity organisations and even communities reserving large plots of land in the cemetery. For example in 1857 the company reported that the Swedish community bought one acre of land to bury Swedish nationals that died in Britain. The Dramatic, Equestrian & Musical Sick Fund Association bought one acre too for the burial of actors (*The Standard* 1857, 6). Victorian actor John William Anson was the founder and secretary of the Fund. The organisation was also behind the foundation of the Royal Dramatic College, of which we will see more later. Anson is buried in the plot at Brookwood Cemetery along with some of the former residents of the College. (Clarke 2004, 211) .

Since its inception, the company directors had difficulties keeping the administration in balance. Clarke researched and reported on the processes of getting the cemetery established. The company was also troubled by internal politics, as some members belonging to the board of directors were reported for fraud (2004, 4–8). There were also compensations to be paid to the commoners for the loss of the use of Woking Common (*The Sussex Advertiser* 1853, 7). There were also extra costs (from those initially budgeted for) that the company had to face for the construction of their private station near Waterloo as well as drainage for the cemetery. Once the cemetery opened for burials, on 13 November 1854, the business was slow to start. Between its opening and 31 January 1855, the company reported only 325 funerals, which was a very small number considering that at the time weekly burials in London were 1,400; the company was conducting very little business. However, the company directors worked hard at securing the sign-up of more parishes, such as those of St. Luke, Chelsea, Bermondsey and Chiswick among others, with an undertaking to use Brookwood for burials. Although some churchyards were closed due to the unsanitary conditions, others needed to wait until those parishes would run out of their current burial space to then start using their reserved plots in Brookwood (*The Daily News* 1855, 2). Along with the above-mentioned problems, the company had obligations to the Government with regard to the land they could sell for profit under the 1852 Act.

As soon as the cemetery was opened for business, a draft to amend the clauses that regulated the selling of its land was prepared and submitted to the government. It was eventually passed on 23 July 1855 (Clarke 2004, 14–6), and the company was granted permission to sell 1,200 acres of land of which 420 were in the vicinity of Woking station and more suitable for building than a cemetery. The Act also granted the company the possibility to sell some of the most valuable parts of their properties too, such as the Hermitage Estate as well as existing brickfields. From the annual reports it appears though that the company did not sell the brickfields, as they were actually providing it with rent and royalties for the bricks made and sold (*The Morning Advertiser* 1856, 5). Although the London Necropolis Company managed to have the amended act approved by Parliament, there were still restrictions to what it could sell. The amendments following those in 1855 and 1864 only reviewed the timespan for land sales, which allowed the Company to sell land only within a specific time period. It was only with the 1869 Act that eventually the London Necropolis Company was finally free to sell surplus land (Clarke 2004, 14–6). It was also for this reason that the company directors were constantly trying to reassure their investors, as they were not seeing great returns for their money.

After the first few years of difficulties, a clearer sense of direction of travel was set for the company. In a general meeting, published in a London newspaper in 1859, the company's three top objectives, among others, were stated: "1. Keep down the expenses of the undertaking; 2. Increase their funds; 3. Sale of a large estate in land" (*The Standard* 1859, 5). From this statement we can gather that the company's priority wasn't to have a direct input in the actual planning and development of Brookwood and Woking but to secure sales of large plots of land. This was something the company managed to achieve in the early years, as we will see later, for example with the coming of a new prison and asylum to Brookwood. These opportunities were also driven by the Government's policy reforms on public health and security. The results of the policies manifested in a new, large-scale institutional building. This provides us with some evidence that although the company was not directly interested in the overall planning and development taking place in Woking and Brookwood, they had however a vested interest in the local building industry and therefore wanted to see buildings going up in the area, as they were able to provide the main construction material at competitive costs. The sites were not only appealing because they could be reached by train from London but also because the main building materials were locally produced. This would have cut the cost of transport and therefore reduced the cost of the building overall. The coming of a new, large institution to the area provided the company with more financial returns as they were able to sell land as well as secure royalties from the production of bricks needed for the construction of the institutions, which were actually made from the brick fields in their portfolio of properties.

Crosby criticised the company as their myopic politics had direct consequences on the poor quality of Woking's planning. In a passage he states that "Given that the speculation was at the heart of the project the directors could have imposed a rational plan, provided public buildings, and sought to bring into being a town which was worthy and of high quality" *(2003, 78)*. Although Crosby has a point, considering the level of influence the company had due to his authority as landlord in the area, it is also clear that in the early years that was not a priority. The directors had to keep the company and shareholders happy and were preoccupied to generate incomes to distribute dividends to their investors. It is also worth reminding ourselves that the notion of urban planning as we understand it today was not known at the time, as in Britain, urban planning only started to be formalised in the early twentieth century with the experiments related to the Garden City Movement. Indeed, existing examples of enlightened urban planning such as Saltarie and New Lanark could have inspired the London Necropolis Company. However, those pioneering developments were designed for mono industries such as the production of wool. The situation in Brookwood and Woking was different, as these were mainly agricultural areas that with the implementation of the Enclosure Acts were supposed to give new use and value to the land.

It's application however proved complex as it put capitalist speculators in front of issues related to land properties, local contexts in which they did not have personal interest but only wanted capital returns. Also, a person was replaced by a faceless institution, namely the local landlord was replaced by the company's board of directors. Although the company did not know everything about the local context when they took over from the previous landlord, over time they were able to build a knowledge of the context. Even if not always the company directors lived on site or in the vicinity, their staff did, in the accommodation provided by the company near the cemetery. The company's extensive land properties, conveniently connected to transport networks such as road and rail, were ideal locations to accommodate the establishment of any kind of development from residential to institutions that were either newly established or relocating from London and looking for cheaper land options beyond the metropolitan area, connected to the capital by reliable transport links. We have seen in the previous chapter how this took place in the context of Highgate, where the coming of the cemetery was followed by the opening of new hospitals – and other institutions – and only later by residential developments. A similar pattern of development took place between Brookwood and Woking, where institutions arrived first and later were followed by residential developments.

The first institution to be constructed in the area was the Woking Invalid Convict Prison (also known as Knaphill Prison). It was completed only five years after the opening of the cemetery and opened in April 1859. Designed by Joshua Jebb – buried at Brookwood Cemetery (Clarke 2004, 82) – and Arthur Blomfield, this institution had its own gas works to produce the fuel used to light and heat the buildings (Crosby 2003, 126). The complex occupied 64 acres of land (see Figure 5.4), which the London Necropolis Company sold to the government. The prison was extended in

Figure 5.4 Woking Invalid Convicts Prison, and from 1889 Inkerman Barracks. Note the public lighting featured in the postcard. Undated. Author's collection.

1870 with the construction of a section for convicted women. It was the first prison to be designed for convicts suffering mental illnesses (Johnston and Turner 2017, 13). At this time the prison had about 1,400 detainees, which required a large number of staff, from gatekeepers to carpenters and bakers. The Home Office provided housing for the prison workers nearby, between St. John's and Knaphill. By 1886, the Government had decided to close the prison over the next ten years and, by March 1889, the invalid prison was defunct and the property was transferred to the War Department. The portion of the prison that housed women convicts continued to be used until October 1895, when they were transferred to Holloway Prison.

The construction of the waterway and railway, and the Invalid Prison, was possible because of the brick yards nearby. This was also the case when the County Lunatic Asylum (Figure 5.5) was completed in 1867 on 150 acres of land previously owned by the London Necropolis Company (Clarke 2004, 15). The coming into force of the County Asylum Act in 1845 addressed the questions about mental health and care for the less fortunate. The legislation made the individual counties responsible to provide shelter, care and moral treatment to its patients (as mentioned on the County Asylums website www.countyasylums.co.uk/history/).

Figure 5.5 Aerial view of Brookwood Mental Asylum. Postcard. Undated. Author's Collection.

It is worth mentioning that the London Necropolis Company also must have made money from both institutions from subsequent burials of prisoners or inmates from the asylum. As we have seen in the case of the hospitals in Highgate, the Woking Invalid Convict Prison and the County Lunatic Asylum were a landmark of change in terms of wellbeing. These new institutions were also pioneering unprecedented ways to programme space and functions, through architecture and landscape design as well as engineering. With the availability of land in the area, there was no limit to what was possible to build, in terms of scale and ambition. These large-scale developments were a sign of the new typologies of institutions that were emerging in the mid and late Victorian times. They could be compared to self-sufficient small villages. They also had their own rules, systems, they were economic activators, as they gave work to many people in the local area. As they were so isolated, they were like islands in the large sea of green that surrounded them. They were a visual landmark in landscape, and as they were very large, they could be seen from afar. Towers such as the one at the Brookwood Lunatic Asylum doubled as a water tower as well as a clock tower that regulated the rhythm of the day and night, like a bell tower in a village. They needed to be self-sufficient so they had to produce their own energy, store the necessary water and have their own sewage systems.

From a map of the area dated 1897 it is possible to notice the asylum main building and the ancillary structures dedicated to services including a hospital, a church, a mortuary (but not a burial ground), a dairy farm, gas works and a gasometer. The asylum also had its own water supply and vegetable and fruit gardens as well as a landscaped park that was open to visitors during the flowering season. Gardening in particular was adopted as part of the therapies for the inmates. Sarah Rutherford has been researching this aspect of these institutions and also wrote about Robert Lloyd the head gardener at the Brookwood Asylum. Rutherford theorised that the design formula for private asylums was "largely based on the aristocrat's landscape park and garden. This model was adopted because it addressed the needs of an extensive building in a rural setting, which required ornamental grounds and an element of agricultural self sufficiency" (2005, 62). A part of the self-sufficiency aspects to consider were the housings for the workers employed by the institutions. They were often accommodated in dwellings especially constructed for them, as the cottages the London Necropolis Company constructed for their workers were within walking distance to the cemetery (Figure 5.6).

Along with the land sales to accommodate large institutions, the company was also approached by the developers looking for small parcels of land. In 1878 the company sold one acre to the Cremation Society, and the first crematorium was established in St. John's (Figure 5.7). The location was chosen for its strategic position being in close proximity to the large cemetery and the company's private existing railway link to London. The society built the crematorium there to test and develop the new technology.

Figure 5.6 Houses for the London Necropolis Company workers at Brookwood Cross Roads. Postcard. Undated. Author's collection.

Figure 5.7 St. John Crematorium, Woking. Postcard. 1906. Author's collection.

In 1885 the St. John Crematorium in Woking was completed and officially opened for business (Parsons 2018, 82). From the existing documentation of the London Necropolis Company, in particular their prospectuses, one can assume that the directors of the cemetery company and the cremation society had reached a definitive agreement to work together. In a pamphlet published by the London Necropolis Company, in 1898, cremation charges and details about Woking Crematorium form an integral part of the company's offerings of burial services.

In 1858 the Dramatic, Equestrian & Musical Sick Fund Association was looking to establish a purpose-built retirement home for actors. The organisation approached the London Necropolis Company for a site in Woking and eventually the company donated five acres of land for the construction of the building. In return the Society was to buy within two years the equivalent amount of land, adjacent to the donated site. The given land was by Woking station and therefore the new institution was in a prominent and visible position. This was seen as a positive by the company's directors, as they felt it would have improved the neighbourhood as well as the value of their estate *(The Standard* 1859, 5). However, the initiative was not as long lasting as expected by the Royal Dramatic Society, and by 1880 the sale by auction of the building appeared in local and national newspapers. The main building, alongside a central hall, library and galleries, featured 20 individual dwellings (with bedroom, sitting room, kitchen and services) across the east and west wings. The property also included extensive landscaped grounds featuring among others a kitchen garden, walks and parterres. The advert also indicated that the property was particularly suited for an institution or school (*The Daily News* 1880, 8). However in 1884 when it was eventually purchased by linguist and academic Gottlieb Wilhelm Leitner, the building was adapted to suit his Oriental University Institute (Figure 5.8). His objective was to create a centre for the study of the culture and history of India and the Islamic world, and for the linguistic preparation for those attending posts in various locations and countries in the East. Later, in 1889, Leitner commissioned William Isaac Chambers to design the Shah Jahan Mosque. Constructed near the Institute, this was the first purpose-built mosque ever built in Britain (as stated by the King's College London website on 28 March 2018, www.kcl.ac.uk/the-kings-professor-who-founded-the-uks-first-purpose-built-mosque). The building was part of a larger visionary plan Leitner had for the Oriental Institute and included the commissioning and construction of a Hindu temple, a Synagogue and an Anglican Church all on the land adjacent to the Institute (as stated by The Lightbox on June 18, 2021 website, www.thelightbox.org.uk/blog/wilhelm-leitner). Brookwood Cemetery was also the location of Britain's first Muslim cemetery (as reported by Clarke on his website on 25 July 2019, www.john-clarke.co.uk/news_2019.html#trails).

Despite the success in selling large portions of land to accommodate large-scale institutions in the areas between Brookwood, Knaphill and

Suburbs/Brookwood and Woking 133

Figure 5.8 The Oriental Institute, Woking. Postcard. 1906. Author's collection.

Woking, the London Necropolis Company was not able to attract residential developers to that part of Surrey, despite the direct train connections to London Waterloo Station. For example, in 1888 the Company tried to auction the land on a prime site, near Woking station (Woking Common Freehold Building Estate). The sale was not successful and indicated that there was no market yet for this premium suburban land within commuting distance from London (at the time, 40 minutes from London Waterloo Station).

By the early 1890s, Woking made a step forward towards urbanisation, with the coming of public lighting. This was possible as the new gas works were established in Boundary Road (see Figure 5.11). The site was conveniently located near the Basingstoke Canal. Woking local historian, Iain Wakeford, in *A Guide to the Industrial History of Woking and its Borough* explains that Woking District Gas Company purchased 1.5 acres of land from the Necropolis Company and that "a 60ft high gasometer was built and the works opened on 9th June 1892" (1995, 26–7). According to Wakeford, the Gas Works quickly prospered, and in 1901 and 1905 the works were extended, and later, in 1909, a tramway was built to transport the coal needed for the production of gas from the nearby Basingstoke Canal to the works (26–7). We saw a similar arrangement in Chapter 3, when discussing the development of the Kensal Green areas and the coming of the gas works there in 1845, on a site (previously owned by the

General Cemetery Company) located between the Grand Union Canal and the cemetery.

The development is also mentioned in a small publication dated 1907 and titled "Woking as a Residential District" produced by local builders and contractors Drowley & Co., one of the builders and contractors of the development. There were also others such as Harris & Company who constructed in 1899 the chapel in the Roman Catholic section of Brookwood Cemetery (Clarke 2004, 22). The stylised shamrock on the title page may suggest that the company had Irish origins or connections. The text in the brochure features a selection of completed projects such as country houses and other residential buildings, shops, golf courses, church buildings and even the Woking Council offices (Figure 5.9). Most of the buildings illustrated in the publications were designed by Tubbs and Messer. The text also points out the favourable position of Woking due to its connections to London and clean air and access to countryside (*Woking as a Residential District* 1907, 1).

Beyond the developments in Woking and the estates, other residential developments were also taking place in the west end of Brookwood. In a period photo from the early twentieth century, it is possible to see town houses on both sides of Connaught Road, towards Pirbright (Figure 5.10).

Figure 5.9 View of Commercial Road. From the left: The Water Co. office, the Grand Theatre, the Woking Council offices and the Wesleyan church (these last two were built by Drowley & Co.). These formed the core of the civic heart of Woking. Postcard. 1906. Author's collection.

Suburbs/Brookwood and Woking   135

Figure 5.10 Houses in Connaught Road, Brookwood. Postcard. Undated. Author's collection.

In 1909 a new institution was established in Woking and was located to the west of the Oriental Institute. The London & South Western Railway Servants' Orphanage (Figure 5.11 and Figure 5.12) occupied seven and a half acres of land purchased from the Necropolis Company. Its foundation and completion were reported in local and national newspapers and magazines. On 28 June 1909 a short article appeared in *The Sphere* explaining that the object of the orphanage was to:

> "House, feed, clothe, and educate the fatherless children of those who, regardless of grade or position, were at the time of their decease in the employ of the London and South-Western Railway Company"
>
> (28)

Clarke reports that the new orphanage in Woking replaced earlier and smaller premises in Clapham. The institution was managed by employees ("servants") of the London & South Western Railway and not by external management or directors. The railway company also reserved plots at Brookwood which contain upwards of 1,000 former railwaymen and their families. (2021, 6–8).

From a 1938 map it is also possible to get a sense of the arrangement of the institutional buildings, the crematorium and developments in the Brookwood, St. John's as well as Knaphill areas (see Figure 5.13). It is

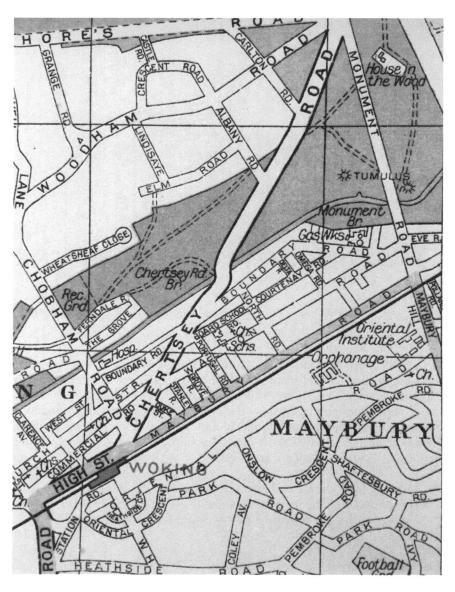

Figure 5.11 Map of Woking showing Gas Works, Oriental Institute and London & South Western Railway Servants' Orphanage. 1932. Author's collection.

Figure 5.12 Undated postcard featuring the boys' gymnastic activities at the London & South Western Railway Servants' Orphanage. Note in the background the Shah Jahan Mosque. Author's collection.

possible to see how the presence of golf courses between the west end of the cemetery, and Hook Heath formed a continuum between the cemetery, sports amenities, and the low density residential developments and the urbanised and higher density areas of Woking centre. In this respect the cemetery, instead of remaining isolated, became an integral component of what effectively became a new satellite town to London, providing both housing for the living and resting places for the dead.

The arrival of the London Necropolis Company to the area had a deep influence in the shaping of the local economy and indeed the spatial arrangements of the areas in the vicinity of the cemetery. This happened both directly and indirectly; directly, through their own operations such as the establishment of the cemetery and the private railway line, and the establishment of other services related to the cemetery, such as dwellings for the workers or contractors responsible for the establishment and maintenance of the cemetery. The Company also indirectly influenced developments of the area, due to the control they had through the land ownership. Indeed the Company, as we have seen, also struggled to stay afloat as a commercial enterprise. However, by the end of the century, the area between Brookwood and Woking became one of the satellite towns to London, that although not formally planned, featured, alongside the cemetery, a crematorium, new institutions, new housing stock and amenities. In the Greater

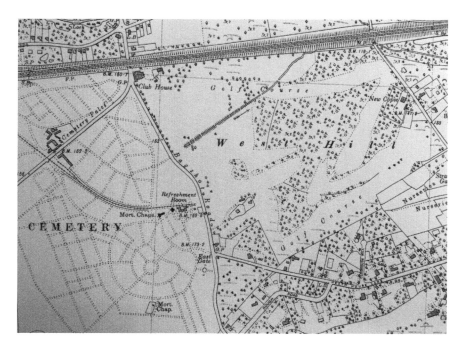

Figure 5.13 Map of Brookwood, Knaphill and St John's. 1938. Author's collection.

London Plan devised by Patrick Abercrombie 1944 (Figure 5.14), Woking features just beyond the border of the proposed green belt.

To conclude we can say that what we have seen above are innovative typologies of buildings and pioneering building technologies and architecture in their own ways, that urbanised the area and turned a district that was otherwise out of London's metropolitan area into a new town. The connection between the existing local industry (nurseries and brick yards) was enhanced by the coming of the London Necropolis Company to the area. Towards the end of the century, Woking was at a convenient and commutable distance from London, therefore accessible. The presence of open spaces in the surroundings, including the canal, the golf courses and indeed the cemetery, became a feature to the area that became desirable for people looking to move out of London to a less congested area, but still being able to commute to the city.

5.3 New century, new beginning

A major turning point in the history of the London Necropolis Company came about in 1899, when the plans for the expansion of Waterloo Station were approved and due to be implemented in the first two decades of the twentieth century. The scale of the project was unprecedented and aimed

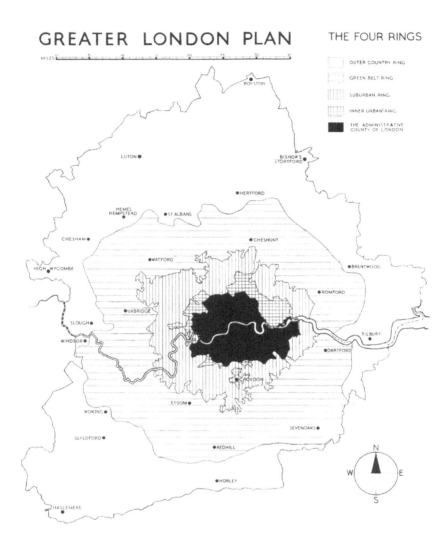

Figure 5.14 Abercrombie Greater London Plan: the Four Rings. 1944. Author's collection.

at making train transport more efficient and the station more user friendly. The new upgraded terminus was eventually officially opened on 21 March 1922. As part of the renovation, the Necropolis Company was forced to relocate its offices, workshops and their private station (that connected London to Brookwood Cemetery by rail) from its original premises on the west side of the station (at the junction of York Street and Westminster Bridge Road) to a new site located on the east side of the station. In the original Necropolis Company offices as seen in a brochure dated 1898 (on the left hand side of the railway station access), the building did not have distinctive features, but the archway access to the private station was heavily decorated and featured very large-scale advertising that was probably possible to see by train travellers going to and from Waterloo Station. These relatively small premises however were able to cope with some large-scale public funerals. In his book *London's Necropolis: A Guide to Brookwood Cemetery* Clarke explains that in 1895 for the funeral of German philosopher Friedrich Engel, the station managed to fit over 120 people attending the funeral (2004, 22–3).

To obviate the relocation issue, the London & South Western Railway (LSWR) company offered to the London Necropolis Company the opportunity to select a suitable new plot of land where to build new offices and service buildings, including a new station. A suitable plot of land was eventually identified and purchased by the LSWR. Tubbs prepared the designs and specifications for the office block, workshops and Necropolis Station, and the building constructions were completed and in use by 1902. The London Necropolis were undertakers as well as cemetery proprietors, so they were able to provide one-stop-shop services, from the preparation of the corpse to funeral and disposal. The new site was distinctively shaped as the letter "S", with a narrow street front at one end and access to Waterloo rail tracks at the other end that would be suitable to accommodate a new private station. Tubbs cleverly also managed to fit on the site workshops, mortuaries, a chapel and a separate entrance block for 3rd class funerals.

According to Clarke, Tubbs was the man that gave the London Necropolis Company a sense of vision (2004, 22–3). Beyond being a versatile commercial surveyor and architect, Tubbs was able to design and specify complex buildings, as the new company premises, as well as design country houses in Surrey inspired by the Arts & Crafts design canons. Tubbs' attentive eye for detail is evident in the 57 pages specification document he prepared in April 1899 (part of the archives at the Surrey History Centre, Woking. Ref No: 6852/8/1/3), where one can get a sense of the materiality of the building and the finishes of its spaces. From this document it is possible to gather that the facade was finished in granite, terracotta and bricks. Tubbs specified that the granite for the bricks was to be laid in "Old English" bond (8). The internal walls of the passageways were finished in white glazed bricks (ground floor and first floor, also to walls of stairs, WC and lobby on station level (42). The roof was to be covered using green slates (14). Teak wood (of Burmese growth) and English oak was specified by Tubbs for the interior flooring of the offices and waiting room. The building had electricity and internal communication consisting of electric bell services and speaking tubes fitted in offices and workshops (37). The chapel had fine pilasters made in Parian cement with flutings on the surface and moulded bases and polished finishes

(55). The architectural aesthetics adopted by Tubbs for the office building facade include materials such as granite and specifically designed and casted terracotta ceramic, the latter of which featured in other buildings completed near the time in London, such as the Whitechapel Gallery in the East End, designed by Charles Harrison Townsend and opened in 1901, as well as The Bishopsgate Institute near Liverpool Street Station completed in 1895 and the Hotel Russell by Charles Doll completed in 1898 (see Figure 5.15 and Figure 5.16).

Tubbs' design solutions made the most of an otherwise narrow and awkwardly shaped site. There, beyond the offices, he accommodated a diverse range of space needed for the running of the Company's funeral services: from preparing the corpses for burial to the coffins workshop. Within the site, Tubbs also integrated a funerary chapel and a private railway station, which connected the company's London premises to Brookwood Cemetery. Every aspect was thought through and designed by Tubbs, including signage for the circulation and way-finding, and as we can read in the specification document he allocated a sum of £20 (roughly £1,400 in today's money) to design and produce notice boards and names on doors and fixings. A sum of £100 (roughly £7,000 in today's money) was allocated to the ventilation of the building, including flues, gratings, inlets and exhaust ventilation to the mortuaries (37). Two hydraulic lifts were fitted in the building complex. Semi-prism pavement lights on the station platform were fitted to bring natural light into the workshops located under the stations' platform (57).

5.4 The Woking residential estates

Following the completion of the building, the London Necropolis Company produced a pamphlet in 1904 to introduce its new premises at 121 Westminster Bridge Road (*The London Necropolis* 1904). Two-thirds of the publication explained in great detail the new offices, workshops and station, and emphasised how the same attention to detail was applied to their funerary designs and services. Especially commissioned photographs illustrated the publication and provided a visual tour of the new premises and the cemetery. The real innovation to the company's new image and outlook, however, was featured in the last part of the pamphlet, where the company introduced "The Woking Residential Estates" and outlined their vision to develop the areas in the vicinity of Brookwood Cemetery.

It was only with the appointment of Tubbs, first as a surveyor and land agent, and later as the company's architect, that the management of the company's landholdings changed. Tubbs advised the company on subdividing the administration of the estate into three parts: Woking Station, Knaphill and Hook Heath. Two agents were appointed for the Woking Station area and Knaphill, while Tubbs was responsible for Hook Heath (Clarke 2004, 22–3). From 1898, Tubbs entered a professional partnership with Messer and together they designed houses for the estates and in the

142 Suburbs/Brookwood and Woking

Figure 5.15 Front facade. London Necropolis Company offices at 121 Westminster Bridge Road designed by Cyril B. Tubbs. Early 1900. Author's collection.

Figure 5.16 The platforms of the new private Necropolis Station. Note that a partition separated the first-class platform (left) from the second-/third-class departures to Brookwood Cemetery. Early 1900. Author's collection.

Weybridge area of Woking. Arthur Albert Messer trained in Birmingham and in 1888 moved to New York where he worked for Withers & Dickson and then for Frederick Clarke Withers. Later that year, he set up his own practice with his brother Howard Messer in Fort Worth, Texas, specialising in large family houses. On returning to England in 1898, Messer established an architectural practice with Tubbs. Together they completed the chapel in Brookwood Cemetery and other residential projects on the estates in 1899.

The land allocated to the development of the estates was set east of the existing cemetery and south of the railway line, which connected Brookwood and Woking to London. Brookwood Cemetery was already self-contained, as the majority of the funerals arrived by rail from London directly into the cemetery, and interfered little with the day-to-day life on the estates and nearby areas. The architectural style Tubbs and Messer adopted for the estates was infused with the subdued rustic qualities of the Surrey vernacular style embodied by timber-framed houses with pitched roofs and terracotta hanging tiles. Overall, the development was formed by four estates with distinctive characters and aimed at different typologies of residents. These included influential politicians such as Gerald Balfour, who commissioned architect Edwin Lutyens to design his residence (Fishers Hill) in Hook Heath, as well as composer and suffragette Ethel Smyth. The Hook

144 *Suburbs/Brookwood and Woking*

Heath Estate and the Hermitage Woods developments were very low density and included the largest plots of land. This can be gathered from newspaper adverts showing the side of some of the properties (see Figure 5.17).

We have seen in Chapter 4 how the local community in Highgate attempted to resist the coming of the cemetery when first established because of the close proximity to residences, so how was the London Necropolis Company going to promote a new development which was located in close proximity to the cemetery? Who were they hoping to attract to live near a cemetery? And why? Was there a masterplan for the area? What role did Brookwood Cemetery have in the context of the ambitious Woking Estates project? How did it happen that the London Necropolis Company came up with this idea?

The directors knew that most people associated Woking with Brookwood Cemetery, and anticipated that some people would be concerned about the close proximity between the newly developed estates and the cemetery, therefore they clarified that from the start. In one of the opening passages of the 1904 pamphlet, they reassured the public by stating that for "Those who are seeking a home can visit Woking for themselves, and if they expect a wilderness of gravestones they will be agreeably surprised" (The London Necropolis Company 1904, 39). Indeed the intention was to gauge the attention of a certain type of clientele, and tap into their aspirations: "The young and busy man who catches the 8.14am [from Woking] will be in the office at Lombard Street at 9am" (40).

The relatively short commute from Woking to London's business heart was possible by the integration of railway connections beyond the metropolitan districts, to the fast urban transport network of the capital. The opening of the Waterloo and City Railway in 1898, for example, not only reduced the distance between Waterloo Station and the financial district of

Figure 5.17 Newspaper advertisement of a property for sale in Hook Heath. 1935.

the capital but also the commuting distance from counties such as Surrey or Hampshire. A new generation of Londoners were able to consider a healthier lifestyle beyond the metropolitan districts, in less densely populated areas such as Woking, with easy access to open spaces in the countryside and to fresh air. As well as highlighting the easy access to the city via fast and reliable railway connections, the publication made a feature of the cemetery and its surroundings by highlighting the beauty of the natural landscape. Amenities such as golf courses, cricket grounds and playing fields, as well as woodlands, were all available in the estates too. Instead of showing all this in a plan, the company promoted their residential developments with the image of a golf course and a nearby lake, which set the tone for the type of residents they wanted to move into the area. Hermitage Woods had a similar arrangement to Hook Heath in terms of setting, but the plots of land offered here were smaller, and there was also land available for farming within the vicinity. The Knaphill and Maybury estates were higher density (semi-detached houses mostly) and closer to Woking Station for easier access to the city (see Figure 5.18).

The London Necropolis' pamphlet did not feature any plans of the estates. Had these been included, it would have given the reader a better understanding of each geographical location and context and their relationship to one another. The only visual references provided are photographs of the houses on the estates, from which it is possible to gather the

Figure 5.18 Developments in Chertsey Road, one of the roads in the centre of Woking. Author's collection.

architectural style and variety of scales from mansions to cottages. Perhaps committing to a plan would have restricted the directors in their operations, and this approach instead gave them a range of flexibility in the development of the estates. Although this was a commercial enterprise, the directors employed a strict policy of control over the architecture of the buildings on the estates, which showed their little interest in rows of semi-detached houses, but rather an inclination to obtain a diverse visual arrangement in terms of scale and architectural languages which might also reflect social variety. To encourage new residents to move to the area, the company also offered mortgages for first-time homebuyers. The directors specified that no trees would be cut down to make space for new houses, particularly in the Hook Heath Estate. This was in line with the residential qualities of the estate. It was not permitted to build shops, public houses, reading rooms or concert halls in the area; however, some were located in the fringes of the estate. An extract from the company's pamphlet reads:

> The Agent of the Estate has laid down certain broad lines which, while making Hook Heath sites equally desirable purchases for the rich or people of moderate means, will preserve it for many years as a delight for those whose refinement revolts at the sordid results of modern building schemes. In fact the line has been rigidly drawn at that absolute abomination the suburban villa, and there are many who will be thankful to know that they can come and build either a mansion or a cottage, as their circumstances require, with no fear of their neighbours surrounding them with rows of jerry-built dwellings.
> (The London Necropolis 1904, 43)

To promote its estates, the London Necropolis Company also compared Woking to Hampstead Garden Suburb (see Figure 5.19), highlighting how the connecting railway services available between Woking and London were just as frequent as the ones from Hampstead. Although the company's aim was to attract potential new residents, there were already settlers in Hook Heath by the time the pamphlet was distributed. This was a calculated move by the company's directors to tell their readers the calibre of residents already living in the neighbourhood. The intention here must have been to convey to the reader that the estates were already established, at least socially, and therefore trustworthy.

Looking at the 1938 map of the area (see Figure 5.20), it is possible to see that the two large-scale developments and the crematorium were located on the north part of the railway and the Basingstoke Canal, while the cemetery was located in the south part of these. The canal and the railway created a double separation between the two. The north part contained the two institutions and brick yards, of which we will see more later in this chapter. In the south part, where the cemetery was, there were more farms, nurseries

Figure 5.19 Aerial view of Hampstead Garden Suburb. 1907. Author's collection.

and heathland; it was less dense. This is the area where Tubbs and Messer started to develop their Woking Residential Estates mentioned in the 1904 brochure.

One could say that the plan envisaged for the estates was based on aspirations and commercial interests, rather than the pioneering experimentation that was taking place in North London with the Hampstead Garden Suburb near Golders Green. Although Tubbs and Messer did care about the aesthetics of the estate, the results were mixed in terms of architectural range as in the case of the golf club house in Hook Heath. However, they put careful attention into the preservation of the natural features of the area, a strategy to regulate density of population and of farming, industry and businesses, and lastly, the idea of building the estates around an existing community in the area. With regards to density, we saw how the estates were organised in a radiating system: density was high in the areas which were closest to the station – such as Maybury – and gradually lowered in those further away, as in the case of Hook Heath. There was an inverse proportion between density and plot sizes. In areas where the density was higher, plots were reduced in size. In those areas in which density was lower, the plots of land were larger. The larger properties were located on the fringes of the estates, and like Hook Heath, were secluded among open spaces, golf grounds and farmland. In the estates we also saw that a core community was already

148 Suburbs/Brookwood and Woking

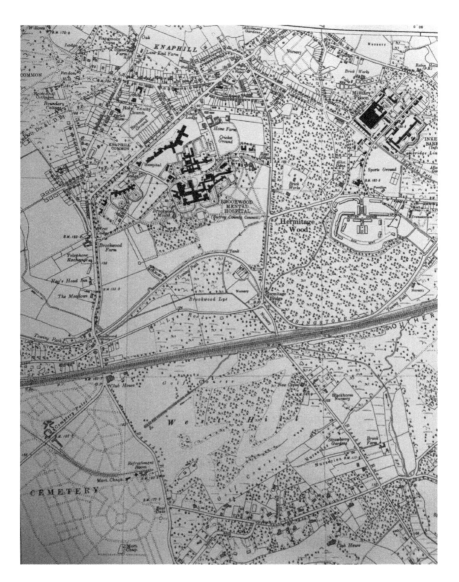

Figure 5.20 Map of Brookwood, Knaphill and St John's. 1938. Author's collection.

established in the area. This element helped set the tone for the actual development, giving it a strong identity.

But why did an established cemetery company suddenly decide to move into an uncharted area such as building development? As we saw earlier in this chapter, since its early years the company had diversified their objectives to create new income streams. One could argue that this new role for

Figure 5.21 Poster promoting Golders Green new houses. 1907. © TfL from the London Transport Museum collection.

Figure 5.22 View of Golders Green prior to its development and station. Note Golders Green Crematorium in the distance (above road sign). Postcard. 1904. Author's Collection.

the company was not new. Although little documentation is available about their activities, it is possible that their combined experience must have been key to the company's new venture. As we saw, Messer in the United States was directly involved in the development of Fort Worth in the suburbs of Dallas, and Tubbs in Britain worked as surveyor and architect. Perhaps the directors were also aware of Howard's book *Garden Cities of To-morrow*, which by coincidence was published in 1898, the same year Messer returned from abroad. Certainly there was an aspiration of the London Necropolis Company that was connected to the prospects of commercial returns, but also the opportunity to be associated with a movement that, at the time, was promoting suburban living. The opening of new stations particularly in the north areas of London such as Golders Green was already promising new prospects for the middle-classes that wanted to escape the city (see Figure 5.21 and Figure 5.22). The London Necropolis Company and the Woking Residential Estates were equally echoing this new tendency.

5.5 Conclusions

In this section I will draw some conclusions on how the influence of Brookwood Cemetery and the London Necropolis Company radiated beyond the physical boundaries of the cemetery. We have seen how even before the opening of the cemetery for business, the internal political battles within the board of directors and the complex bureaucracy of the company along with the expenses needed to set up the cemetery destabilised the company from the start. This situation, combined with the limitations imposed by the government in terms of land ownership and caps in terms of burial fees, pushed the company directors to look for alternative business opportunities related to their cemetery such as undertaking, funeral insurances and later building developments. The balancing act between carefully developing the estate in the company's portfolio and diversifying their business to secure streams of income was at times precarious and not always successful. Considering that in the early years the company's priority was to sell large portions of land to developers, it was not a surprise to see that large institutions were eventually built in the area such as the prison and the asylum. The returns they reported over the years, of the brickfields' royalties received for the production of bricks, provides an indication of how they connected to the local building industry. Although more research is needed, it is evident that the sale of large plots of land to accommodate large-scale building projects proved convenient to the company, as they had a two-fold return: from the land sale and from the royalties from the brickfield where the building material for the construction of the institutions was generated, as well as from burials for these institutions.

Although Crosby (2003, 74–9) suggested that the company could have taken a leading role in drawing a more cohesive urban plan for the development of Woking, there is evidence from the reports they made public in the press that this was not necessarily one of the company's priorities. Although the company may have missed an opportunity to draw a cohesive plan for the development of Woking, they facilitated its development in the long term and managed as well as connected with local industries and let them flourish and grow. It is clear however that the company had vested interests in attracting building developers to buy their land in the area, as new builds would have increased the value of their land and estate overall, as well as giving them an opportunity to increase their royalties if the developer was going to use the locally produced bricks for their buildings.

For sure, the presence of the company as landlord allowed the local brick workers to gain work through the new buildings that were getting established in the area. Similarly, the local nurseries received work not only from the cemetery but also from the institutions present in the area. There was also another value to the land that eventually came to fruition, which was the fact that in the late nineteenth century, the company started to establish amenities to attract wealthy residents to the area. Golf courses were designed and landscaped by local nursery businesses that also specialised in their maintenance. The vision of an estate in Hook Heath of residences with gardens, mostly destined for the wealthier classes, also brought business to the company via the brickfield part of their portfolio as well as nurseries that specialised in exotic planting and garden landscaping.

The ability to diversify their business was somehow in the DNA of the company since the beginning (undertaking, insurance), so the fact that it branched out to provide architecture and design services by the end of the century was not by accident. Although the company proved adventurous in terms of risk-taking in business, it was also very sensible in taking decisions, as the expectations of the many stakeholders, from the government to the locals and from the potential developers to the London parishes, had to be managed. What was transformative about the vision of the company's directors was their acknowledgement of Brookwood Cemetery as part of the bigger picture of what the company was about, particularly in the early twentieth century when they included it as one of the assets of the Woking Residential Estates, to attract new residents to the area. This was a departure from the Victorian idea that the presence of a cemetery was seen as a limitation to attract new residents to the area. Considering that the origins of Brookwood Cemetery are closely intertwined with the Enclosure Acts, it is possible to say that ultimately the arrival of the cemetery provided an opportunity to give new value to what was otherwise considered waste land. Although the London Necropolis Company did not have a cohesive plan for the area, through its ambitions and management of the stakeholders it was able to avoid high density speculative development and retained the open spaces in the vicinities of the cemetery, which are still today an asset for the town of Woking and its local residents.

Bibliography

"Basingstoke Canal Navigation." 1796. *Hampshire Chronicle: And Portsmouth and Chichester Journal* 25, no. 1216 (June 4): 1. Accessed May 16, 2021. https://www.britishnewspaperarchive.co.uk/viewer/BL/0000230/17960604/011/0001?browse=False

Byrne, Richard. 1989. *Prisons and Punishments of London*. London: Harrap.

Chadwick, Edwin. 1843. "Report on the Sanitary Condition of the Labouring Population of Great Britain. A Supplementary Report on the Results of a Special Inquiry into the Practice of Interment in Towns." London: Clowes and Sons.

Cherry, Gordon E. 1974. *The Evolution of British Town Planning*. Leighton Buzzard: Leonard Hill Books.

Clarke, John M. 2021. "Thomas Higgs (1835–1913)." Friends of West Norwood Cemetery. Newsletter. No. 100 (January): 6–8.

Clarke, John M. 2005. *The Brookwood Necropolis Railway* (4th edition). Usk: The Oakwood Press.

Clarke, John M. 2004. *London's Necropolis. A Guide to Brookwood Cemetery*. Stroud: Sutton Publishing.

Creese, Walter L. 1966. *The Search for Environment. The Garden City Before and After*. New Haven and London: Yale University Press.

Crosby, Alan. 2003. *A History of Woking*. Chichester: Phillimore & Co Ltd.

Crosby, Theo. 1969. *Architecture: City Sense*. London: Studio Vista Limited.
Crosby, Theo. 1967. *Urban Structuring, Studies of Alison & Peter Smithson*. London: Studio Vista Limited.
Curl, James Stevens. 2004. *The Victorian Celebration of Death*. Thrupp: Sutton Publishing.
Curl, James Stevens. 2001. *Kensal Green Cemetery. The Origins and Development of the General Cemetery of All Souls, Kensal Green, London, 1824–2001*. Chichester: Phillimore & Co.
Curl, James Stevens. 1984. "The Design of Early British Cemeteries." *Journal of Garden History* 4, no. 3: 223–54.
Darling, Elizabeth. 2001–2. "Exhibiting Britain: Display and National Identity 1946–1967." Accessed August 24, 2020. https://www.vads.ac.uk/customizations/collection/DCADB/pages/html/esd.html
Dawes, Martin C. 2003. *The End of the Line: The Story of the Railway Service to the Great Northern London Cemetery*. London: Barnet & District Local History Society.
Dennis, Richard. 2008. *Cities in Modernity. Representations and Productions of Metropolitan Space, 1840–1930*. Cambridge: Cambridge University Press.
Fishman, Robert. 1982. *Urban Utopias in the Twentieth Century: Ebenezer Howard, Frank Lloyd Wright and Le Corbusier*. Cambridge, Massachusetts: MIT Press.
Geddes, Patrick. 1968. *Cities in Evolution*. London: Ernest Benn Limited.
George, Juliet. 2010. *Fort Worth's Arlington Heights*. Charleston: Arcadia Publishing.
Gorer, Geoffrey. 1963. *Death, Grief and Mourning in Contemporary Britain*. London: The Cresset Press.
Gilles, John R. 1993. *Commemorations: The Politics of National Identity*. Princeton: Princeton University Press.
Gillon, Edmund V. 1972. *Victorian Cemetery Art*. London: Constable.
Haden, Francis S. 1875. *Earth to Earth: A Plea for a Change of System in Our Burial of the Dead*. London: Macmillan & Co.
Burial Space Needs in London. 1997. Halcrow Fox, Cemetery Research Group, The Landscape Partnership. London: London Planning Advisory Committee.
"Highgate Cemetery." 1881. *Hampstead & Highgate Express*. No. 1053 (January 15). Accessed June 30, 2021. https://www.britishnewspaperarchive.co.uk/viewer/bl/0001981/18810115/065/0004
Heffer, Simon. 2013. *High Minds: The Victorians and the Birth of Modern Britain*. London: Random House Books.
Hill, Octavia. 1883. *Homes of the London Poor*. London: Macmillan & Co.
Holmes, Isabella. 1896. *The London Burial Grounds. Notes on Their History from the Earliest Time to Present Day*. London: T. Fisher Unwin.
Johnston, Helen, and Joanne Turner. 2017. "Disability and the Victorian Prison: Experiencing Penal Servitude." *Prison Service Journal*, no. 232 (July): 11–6. Accessed May 4, 2021. https://www.crimeandjustice.org.uk/sites/crimeandjustice.org.uk/files/PSJ%20232%20July%202017.pdf
Jupp, Peter C. 2006. *From Dust to Ashes: Cremation and the British Way of Death*. London: Palgrave Macmillan.
Jupp, Peter C., and Hilary J. Grainger. 2002. *Golders Green Crematorium 1902–2002. A London Centenary in Context*. London: London Cremation Company.

Kilburn Times and Western Post. 1882. "General Cemetery Company. Kensal Green Cemetery Extension". No. 733 (March 31): 4.. Accessed May 28, 2021. https://www.britishnewspaperarchive.co.uk/viewer/bl/0001813/18820331/088/0004

Masterman, Charles Frederick Gurney. ([1902] 1980). *From the Abyss: Of Its Inhabitants, by One of Them.* London: Garland.

Matless, David. 1998. *Landscape and Englishness.* London: Reaktion Books.

Mayhew, Henry. ([1861–2] 2010). *London Labour & the London Poor.* Oxford: Oxford University Press.

McKellar, Elizabeth. 1999. *The Birth of Modern London. The Development and Design of the City 1660–1720.* Manchester: Manchester University Press.

Meller, Hellen. 1980. "Cities in evolution: Patrick Geddes as an international prophet of town planning before 1914." In *The Rise of Modern Urban Planning 1800–1914*, edited by Anthony Sutcliffe, 199–223. London: Mansell.

Miller, Mervyn, and A. Stuart Gray. 1992. *Hampstead Garden Suburb.* Chichester: Pillimore.

Morley, John. 1971. *Death, Heaven and the Victorians.* London: Studio Vista.

Morris, Susannah. 2001. "Market Solutions for Social Problems: Working-Class Housing in Nineteenth-Century London." *The Economic History Review* 54, no. 3 (August): 525–45. Accessed June 30, 2020. http://www.jstor.com/stable/3091763

Morrison, Kathryn. 1999. *The Workhouse. A Study of Poor-Law Buildings in England.* Swindon: English Heritage and the National Monuments Record Centre.

Mulkay, Mike. 1993. "Social Death in Britain." In *The Sociology of Death*, edited by David Clark. Oxford: Blackwell/Sociological Review.

Mumford, Lewis. 1947. *Technics and Civilization.* London: George Routledge & Sons Ltd.

Mumford, Lewis. 1967. *The Myth of the Machine. Technics and Human Development.* London: Secker & Warburg Limited.

Mumford, Lewis. 1974. "The Garden City Idea and Modern Planning." In *Garden Cities of To-Morrow*, edited by E. Howard, 29–40. London: Faber and Faber.

Mumford, Lewis. 1991. *The City in History.* London: Penguin Books.

Mumford, Lewis. 1996. *The Culture of Cities.* San Diego: Harcourt Brace & Company.

North East London Polytechnic. 1976.*Have Our Cemeteries a Future?* London: Faculty of Environmental Studies.

Olsen, Donald J. 1976. *The Growth of Victorian London.* London: B.T. Batsford Ltd.

Otter, Christopher. 2004. "Cleansing and Clarifying: Technology and Perception in Nineteenth-Century London." *Journal of British Studies* 43, no. 1 (January): 40–64. Accessed May 27, 2021. https://www.jstor.org/stable/10.1086/jbs.2004.43.issue-1

Parton, A. G. 1985. "Parliamentary Enclosure in Nineteenth-Century Surrey – Some Perspectives on the Evaluation of Land Potential." *The Agricultural History Review* 33, no. 1: 51–58. Accessed May 16, 2021. https://www.jstor.org/stable/40275419

Parsons, Brian. 2018. *The Evolution of the British Funeral Industry in the 20th Century. From Undertaker to Funeral Director.* Bingley: Emerald Publishing Limited.

Parsons, Brian. 2005. *Committed to the Cleansing Flame. The Development of Cremation in Nineteenth-Century England.* Reading: Spire Books Ltd.

Paxman, Jeremy. 2011. *Empire: What Ruling the World did to the British*. London: Penguin Books Ltd.
Rutherford, Sarah. 2012. *The Victorian Asylum*. Oxford: Shire Publications Ltd.
Rutherford, Sarah. 2005. "Landscapers for the Mind: English Asylum Designers, 1845–1914." *Garden History* 33, no. 1 (Summer): 61–86. Accessed May 20, 2021. http://www.jstor.com/stable/25434157
Surrey Comet and Kingston Gazette. 1855. No. 43 (June 2): 2. Accessed May 20, 2021. https://www.britishnewspaperarchive.co.uk/viewer/BL/0000684/18550602/038/0002?browse=False
Taylor, Jeremy Reginald Buckley. 1991. *Hospital and Asylum architecture in England, 1840–1914 Building for Health Care*. Book. English. London: Mansell.
The Basingstoke Canal. Website. Accessed June 30, 2021. https://basingstoke-canal.org.uk/about/the-canal/
The Daily News. 1880. "Sales by Auction". No. 10684 (July 15): 8. Accessed June 18, 2021. https://www.britishnewspaperarchive.co.uk/viewer/BL/0000051/18800715/098/0008
The Daily News. 1855. "London Necropolis and National Mausoleum Company." No. 2727 (February 14): 2. Accessed June 18, 2021. https://www.britishnewspaperarchive.co.uk/viewer/BL/0000051/18550214/006/0002?browse=False
The Era. 1856. "London Necropolis and National Mausoleum Company." Vol. 18, no. 908 (February 17): 11. Accessed June 17, 2021. https://www.britishnewspaperarchive.co.uk/viewer/BL/0000053/18560217/040/0011?browse=False
The Field: The Country Gentlemen Newspaper. 1871. Vol. 38, no. 989 (December 9): 32. Accessed May 20, 2021. https://www.britishnewspaperarchive.co.uk/viewer/BL/0002446/18711209/003/0001
The Globe. 1880. No. 26542 (June 15): 8. Accessed May 20, 2021. https://www.britishnewspaperarchive.co.uk/viewer/bl/0001652/18800615/056/0008
"The London Necropolis." 1904. London: Joseph Causton and Sons Ltd.
The Morning Post, 1906. No. 41830 (June 20): 1. Accessed May 20, 2021. https://www.britishnewspaperarchive.co.uk/viewer/BL/0000174/19060620/037/0001?browse=False
The Morning Post. 1865. No. 28444 (February 14): 6. Accessed June 17, 2021. https://www.britishnewspaperarchive.co.uk/viewer/BL/0000174/18650213/040/0006?browse=False
The Morning Advertiser. 1856. No. 20174 (February 15): 5. Accessed April 22, 2021. https://www.britishnewspaperarchive.co.uk/viewer/BL/0001427/18560215/085/0005?browse=False
The Sphere: An Illustrated Newspaper for the Home. 1909. Vol. 37. No. 492 (June 26): VI. Accessed June 10, 2021. https://www.britishnewspaperarchive.co.uk/viewer/BL/0001861/19090626/036/0028?browse=true
The Standard. 1857. "London Necropolis Company." No. 10289 (August 5): 6. Accessed June 18, 2021. https://www.britishnewspaperarchive.co.uk/viewer/BL/0000183/18570805/037/0006?browse=False
The Standard. 1859. "London Necropolis and National Mausoleum Company." No. 10767 (February 16): 5. Accessed June 18, 2021. https://www.britishnewspaperarchive.co.uk/viewer/BL/0000183/18590216/027/0005?browse=False

The Sun. 1868. "London Necropolis Company." No. 23614 (February 17): 7. Accessed June 17, 2021. https://www.britishnewspaperarchive.co.uk/viewer/BL/0002194/18680217/140/0007?browse=False

The Surrey Comet and Kingston Gazette. 1855. "London Necropolis Company." No. 43 (June 2): 2. Accessed April 22, 2021. https://www.britishnewspaperarchive.co.uk/viewer/BL/0000684/18550602/038/0002?browse=False

The Sussex Advertiser. 1853. "Enclosure of the Common at Woking by the Necropolis Company." No. 8011 (October 25): 7. Accessed April 22, 2021. https://www.britishnewspaperarchive.co.uk/viewer/BL/0000257/18531025/047/0007?browse=False

Wakeford, Iain. 1995. *A Guide to the Industrial History of Woking and its Borough*. Guildford: Surrey Industrial History Group.

Ward Richardson, Benjamin. 1876. *Hygeia, A City of Health*. London: Macmillan & Co.

Williams, Michael. 1970. "The Enclosure and Reclamation of Waste Land in England and Wales in the Eighteenth and Nineteenth Centuries." *Transactions of the Institute of British Geographers*. No. 51 (November): 55–69. Accessed May 16, 2021. https://www.jstor.org/stable/621762

"Woking as a Residential District." 1907. Woking: Drowley & Co. Accessed 20 May 2021. https://wokinghistory.org/1907%20Drowley%20&%20Co.pdf

6 Rethinking

6.1 Open spaces

Towards the end of the nineteenth-century London's organic suburban growth integrated the once rural or semi-rural settings into the capital's metropolitan area. In 1800, London had a population of around one million, by 1881 it had grown to 4.5 million, and by the beginning of the twentieth century (1911) it had reached over seven million. This sudden growth highlighted a startling contrast of how slowly other central districts developed, such as the West End, which emerged in the Georgian era (Porter 2000, 249). The fragmented ownership of land, together with the equally complex local administration of London, made it difficult to control the development of the city and its outwards expansion into the suburbs. This was also prevented by a laissez-faire attitude of the government at the time, which with a very light hand supervised private speculative initiatives. One of the key issues connected with London's urban growth was housing the lower classes (as we also saw in Chapter 3). This problem was yet not addressed on a large scale and was left to the charity of individual benefactors and philanthropists, who embraced it as an opportunity to pioneer and test their own ideas in providing affordable housing. According to geographer and urban studies specialist Gordon Cherry, the private sector, "with or without philanthropic support, could no longer adequately provide the conditions for accommodating its labour force in dwellings of acceptable numbers" (1979, 317). It was with the formation of the London County Council in 1888 that the problem of social housing was finally taken under the administrative wing of a local authority.

A further consequence of the suburban sprawl was the lack of open spaces both in the new suburbs (high density due to speculation) and inner parts of the city. We saw how the suburban expansion of London in the course of the nineteenth century affected the areas surrounding Victorian cemeteries, and how diverse the effects and results were, both in terms of the quality of the built environment and diversity in terms of services and architectural styles across each one of the case studies. In some areas that

DOI: 10.4324/9781003178934-7

lacked open spaces or recreational grounds in parts of the city, a cemetery or a disused graveyard became the only open green space available. Social reformer Octavia Hill addressed this issue publicly with a paper entitled *Open Spaces* (Special Collections: Cremation Society – Durham University. Reference: CRE/H5), that she presented to the National Health Society on 9 May 1877, and proposed to transform the once poisonous parish churchyards of inner London into public gardens or, as Hill suggested, into "outdoor sitting rooms" for the poor. In an extract from her essay she outlines the visionary project:

> There are, all over London, little spots unbuilt over, still strangely preserved among this sea of houses – our graveyards. They are capable of being made into beautiful out-door sitting rooms. They should be planted with trees, creepers should be trained up their walls, seats should be placed in them, fountains might be fixed there, the brightest flowers set there, possibly in some cases bird cages might be kept to delight the children. To these the neighbouring poor should be admitted free, under whatever regulations should seem best.
>
> (64)

Hill saw in London's disused graveyards the opportunity to give to the poor an urban version of the traditional village green found in rural areas in the British countryside. Hill's idea eventually came to fruition over the following years, as a selection of disused graveyards converted into gardens. These featured in the book *The London Burial Grounds: Notes on Their History from the Earliest Times to the Present Day* (1896) written by Isabella Holmes. The author endorsed Hill's proposal for the conversion of London's disused graveyards into public gardens (see Figure 6.1).

Holmes' interest in the issue was sparked by research she conducted for the London Metropolitan Public Gardens Association (founded in 1882 and which also advocated the initiative, and encouraged the enactment of the 1884 Disused Burial Ground Act). In her book Holmes airs her own views on the issue:

> The more public interest is brought to bear upon the burial-grounds, the more likely it is that they will be preserved from encroachments. The London County Council has special powers to put in force the provisions of the Disused Burial Ground Act [1884], and it has the record of their actual sites on the plans prepared by me. It is for the public to see that these provisions are carried out not only for historical, sentimental, and sanitary reasons, but also because each burial-ground that is curtailed or annihilated means the loss of another space which may one day be available for public recreation; and considering that land, even in the poorest part of Whitechapel, fetches about £ 30,000 per acre, it

Figure 6.1 The former churchyard of St. John's Church Waterloo Road used as a public garden. *The Graphic*. 1887. Author's collection.

is easily understood of what inestimable value is a plot of ground which cannot be built upon.

(22)

In another section of her book, Holmes gives guidelines on how to proceed for the acquisition and conservation of a churchyard, which steps to take and which offices to consult. Her crusade was against ruthless speculative developers that were looking to build on any pocket of land available, and she reinforces this statement more than once in the book. In one instance, Holmes describes the disused graveyards as a new kind of village green and makes a comparison between the two:

> A playground such as Spa Fields is about as different from an ordinary village green, where country boys and girls romp and shout, as two things with the same purpose can well be. For the soft, green grass, you have gritty gravel; for the cackling geese who waddle into the pond, you have a few stray cats walking on the walls; for the picturesque cottages overgrown with roses and honeysuckle, you have the backs of little houses, monotonous in structure, in colour and in dirt; and instead of

resting "underneath the shadow vast of patriarchal tree", you must be content with a wooden bench close to the wall, bearing on its back the name of the association which laid out the ground. But it is only necessary to have once seen the joy with which the children of our crowded cities hail the formation of such a playground, and the use to which they put it, to be convinced that the trouble of acquiring it, or the cost of laying it out, is amply repaid.

(277)

Holmes was also very vocal about the entire funeral system at the time, and defined it as "an extravagant imposition". She was a supporter of cremation and even considered burial at sea as an alternative to the construction of new cemeteries, which she abhorred, especially Kensal Green. In a passage the author states:

But Kensal Green Cemetery is truly awful, with its catacombs, its huge mausoleums, family vaults, statues, broken pillars, weeping images, and oceans of tombstones, good, bad, and indifferent. I think the indifferent are to be preferred, the bad should not be anywhere, and the good are utterly out of place. It is also the largest in the metropolis, and as the Roman Catholic ground joins it there are in this spot, or there very soon will be, 99 acres of dead bodies. There are many sad sights in London, but to me there are few so sad as the one of these huge graveyards.

(256)

The criticism addressed by Holmes to cemetery companies was not only questioning the possibility of burial overcrowding and its related hygienic concerns, but also arguing that the practice of earth burial wasn't suitable anymore to the modern city. Holmes expresses her anxiety over the future of London burial spaces, and questions if more precious space should be allocated to new burials, or if the existing cemeteries should be reused over and over:

But the question of paramount importance is how to stop the increase of cemeteries. Are we ever to allow England to be divided like a chessboard into towns and burial-places? What we have to consider is how to dispose of the dead without taking so much valuable space from the living. In the metropolitan area alone we have almost filled (and in some places overfilled) 24 new cemeteries within 60 years, with an area of above six hundred acres; and this is nothing compared with the huge extent of land used for interments just outside the limits of the metropolis. If the cemeteries are not to extend indefinitely they must in time be built upon, or they must be used for burial over and over again, or the ground must revert to its original state as agricultural land, or we must turn our parks and commons into cemeteries, and let our cemeteries be our only recreation grounds – which Heaven forbid!

(269)

The sense of urgency that can be detected in Holmes's writing could be compared to that of Walker in his 1839 survey of London's graveyards. Although less graphic in her descriptions than Walker, Holmes is equally incisive and expressive in her statements. The author's concerns over the future of London's burials was a sign that a new awareness was starting to emerge at the turn of the century. Holmes was calling for a substantial rethinking of disposal and burial solutions for the long term and framed within the broader context of the fast city expansion. In this respect the solution was not about extending the existing Victorian cemeteries, where possible, or creating new ones. New strategies of disposal had to consider complex issues such as overcrowding, housing and hygiene in a more holistic way, and not only in relation to economics or private enterprise.

But how were the privately owned Victorian cemeteries, established in the first half of the century, going to survive in such a critical time of change? Kensal Green (Chapter 3) and Highgate (Chapter 4) by the end of the century were surrounded by new transport networks of roads and railway systems, new buildings and even new parks. This was both an asset – as they became easier to reach by mourners and visitors – and a limitation, as they could not expand beyond their existing boundaries. Particularly the early Victorian cemeteries by this time were running out of available burial space.

The situation was very different from cemetery to cemetery due to location, topography and even geology. The General Cemetery Company, for example, expanded Kensal Green Cemetery by 22 acres in 1882 (*Kilburn Times and Western Post* 1882, 4). However, the London Cemetery Company, which owned Highgate Cemetery, not only was at risk of becoming overcrowded, but also did not have the possibility to expand beyond its boundaries. Highgate, at the time, also faced structural issues due to its poor drainage system. In the East part of the cemetery, the clay subsoil was provoking problems with the interments in that part of the cemetery. In the article, a correspondent of the Daily Telegraph pointed out "the fearful state of the grounds at Highgate Cemetery". From the description it appears that the new portion of the cemetery (East) had problems with drainage as some of the graves were engulfed in wet clay. The correspondent noted that drainage was one of the first aspects the London Cemetery Company should have considered as part of their business (*Hampstead & Highgate Express* 1881, 4).

A completely different arrangement, however, was that of the London Necropolis Company, as Brookwood Cemetery was located beyond London's metropolitan area, and not integrated in any way to the city's urban fabric, yet it was directly connected to it by a train link that connected the company's private station to the cemetery. At the turn of the century, as we have seen in

Chapter 5, the London Necropolis Company landholding in Surrey was an asset that not only allowed them to accommodate future burials, but also to explore new commercial ideas beyond funeral services. The company's inclination towards alternative solutions beyond earth burial was already evident in their 1887 pamphlet, where the company offered to its potential clients the so-called "earth-to-earth" burial method and the Thompson's cremation technique, which we will see in more detail in the next section.

6.2 New alternatives to earth burial

In Chapter 1 we saw how overcrowding and lack of space were affecting the living conditions of Londoners and how the issue of overcrowding and the hygiene of burial spaces came to the fore once again. New ideas were indeed needed to rethink future burials, as cemetery companies just partially relieved the problem of overcrowding when they established their new suburban cemeteries. New disposal methods therefore, to be effective in the longer term, needed to foresee the future development of London.

This section studies how a selection of new disposal methods emerged in the late nineteenth century. As we will see, some focused primarily on technological aspects, others envisaged in a utopian way a deeper sociocultural revolution which also involved a transformation of burial practices. Prior to Holmes' critique on Victorian cemeteries and the funeral industry at large, thinkers were already at work on proposals that would in some cases address specifically new typologies of burial in isolation. In other cases, however, they were also part of new and holistic suggestions for the future urban growth of cities.

Earlier on in this book we saw how the medical profession was directly involved in the reformation of burials, first in 1839 with Walker's survey of London's graveyards and then with Southwood Smith's involvement in Chadwick's 1843 report, which contributed to the shaping of new sanitary and burial laws. As we will see here, disposal and burial practices carried on being of interest to the medical profession later on in the century. This was the case of Sir Henry Thompson, a surgeon and physician to Queen Victoria, who became a key figure in the promotion of cremation. In 1873 Thompson visited the Universal Exhibition in Vienna and was impressed by the research on a cremation apparatus presented by scientist Paolo Gorini and anatomist Lodovico Brunetti. As a result of this visit in January 1874 Thompson initiated the Cremation Society of Great Britain with the aim of promoting cremation as a new solution to the hygienic and spatial issues related to disposal and burial. As we will see in more detail later, the Cremation Society established the first crematorium in Woking in 1878, near Brookwood Cemetery, on land bought from the London Necropolis Company. Eventually, in 1884, Thompson made a stronger case for cremation with his book *Cremation, the Treatment of the Body after Death*. Here the author outlines the reasons for the need to implement cremation, without going into technical details, but amplifying the benefits of the new method in the broader context of the unprecedented growth of the urban population. In an extract he explains:

> When the globe was thinly populated and when there were no large bodies of men living in close neighbourhoods, the subject was an inconsiderable one and could afford to wait, and might indeed be left for its solution to sentiment of any kind. But the rapid increase of population forces it into notice, and especially man's tendency to live in crowded cities. There is no necessity to prove, as the fact is too patent, that our present mode of treating the dead, namely, that by burial beneath the soil, is full of danger to the living. Hence intramural interment has been recently forbidden, the first step in a series of reforms which must follow.
>
> (5–6)

Thompson reinforces his point on the necessity of switching from earth burial to cremation, by stating that in the modern context man should be able to remove the dead from the city, by adopting an appropriate and hygienic method of disposal. He maintains that:

> Modern science is equal to the task of thus removing the dead of a great city without instituting any form of nuisance; none such as those we tolerate everywhere from many factories, both to air and streams.
>
> (9–10)

Although Thompson strongly believed in the benefits of cremation, he is also aware of the resistance towards it that other practitioners and society at large have expressed and therefore uses his book to clarify that the scepticism towards cremation could be overcome. One of the major concerns associated with cremation had to do with premature death, as at the time there was no medical procedure to declare a person officially dead. Thompson therefore proposed to introduce an inspection of the whole body by an appointed health officer, before proceeding to the actual cremation of a corpse. The author also is aware that time was needed for cremation to be accepted by the wider society; in a passage he states:

> Perhaps no great change can be expected at present in the public opinions current, or rather in the conventional views which obtain, on the subject of burial, so ancient in the practice and so closely associated is it with sentiments and affection and reverence for the deceased. To many persons, any kind of change in our treatment of the dead will be suggestive of sacrilegious interference, however remote, either in fact or by resemblance to it, such change may be.
>
> (13)

If cremation in Thompson's view would have taken time to be accepted by society because of its association with technology and rational thinking, there were alternative disposal methods that instead celebrated the more natural, yet perfectly engineered process of decomposition and regeneration of the earth such as the "earth-to-earth" burial method. This was the brainchild of Francis Seymour Haden, also a surgeon like Thompson, who theorised and promoted this new method of disposal in his 1875 publication titled *Earth To Earth: A plea for a change of system in our burial of the dead*. This booklet contains three letters the author wrote to the then editor of *The Times*, which were a response to:

> The proposal of certain German and Italian writers in their own country, and of an eminent surgeon in this, to substitute the burning of the dead for their interment.
>
> (5)

Haden was referring here to Gorini and Brunetti, whom, as we saw earlier, Thompson had met in Vienna in 1873. Friedrich August Siemens was also developing a cremation technology. Haden was fundamentally against any technological intervention in the disposal process and argued that the dead were improperly buried and that wooden coffins slowed down the process of decomposition. His suggestion therefore was to bury corpses in shrouds or coffins materials lighter than wood:

> No coffins at all would, of course, be best, or a coffin of the thinnest substance which would not long resist the action of the earth, or a coffin the top and sides of which admitted removal after the body had been lowered into the grave, or a coffin of some light permeable material, such as wicker or lattice-work, open at the top, and filled in with any fragrant herbaceous matters that happened to be most readily obtainable.
>
> (16)

The author also reinforces the competence of nature in finding its way to regenerate itself through a process of transformation which starts from decomposition, a process so perfect that not even a technologically advanced method such as cremation could supersede it:

> To question the competency of the earth, thus endowed, to effect the resolution and conversion of its dead, or to fail to perceive and profit by that competency, would pass comprehension if habit had not taught us to shut our eyes to it, and if the advocates of Cremation had not stepped in to tell us that we may improve upon it.
>
> (8)

As well as criticising cremation, Haden also expresses his disapproval of cemetery companies and the government that let commercial enterprises make a business of death and burial.

It is neither to the interest nor the dignity of a great nation to entrust the burial of the dead to speculative associations – ignorant of their duties as we have seen them to be, and animated by no higher impulses than such as arise out of a spirit of trade – it is also inadmissible. If the Burial of the Dead, in short, may not unreasonably be compared in importance with the main drainage, is it not at least as fit – would it not be much fitter – that so serious a trust should be undertaken either by the Board of Works, or by a special department under its immediate supervision?

(63)

Haden's criticism towards cemetery companies however was not paramount, as the author indicates that the best suitable cemetery for "earth-to-earth" burials, in terms of availability of both space and of geology, was Brookwood Cemetery.

The Woking Cemetery is also the only existing cemetery in which the burial of a body can be effected with the present certainty that it will not be disturbed for ten years. In the absence, therefore, of any ameliorations whatsoever of our present cemeterial system being obtainable, it is plainly to the interest of every class, high and low, to avoid seething suburban cemeteries and to bury their dead in Woking.

(66)

If Thompson and Haden researched specifically into finding new ways to dispose of corpses, more holistic visions that combined nature, landscape and architecture started to be outlined, as the one proposed by William Robinson. Known primarily for introducing the idea of the "wild garden" – a movement that rejected the regimented Victorian formal gardening, Robinson was also a journalist and friend of Ruskin and William Morris among other notable figures at the time. In his 1880 book *God's Acre Beautiful; Or The Cemeteries of the Future* he warned that the commercial scope of the funeral industry would lead to overcrowding in the suburban cemeteries. One extract from the book reads:

So large and so important a question as the burial of the dead should never be in the hands of those who merely regard it from the point of view of money making. It is well known that the profits from certain cemeteries in some of the pleasantest suburbs of London are very large; the temptation to continue burial in them, longer than decency or sanitary reasons would permit, will probably lead to danger in the future from pollution of air and water. The present state of some of our cemeteries close to London is already dangerous and offensive.

(59)

What Robinson envisaged for the future cemetery in London was to shift the focus from gravestones dotting the landscape to buildings (columbaria) containing thousands of urns. In this way the landscape remains undisturbed and the overall feeling is that of a communal garden.

> The cemetery of the future not only prevents the need of occupying large areas of ground with decaying bodies, in a ratio increasing with the population and with time, but leaves ample space to spare for those open green lawns, without which no good natural effect is possible in such places. It is to be a national garden in the best sense; safe from violation as the via sacra, and having the added charms of pure air, trees, grass and flowers. The open central lawns should always be preserved from the follies of the geometrical and stone gardeners, so as to secure freedom of view and air, and a resting place for the eye.
>
> (28)

In *God's Acre* Robinson also explains in detail how society should rethink the approach to burial and funerary architecture. His vision of cremation and urn-burial was broad – hinting at the possibilities of re-integrating the cemetery into the city by suggesting that, "Buildings, sacred or otherwise, may be adapted for urn-burial" (17). In Robinson's view, any building could be suitable for an urn-burial on the basis that the cremation of the remains would need to happen in a separate place due to health considerations. Robinson also touches on how his proposal would not only be safe but also more affordable and less disruptive than earth burial.

> A single burial in such an urn-tomb need not be so expensive as one in the commonest of the graves with which such large areas in our cities are now covered. The disturbance of the ground would not be necessary, as it is now; not to speak of the abolition of other onerous charges. The question of space is settled by the fact that one hundred of the simple forms of urn could be placed in the space necessary for the burial of a single body in the ordinary way.
>
> (15)

Following the first publication of *God's Acre*, Robinson's enthusiasm and support for him evidently grew, and the republication of his book (in 1883 and 1889) must have supported the cause and helped establish the practice. Some of the theoretical ideas Robinson put forward in *God's Acre* eventually were tested in real life, as he was commissioned to design the landscape of London's first crematorium in Golders Green (1902).

Robinson's idea was to make the land available for the scattering of the ashes, a landscaped garden of remembrance, freed from any tombstone, memorial or monument dedicated to individuals. What Robinson advocated for the crematorium was therefore completely the opposite of what was to be seen in any of London's Victorian necropolises at the time. The ethos of Golders Green Crematorium was quite different from the one promoted by the Victorian necropolises, which as we saw, were more about individuality and social status.

Areas within the landscape in Golders Green Crematorium (see Figure 6.2) were allocated to the scattering of the ashes based on a rotation calendar system, which allowed for the soil to absorb the ashes and regenerate. The innovations Robinson introduced, however, were a separation between the actual place where the ashes were scattered and where the memorial plaques were located. The landscaped garden was the place where the ashes were scattered, but the memorial plaques were located in an especially designed covered space (see Figure 6.3).

This solution allowed for the plaques to be protected from direct exposure to the elements (such as rain, frost and strong sunlight) and preserved them for longer. Because of their size, they were also less expensive to maintain, unlike traditional tombstones, graves and memorials. Robinson's design principles for the landscaped garden of Golders Green Crematorium promoted social equality by removing any visible element that would indicate social status and diversity. This marked a major shift in death culture and funerary architecture. Although it did not immediately phase out the traditional cemeteries or indeed funerary architecture, it provided a more rational, yet democratic solution to hygienic disposal and burial. It also provided a tangible answer to the questions on the future allocation of precious space that could be allocated for burial. This new consciousness also

Figure 6.2 Golders Green Crematorium. View over Robinson's landscape. Postcard. 1904. Author's collection.

Figure 6.3 Golders Green Crematorium. View of the West Columbarium. Postcard. 1904. Author's collection.

demonstrated that the time of cemetery companies was over. Fresh new ideas were raised to address not only the use of space but also funeral and burial charges, to make them more affordable for society at large. Cremation presented itself as the alternative to earth burial, being more hygienic, less expensive and saving on space.

6.3 Future visions

As seen in the previous three chapters, Kensal Green, Highgate and Brookwood are telling stories of new suburban development that clustered around the large Victorian cemeteries in an organic way, without responding to a specific plan. The results are very different from case to case, and the character of locations are the results of a combination of elements and influencing factors. As we have seen so far, public health and hygiene concerns were the fundamental drivers of the urban and suburban change in London and many other large cities in Britain and mainland Europe in the nineteenth century. Often the new interventions had to compromise with what already existed there, or the limitations of space available or resistance of local influencers. Victorian cities were indeed full-scale living experiments. Dyos defined them as "both theatre and laboratory" and reminds us that "no urbanising nation ever proceeded so far with so little knowledge as to the pathological and psychological implications of such high human densities" (1982, 27). There was no time to theorise or elaborate on the consequences, but there was a need to actively intervene by implementing new ideas and finding immediate solutions. In the second half of the century, however, alternative solutions to earth burial practices started to be evaluated in the context of utopian ideas and holistic visions which started to emerge of new cities planned around health and hygiene. The ideas could be seen as the ultimate frontier of the pathological method – as expressed by Foucault – applied to the built environment and possible spatial arrangements of the city or quarters of the future. One example is the outline for *Hygiea: A City of Health*, written by sanitary reformer Benjamin Ward Richardson, in 1876.

In the first few pages, Ward Richardson explains that his intention is to draw up a proposal for a city that would show the lowest mortality. He felt that this could be easily achieved by taking into account the scientific knowledge gathered in the last two generations. One of the advantages, Ward Richardson explains, is that of "being a new foundation, but it is so built that existing cities might be largely modelled upon it". Ward Richardson imagined Hygeia to be a city with a population of 100,000 dwellers, 20,000 houses over an extent of 4,000 acres of land, which would make an average of 25 people per acre (17–8). Ward Richardson envisaged that

> churches, hospitals, theatres, banks, lecture-rooms, and other public buildings, as well as some private buildings such as warehouses and stables, stand alone, forming parts of streets, and occupying the position of several houses. They are surrounded with garden space, and add not only to the beauty but the healthiness of the city. The large houses of the wealthy are situated in a similar manner.
>
> (19–20)

Detailed considerations were given about hygiene in the context of the home interiors, even down to the materials, design and arrangements of living spaces.

> Considering that a third part of the life of man is, or should be, spent in sleep, great care is taken with the bed-rooms, so that they shall be thoroughly lighted, roomy, and ventilated. Twelve hundreds cubic feet of space is allowed for each sleeper, and from the sleeping apartments all unnecessary articles of furniture and of dress are rigorously excluded. Old clothes, old shoes, and other offensive articles of the same order, are never permitted to have residence there. In most instances the rooms of the first floor are made the bed-rooms, and the lower the living rooms. In the larger houses bed-rooms are carried out in the upper floor for the use of the domestics.
>
> (26)

Ward Richardson's visionary plan also included a revisited version of the cemetery, which is carefully engineered, so to make earth burial safe:

Thus the cemetery holds its place in our city, but in a form much modified from the ordinary cemetery. The burial ground is artificially made of fine carboniferous earth. Vegetation of rapid growth is cultivated over it. The dead are placed in the earth from the bier, either in basket work or simply in the shroud; and the monumental slab, instead of being set over or at the head or foot of a raised grave, is placed in a spacious covered hall or temple, and records simply the fact that the person commemorated was recommitted to earth in those grounds. In a few months, indeed, no monument would indicate the remains of any dead. In that rapidly resolving soil the transformation of dust into dust is too perfect to leave a trace of residuum. The natural circle of transmutation is harmlessly completed, and the economy of nature conserved.

(43)

Ward Richardson's design proposal for the cemetery was both practical and achievable, it was a combination of Haden's "earth-to-earth" and Robinson's proposal outlined in his *God's Acre* book. Considering that Ward Richardson promoted cremation in its early days (Parsons 2005, 41) is curious to see that he did not contemplate the use of cremation as a way of disposing of the dead in his utopian vision for a city of the future. Ward Richardson reframed earth burial practices through the engineering of the soil of the area allocated to the cemetery. The process of decomposition is completely natural and not mechanised in any way as cremation was.

Ward Richardson's plans for a utopian city of health not only directly inspired Howard's theoretical framework for the Garden City movement, but also contemplated a new typology of the cemetery and disposal process. The urban utopias of both Ward Richardson and later by Howard marked a turning point in the vision of how the city could look and how humans, nature and social activities could be engineered into a cohesively planned built environment.

Although, as sustained by Briggs, British cities still at the end of the nineteenth century "remained confused and complicated, a patchwork of private properties, developed separately with little sense of common plan, a jumble of sites and buildings", changes were underway across society at large. For London School of Economics scholar Susannah Morris towards the end of the nineteenth century, "Public perception began to turn away from considering how society might cope with an urbanized and industrialized nation to planning how this society might be shaped in the future" (2001, 520). It was not anymore only about public health or education or housing the poor, or where and how to dispose of the dead, but simultaneously about all of those aspects together. As pioneering urban planner Patrick Geddes stated in the opening page of his seminal 1915 book *Cities in Evolution*, "Despite our contemporary difficulties industrial, social, and political, there are available around us the elements of a civic uplift, and with this, of general advance to a higher plane of industrial civilisation" (v).

Somehow the suburbs that emerged in the vicinity of the Victorian cemeteries, despite being unplanned or chaotic in their arrangements of their physical space, through the institutions, housing, industry and other services were the manifestation of a new and emerging civic life. From the model housings of Kensal Green to the new hospitals of Highgate and the institutions of Brookwood, and indeed to the cemeteries themselves, they all embodied an evolution of the notion of civic life and ethics of a society that addressed unprecedented complex issues through architectural form, spatial organisation, engineering and indeed capitalist entrepreneurship, and fundamentally courage and vision, that are still inspiring to this day. The growing criticism expressed on the large scale of Victorian cemeteries (as seen earlier with Hill and Holmes) combined with the need to solve social and spatial issues such as housing, transport and other civic functions as well as simultaneously retain open spaces in cities was indeed a complex question that required coordination and an integrated approach. However, the question (and indeed visions) of cemeteries was not contemplated as one would have imagined, considering their relevance. For example, Howard's vision for the Garden City only marginally investigated and contemplated cemeteries (and indeed disposal of human remains) for their contribution to the civic space of the city or indeed its suburbs. However, he does not even make a proposition to adopt cremation either, or other alternatives such as the one put forward by Ward Richardson. It was simply not addressed, as if it did not have relevance to the city of the future. As we have seen in this book, the influence of a cemetery in an area not only impacted its character but its economy, societal and cultural context as well as its natural landscape.

6.4 Conclusions

To conclude we saw that towards the end of the nineteenth century the quality of London's suburban development came under the scrutiny of representatives of the medical profession, philanthropists and thinkers. They expressed concerns over the freedom given to private commercial enterprises to shape the new expansion of the city as a commercial opportunity without paying attention to social and spatial issues such as overcrowding and space management. The relation between space and its functional organisation became prime and urgent, and consequently more rational. Although Victorian cemeteries contributed to the character of an area, their inception contributed to magnifying the above-mentioned issues of overcrowding and lack of open spaces. There were however positive examples, which were initiated by philanthropists such as Hill, who campaigned to transform the once unhealthy and dangerous London's graveyards, into "outdoor sitting rooms". Cemetery companies were criticised for their indiscriminate use of space, for holding a monopoly over the funeral industry and for their poor management of their cemeteries, as they were at risk of overcrowding and about to become a health hazard to local residents. However, the companies also provided the city with open spaces in the metropolitan area of London. Their unique natural landscapes became distinctive features of the suburbs that shaped around each one of them by the end of the century.

As we saw previously in this book, Victorian cemeteries were initially welcomed as a solution to London's burial issues, however, in a short period of time they were already showing signs of their limited potential and failed in addressing the complex issue of burial in the broader context of a growing metropolis. As a consequence, the problem was again discussed by representatives of the medical profession who, just as they did in the first part of the nineteenth century, expressed their concerns over the overcrowding and hygiene of the new cemeteries. In this instance, however, beyond denouncing the issues, they started to research and work on actual solutions, not only on new ways of disposing human remains but also proposing new urban strategies. Ward Richardson was an example of this movement. As we saw in the previous section, his proposal for Hygeia envisaged a new urban arrangement based on hygiene, to improve and safeguard the health of city dwellers. This was a departure from other previous attempts, as it demonstrated a new awareness of how to approach the organisation of the urban space, for the living and the dead. Ward Richardson configured his utopian proposal not strictly from the point of view of its arrangement and aesthetics, but more holistically framing it in the broader context of the city's future development and the harmonious relationship between mankind and nature.

New research also studied ways to make disposal and burial more affordable, less space consuming and hygienic as in the case of "earth-to-earth" burial and cremation methods. These innovations challenged cemetery companies and pushed them to adapt or change. The fast growth of London's suburbs meant that Victorian cemeteries – especially Kensal Green Cemetery and Highgate Cemetery – were soon to be integrated into the urban fabric of the capital, as new buildings encircled them and restricted their possibility to expand and accommodate new burial spaces. However, by contrast, the London Necropolis Company took an active part in the inception and diffusion of new disposal methods. The strategic geographic position of Brookwood Cemetery, its railway connection and the availability of land to be allocated for burial presented the company with an opportunity to expand their commercial horizons beyond graves and into housing. They also had the unique opportunity to control and influence the development of the area, as effectively the company was the largest landholder in that part of Surrey. This unique and unprecedented situation tells us that although cemetery companies were perceived negatively for their stronghold of the funerary industry, with the establishment of their cemeteries they contributed to change not only death culture but the built environment of nineteenth-century London. The case of the London Necropolis Company and its support of innovative ideas for disposal provided not only a commercial opportunity to expand their offering in terms of funeral services, but also to test social attitudes to such an innovation and measure how people would embrace change in death culture.

History says that we are a society obsessed with health and hygiene – Victorian cemeteries arose out of such concerns, as did cremation. Modern society has found a way to turn the human body into a commodity for exploitation when it is alive, and even when dead. The living body, the healthy body, is connected with industry and productivity – a fundamental enabler of capitalist success. The burial of the body, its allocated space and its relationship with the space of the living has been crucial to our understanding of history through archaeological findings, the majority of which are related to burial culture. The aim of this book was also to reiterate that burials are and always will be an important starting point to observe and study human history, social changes and their role in the formation of the built environment of London. It is unlikely that death will ever re-enter the space of the city beyond trophy memorials because the focus of the city project is self-referential and ordered by capitalist principles. However, this status quo could be challenged by society. Perhaps it will be in the form of a self-initiated social project, transforming a disused urban space into a repository for urns. There would not be an issue with sanitation. Indeed, there would also be no need to disguise death with landscaping. Whatever form they might take, perhaps cities are the perfect places to reintegrate death culture back into the cycle of life.

Bibliography

Cherry, Gordon E. 1979. "The Town Planning Movement and the Late Victorian City." *Transactions of the Institute of British Geographers* 4, no. 2, "The Victorian City": 306–19. Accessed 04 June 2021. https://www.jstor.org/stable/i225643
Creese, Walter L. 1966. *The Search for Environment. The Garden City Before and After*. New Haven and London: Yale University Press.
Crosby, Theo. 1967. *Urban Structuring, Studies of Alison & Peter Smithson*. London: Studio Vista Limited.
Crosby, Theo. 1969. *Architecture: City Sense*. London: Studio Vista Limited.
Curl, James S. 1984. "The Design of Early British Cemeteries." *Journal of Garden History* 4, no. 3: 223–54.
Curl, James S. 2001. *Kensal Green Cemetery. The Origins and Development of the General Cemetery of All Souls, Kensal Green, London, 1824–2001*. Chichester: Phillimore & Co.
Curl, James S. 2004. *The Victorian Celebration of Death*. Thrupp: Sutton Publishing.
Darling, Elizabeth. 2001–2. "Exhibiting Britain: Display and National Identity 1946–1967." Accessed August 24, 2020. https://www.vads.ac.uk/customizations/collection/DCADB/pages/html/esd.html
Davies, Douglas J. 1990. *Cremation Today and Tomorrow*. Bramcote (Nottingham): Grove Books Limited.

Davies, Douglas J. 1995. "British Crematoria in Public Profile." Survey for The Cremation Society of Great Britain.
Dennis, Richard. 2008. *Cities in Modernity. Representations and Productions of Metropolitan Space, 1840–1930*. Cambridge: Cambridge University Press.
Fishman, Robert. 1982. *Urban Utopias in the Twentieth Century: Ebenezer Howard, Frank Lloyd Wright and Le Corbusier*. Cambridge, Massachusetts: MIT Press.
Dyos, H. J.. 1982. *Exploring the Urban Past. Essays in the Urban History*. Cambridge: Cambridge University Press.
Geddes, Patrick. 1915. *Cities in Evolution: An Introduction to the Town Planning Movement and to the Study of Civics*. London: Williams and Northgate. Accessed 8 June 2021. https://archive.org/details/citiesinevolutio00geddu0ft/page/n3/mode/2up?ref=ol&view=theater
George, Juliet. 2010. *Fort Worth's Arlington Heights*. Charleston: Arcadia Publishing.
Gorer, Geoffrey. 1963. *Death, Grief and Mourning in Contemporary Britain*. London: The Cresset Press.
Gilles, John R. 1993. *Commemorations: The Politics of National Identity*. Princeton: Princeton University Press.
Gillon, Edmund V. 1972. *Victorian Cemetery Art*. London: Constable.
Grainger, Hilary J. 2005. *Death Redesigned: British Crematoria, History, Architecture and Landscape*. Reading: Spire Books Ltd.
Grainger, Hilary J. 2020. *Designs on Death. The Architecture of Scottish Crematoria*. Edinburgh: John Donald.
Haden, Francis S. 1875. *Earth to Earth: A Plea for a Change of System in Our Burial of the Dead*. London: Macmillan & Co. Accessed 8 June 2021. https://archive.org/details/earthtoearthaple00hade
Halcrow Fox, Cemetery Research Group, The Landscape Partnership. 1997. *Burial Space Needs in London*. London: LPAC – Planning for Greater London.
Hampstead & Highgate Express. 1881. "Highgate Cemetery". Saturday 15 January, No. 1053: 4. Accessed 18 July 2020. https://www.britishnewspaperarchive.co.uk/viewer/bl/0001981/18810115/065/0004
Heffer, Simon. 2013. *High Minds: The Victorians and the Birth of Modern Britain*. London: Random House Books.
Hill, Octavia. 1883. *Homes of the London Poor*. London: Macmillan & Co.
Holmes, Isabella. 1896. *The London Burial Grounds. Notes on Their History from the Earliest Time to Present Day*. London: T. Fisher Unwin.
Jupp, Peter C. 1993. "Cremation or Burial? Contemporary Choice in City and Village". In *The Sociology of Death: Theory, Culture, Practice*, edited by David Clark, 169–197. Oxford: Blackwell Publishers.
Jupp, Peter C. 2005. Foreword to *Death Redesigned: British Crematoria, History, Architecture and Landscape*, edited by Hilary J. Grainger, 7–10. Reading: Spire Books Ltd.
Jupp, Peter C. 2006. *From Dust to Ashes: Cremation and the British Way of Death*. London: Palgrave Macmillan.
Kilburn Times and Western Post. 1882. Friday 31 March. No. 733: 4. Accessed 28 May 2021. https://www.britishnewspaperarchive.co.uk/viewer/bl/0001813/18820331/088/0004

Masterman, Charles Frederick Gurney. ([1902] 1980). *From the Abyss: Of its Inhabitants, by One of Them*. London: Garland.
Matless, David. 1998. *Landscape and Englishness*. London: Reaktion Books.
Mayhew, Henry. ([1861–2] 2010). *London Labour & the London Poor*. Oxford: Oxford University Press.
McKellar, Elizabeth. 1999. *The Birth of Modern London. The Development and Design of the City 1660–1720*. Manchester: Manchester University Press.
Meller, H. 1980. "Cities in Evolution: Patrick Geddes as an International Prophet of Town Planning before 1914." In *The Rise of Modern Urban Planning 1800–1914*, edited by Anthony Sutcliffe, 199–223. London: Mansell.
Miller, Mervyn, and A. Stuart Gray. 1992. *Hampstead Garden Suburb*. Chichester: Pillimore.
Morley, John. 1971. *Death, Heaven and the Victorians*. London: Studio Vista.
Morning Post. 1906. Wednesday 20 June. No. 41830. 1. Accessed 20 May 2021. https://www.britishnewspaperarchive.co.uk/viewer/BL/0000174/19060620/037/0001
Morris, Susannah. 2001. "Market Solutions for Social Problems: Working-Class Housing in Nineteenth-Century London." *The Economic History Review* 54, no. 3 (August): 525–45. Accessed June 30, 2020. http://www.jstor.com/stable/3091763
Morrison, Kathryn. 1999. *The Workhouse. A Study of Poor-Law Buildings in England*. Swindon: English Heritage and the National Monuments Record Centre.
Mulkay, Mike. 1993. "Social Death in Britain." In *The Sociology of Death*, edited by David Clark. Oxford: Blackwell/Sociological Review.
Mumford, Lewis. 1947. *Technics and Civilization*. London: George Routledge & Sons Ltd.
Mumford, Lewis. 1967. *The Myth of the Machine. Technics and Human Development*. London: Secker & Warburg Limited.
Mumford, Lewis. 1974. "The Garden City Idea and Modern Planning." In *Garden Cities of To-Morrow*, edited by E. Howard, 29–40. London: Faber and Faber.
Mumford, Lewis. 1991. *The City in History*. London: Penguin Books.
Mumford, Lewis. 1996. *The Culture of Cities*. San Diego: Harcourt Brace & Company.
Olsen, Donald J. 1976. *The Growth of Victorian London*. London: B.T. Batsford Ltd.
Otter, Christopher. 2004. "Cleansing and Clarifying: Technology and Perception in Nineteenth-Century London." *Journal of British Studies* 43, no. 1 (January): 40–64. Cambridge: Cambridge University Press. Accessed 27 May 2021. https://www.jstor.org/stable/10.1086/jbs.2004.43.issue-1
Parsons, Brian. 2018. *The Evolution of the British Funeral Industry in the 20th Century. From Undertaker to Funeral Director*. Bingley: Emerald Publishing Limited.
Parsons, Brian. 2005. *Committed to the Cleansing Flame. The Development of Cremation in Nineteenth-Century England*. Reading: Spire Books Ltd.
Paxman, Jeremy. 2011. *Empire: What Ruling the World did to the British*. London: Penguin Books Ltd.
Porter, R. 2000. *London, A Social History*. London: Penguin Books Ltd.
Robinson, William. 1880. *God's Acre Beautiful or The Cemeteries of the Future* (3rd Edition with Illustrations ed.). London: The Garden Office. Accessed 8

June 2021. https://www.google.co.uk/books/edition/God_s_Acre_Beautiful/JGRBAQAAMAAJ?hl=en&gbpv=1

Rockey, John. 1983. "From Vision to Reality: Victorian Ideal Cities and Model Towns in the Genesis of Ebenezer Howard's Garden City." *The Town Planning Review* 54, no. 1: 83–105. Accessed 8 June 2021. http://www.jstor.org/stable/40111935.

Rutherford, Sarah. 2012. *The Victorian Asylum*. Oxford: Shire Publications Ltd.

Rutherford, Sarah. 2005. "Landscapers for the Mind: English Asylum Designers, 1845–1914." *Garden History* 33, no. 1 (Summer): 61–86. Accessed 20 May 2021. http://www.jstor.com/stable/25434157

Surrey Comet and Kingston Gazette. 1855. Saturday 2 June. No. 43. Accessed 20 May 2021. https://www.britishnewspaperarchive.co.uk/viewer/BL/0000684/18550602/038/0002

Taylor, Jeremy Reginald Buckley. *Hospital and Asylum architecture in England, 1840–1914 Building for Health Care*. Book. English. 1991. London: Mansell.

The Daily News. 1880. "Sales by Auction". Thursday 15 July. No. 10684: 8. Accessed 28 May 2021. https://www.britishnewspaperarchive.co.uk/viewer/bl/0000051/18800715/098/0008

The Field: The Country Gentlemen Newspaper. 1871. Vol. 38, no. 989. Saturday 9 December: 32. Accessed 20 May 2021. https://www.britishnewspaperarchive.co.uk/viewer/BL/0002446/18711209/003/0001

The Globe. 1880. Tuesday 15 June. 8. Accessed 20 May 2021. https://www.britishnewspaperarchive.co.uk/viewer/bl/0001652/18800615/056/0008

The London Necropolis. 1904. London: Joseph Causton and Sons Ltd.

Thompson, Henry. 1884. *Cremation: The Treatment of the Body after Death*. London: Smith, Elder & Co. Accessed 8 June 2021. https://www.google.co.uk/books/edition/Cremation/xtZbAAAAQAAJ?hl=en&gbpv=1

Wakeford, Iain. 1995. *A Guide to the Industrial History of Woking and its Borough*. Guildford: Surrey Industrial History Group.

Walker, Nathaniel Robert. 2020. *Victorian Visions of Suburban Utopia: Abandoning Babylon*. Oxford: Oxford University Press.

Ward Richardson, Benjamin. 1876. *Hygeia, A City of Health*. London: Macmillan & Co.

Woking History. *Woking as a Residential District*. 1907. Woking: Drowley & Co. Accessed 20 May 2021. https://wokinghistory.org/1907%20Drowley%20&%20Co.pdf

Index

Note: Page numbers in *italics* indicate figures.

Abercrombie, Patrick 138; Greater London Plan *139*
By Accident or Design (Fyfe) 66
Adams, Annmarie 99
Ainsworth, William Harrison 67, 70
All Souls College Oxford 73, 75
All Souls Kensal Green Cemetery 17
anatomy 18
Anatomy Act (1832) 15, 18
Andrews, Malcolm 34, 49, 59; statement 34
Anson, John William 125
Anthony Waterer Nurseries 123, *124*
Antoine, Jacques Denise 32–33
Architecture of Death, The (Etlin) 31, 59
Artisans, Labourers & General Dwellings Estate 75–76, *75*
Ashurst, William 43
Ashurst House 43

Balfour, Gerald 143
Barry, Charles 96
Basingstoke Canal 121; arrival of railway lines 124; construction of 121
Bentham, Jeremy 13–14; donation 14; principle 14; Utilitarian thinking 17, 39
Birth of the Clinic: An Archaeology of Medical Perception, The (Foucault) 99
Bishop of London 50–51
Blanchard, Samuel Laman 63; *The Cemetery at Kensal Green: the grounds & monuments* 63; novelty of cemetery natural landscape 63
Bleak House (Charles) 17
Blomfield, Charles James 51
body snatchers *see* "resurrection-men"
"brick yard" 121, 129, 146
British Medical Journal, The 101, 102, 105
Brompton Cemetery 38, 67
Brookwood Cemetery 44, 161; architectural styles 46; bird's-eye view *46*; burial plots 35; cemetery and town 125–138; cemetery stations at *48*; establishment of 127–128; map of *148*; Necropolis Station 143, *143*; planting 122–123
Brookwood Mental Asylum *129*; first Muslim cemetery 132; gardening 130
Builder, The 105, *106*, *107*
Bunning, James Bunstone 96, 98
Burdett-Coutts, Baroness Angela Georgina 104, 112–113
burial 30; diverse and complex issues 37; as luxury commodity 38; new alternatives to earth 162–168; new paradigm of 37; plots 34, 35; rationalisation of 55; reformation of 162; standards for 37
Burial Act (1852) 51
burying the dead: business of 36–41; private companies 37

capitalism 5, 39–40, 64
capitalist enterprise, defined 40
cemeteries, new 21; architecture and landscape 34, 41; criticised by Loudon 53; emotional role of nature 30; implementation of 24, 91; rational role of nature 30; in Victorian London 59

Cemetery at Kensal Green: the grounds & monuments, The (Blanchard) 63
cemetery companies: administrative system 51–52; architecture and legacy 41–50; commercial strategies 53; consecration 50–51; innovative identity of 50; intrinsic nature of 50; rational minds 50–56; regulation between Church and 51–52; Rugg's view 38; scholars research 38; *see also specific company*
Cester, Harry 44
Chadwick, Edwin 18, 21; concerns about new private cemeteries 24–25; health issues addressed by 25; report 21; sanitary measures 21
"Champs de Repos", Paris 12
Cherry, Gordon 157
Chertsey Road, developments in 145
Chobham Bridge 122
Church of England 51
Cities (Reader) 14
City in History, The (Mumford) 72
City Prison 96, *98*
Clarke, John 122
Comte, Auguste 100
Connaught Road, Brookwood 134, *135*
consecration 50–51
corpse: Bentham's 18; trading 17–18
County Asylum Act (1845) 129
County Lunatic Asylum 129, 130
Coutts, Thomas 113
cremation 54, 132, 166, 170; by Siemens 164; in Thompson's view 163–164
Cremation, the Treatment of the Body after Death (Thompson) 162
Cremation Society of Great Britain 130, 162
Crosby, Alan 121
Curl, James Stevens 42, 53; spatial consequences 64
Cutbush, James 104
Cutbush, William 104

Darbishire, Henry Astley 104
Davis, Alderman 113
Disraeli, Benjamin 67, 74; "Sanitas Sanitatum, Omnia Sanitas" (Health Cures All Health) speech 74
Doll, Charles 141
Donald, Robert 122
Dramatic, Equestrian & Musical Sick Fund Association 125

Dyos, Harold J.: abolition of road tolls 22; centrifugal deployment of population 65; metropolitanisation 65; poor situation of Victorian streets 22; typology of municipal park 60

"earth-to-earth" burial method 164, 165
Eastern burial cultures 25
Ecclesiastical Gazette 68
Economic Life in the Modern Age (Sombart) 40
Enclosure Acts 125
Endangered Lives: Public Health in Victorian Britain (Wohl) 14
England in the Nineteenth Century (1815–1914) (Thomson) 39
Era, The (magazine) 53
Etlin, Richard 59; *The Architecture of Death* 31, 59; dechristianisation 31–32; design proposals 32–33
exhumation 15–16

"Field of Rest" cemetery 11
The Field–The Country Gentlemen Newspaper 123
Foucault, Michel 64; *Security, Territory, Population. Lectures at the Collège de France, 1977–1978* 64; theories 64–65
Frederick, Augustus, Prince 35
funerary architecture 55
future burial spaces 11
Fyfe, Paul: *By Accident or Design* 66; emergence of modern metropolis 66

Garden Cities of To-Morrow (Howard) 150
Garden City Movement 127
Gatherings from Grave-Yards; Particularly Those of London (Walker) 15, 17
Geary, Stephen 41
General Board of Health 18
General Cemetery Company 35, 38, 42, 51, 72, 161; shares 52; *see also* Kensal Green Cemetery
Gentleman's Magazine, The 62
George III, King of Great Britain and Ireland 35
Georgian era 157
Globe Fields Chapel 16
God's Acre Beautiful; Or The Cemeteries of the Future (Robinson) 54, 165

Index

Golders Green Crematorium 54, 147, *149*, 150, 166–168, *167*, *168*; view of *150*
Gothic Revival style 41, 42; Highgate Cemetery 43, 104; Kensal Green Cemetery 42
Graham, James 98
Grand Prix (1799) 11
Grand Union Canal 23
Greater London Plan (Abercrombie) *139*
"greatest happiness principle" 13–14
Great Fire of London (1666) 11, 22
Great Northern Railway 23
Greek Revival style 42
Griffith, John 42; with Kensal Green Cemetery 44
Guide du Voyageur à Londres et aux Environs (Reclus) 99
A Guide to the Industrial History of Woking and its Borough (Wakeford) 133

Haden, Francis Seymour 164; criticism towards cemetery companies 165
Hainsworth's Kensal Lodge 81
Hampshire Chronicle: And Portsmouth and Chichester Journal 121
Hampstead & Highgate Express 111
Hampstead Garden Suburb 79, 113, *147*
Harrow-on-the-Hill 61
Hassell, John 60; Harrow-on-the-Hill 61; *Single Day Excursions from the Metropolis* 60
Health of Towns Association (1839) 18
Highgate Cemetery 17, 34, 35, 38, 42, 161; administrative system 53; admission-ticket to *35*; architecture and landscape 91–92; consecration plan 50–51; East Cemetery 92; gravestones and vistas 95–103; historical map *111*; vs. Kensal Green 95, 111, 116–117; Metropolitan Cattle Market 96, *97*; new hospitals and clean air 103–117, *103*; opening of Waterloo Park 108, *109*; original plan for 42–43; view from London *94*; view from Parliament Hill *94*; village at edge of metropolis 90–95; West Cemetery 92
Highgate Infirmary 104, *108*
"Highgate Infirmary, The" 105
Highgate Mansion House Academy 43
Highgate Past (Richardson) 42

Highgate Smallpox and Vaccination Hospital 23
Hill, Octavia 158; *Open Spaces* 158; suggestion 158
A History of Woking (Crosby) 121
Holly Lodge Estate 113, *114*; Lady Workers' Homes Ltd flats *116*
Holly Village 104, 116
Holmes, Isabella 158; criticism addressed by 160; funeral system 160; guidelines 159; survey of London's graveyards 161
Hook Heath Estate 143–144, *144*, 145, 146, 147
Hour of Our Death, The (Ariès) 30
House of Commons 32
Howard, Ebenezer 78, 143, 150, 170–171
human bones trading 16
Hunter, Robert 112
Hyde Park 19
Hygiea: A City of Health (Richardson) 169

Ideal Entrepreneur 40–41
Illustrated London News, The 66
Improved Industrial Dwelling Company 108
Industrial Revolution 13, 22, 23
Ingen-Housz, John 32
innovation 22, 141; hygienic 103; Robinson's 167; in stylistic language 3; technical and scientific 8, 13
An Introduction to the Principles of Morals and Legislation (Bentham) 13–14

Jacob's Island 20
Jebb, Joshua 96
jobbing mercantile operation 90
John Bull 90
Jones, Gareth Stedman 23; *Outcast London: A Study in the Relationship between Classes in Victorian Society* 23
Journal of the Statistical Society of London 78

Kendall, Edward 42, 70; proposal 42
Kensal Green 34; Coffee Palace and Worksman Hall 76; electric tram services in 79; Harvey's theory 84; Ordnance Survey map of 81, *81*;

Public Library and Reading Rooms 77; reading room interiors of public library 77; as suburb 80–85, *80*; see also Kensal Green Cemetery
Kensal Green Cemetery 36, *36*, 42, 161; 1865 map of 71; 1888 map of 68; consecration plan 50–51; gas works 71–72; Gothic style design for 70; *vs.* Highgate Cemetery 95, 111, 116–117; landscape of 35; metropolitan picturesque 59–66; Plough Tavern in *62*; as point of reference 85; success of 38; testing ground 66–79; two character-defining moments 60; view of Grand Union Canal 73
Kensal Manor House 67, 81
Kensal New Town 67, 71, 73; laundries in 81
Kensington Gardens 19
Kilburn Times and *Western Post* 75
Kip, Johannes 33
Knaphill Prison *see* Woking Invalid Convict Prison

Ladies Workers' Homes 113, *116*
Lady's Newspaper, The 17
laissez-faire attitude, of government 39, 157
Law of Three Stages 100
On the Laying Out of Cemeteries (Loudon) 25
Lefebvre, Henri 83; formation of space 83
Leicester Chronicle, The 17
Leitner, Gottlieb Wilhelm 132
Literary and Scientific Institution 44
London: basic functions of 14; burials 13; cholera outbreaks 20; churchyards 15; churchyard St John's Church Waterloo Road *159*; diverse economy 15; ethical issues 14; graveyards 15; industry 23; medical community 17; overcrowded churchyards 100; population 13, 157; public health 20; socio-cultural context of nineteenth-century 13–14; trade patterns 15; transport 23
London & South Western Railway (LSWR) company 140
London & South Western Railway Servants' Orphanage 135, *136*, *137*
London and Westminster Cemetery Company 38

London Burial Grounds: Notes on Their History from the Earliest Times to the Present Day, The (1896) 158
London Cemetery Company 38, 41, 44; administrative system 52; commercial strategies 53; logbook 52–53; shares 51–52; *see also* Highgate Cemetery
London County Council 157
London Labour & the London Poor (Mayhew) 20
London Metropolitan Archives (LMA) 13, 51
London Metropolitan Public Gardens Association 158
London Necropolis Company 44, 122, 125; burials and funeral services 46, 50; Crosby criticism 127; dividend token 52; establishment of 127–128; front façade *142*; houses for workers *131*; land selling 126; London & South Western Railway company offer 140; money from institutions 130; promotion 146; purpose-built retirement home for actors 132; turning point in history of 138–140; Woking residential estates 141–150; *see also* Brookwood Cemetery
London School of Economics 170
"London That Never Was, The" (exhibition) 13
London's Necropolis: A Guide to Brookwood Cemetery (Clarke) 140
Loudon, John Claudius 11; concerns about London's cemeteries 25–26; criticism on cemetery design 53; extensive theoretical work 25; *On the Laying Out of Cemeteries* 25; long-term plan for future London 26
Lutyens, Edwin 143

Marcus, Steven 64
Mayhew, Henry 20–21; hard reality of Londoners 21; *London Labour & the London Poor* 20; sanitary measures 21
medical gaze 99–100
Medicine by Design: The Architect and the Modern Hospital, 1893–1943 (Adams) 99
Messer, Arthur Albert 150; Tubbs and 134, 143, 147
Metropolitan Association 18
Metropolitan Asylums Board 23
Metropolitan Cattle Market 96, 97

Index 181

Metropolitan Electric Tramways Limited 79
metropolitanisation 65
"Metropolitan Picturesque, The" (Andrews) 34
metropolitan sepulcher 9–13; "Champs de Repos" in Paris *12*; by Willson *10*
"Metropolitan Small-Pox Hospitals, The" 101
Miller, Thomas 66
Molinos, Jacques 11; "Champs de Repos" *12*
Montmartre, Paris 11
Morning Advertiser 73
Morning Chronicle 20, 96
Morning Post (article) 16
Morris, Susannah 170
Mumford, Lewis 72; *The City in History* 72; gas works 73
municipal park, typology of 60

Necropolis Station 46, 47, *143*
Neoclassicism 41
"New Hospitals Versus The Extension Of Old Hospitals For London" 102
94-storey-high pyramid 9
Norwood Cemetery 38
Nunhead Cemetery 38

Old and New London: Volume 5 (Watford) 62
Olsen's theory 82
Open Spaces (Hill) 158
ordering the dead 19–26
Oriental Institute, Woking 132, *133*
Origins & Development of the General Cemetery of All Souls, Kensal Green, London 1824–2001, The (Curl) 42
Outcast London: A Study in the Relationship between Classes in Victorian Society (Jones) 23
overcrowding 13–18, 162, 171–172; consequences of 22; St. Martin's Burial Ground, Drury Lane *16*; in suburban cemeteries 54

Paddington Arm of Grand Union Canal 60
pagan cultures 30
Parisian cemeteries *31*, 34
Parliament Hill *94*
Paul, John Dean 42

Penny Magazine, The 91, *93*
Pentonville Prison 98–99
Père Lachaise Cemetery, Paris 31, *31*; vegetation 34
Philosophical Radicals 14
picturesque 34, 59–62
Plan of London from Actual Survey (1833) 19–20, *19*
Pond Square 110
Priestley, Joseph 32; scientific discovery 32, 33
Primrose Hill 9
Prince Augustus Frederick (Duke of Sussex) 35
Prince George 35
Princess Sophia 35
Pringle, John 32
Pyramid General Cemetery Company 9

Quarterly Review (article) 16
Queen's Park Estate 76, 78, 82; visual impact of 84

Ragon, Michel 30; adorn burial grounds 30; *The Space of Death* 30
rationalisation, of burials 55
Reader, John 14
Reclus, Élisée 99; *Guide du Voyageur à Londres et aux Environs* 99; overview of London 99
Regent Park 19
"resurrection-men" 18
Richardson, Benjamin Ward 169; design proposal for cemetery 170; *Hygiea: A City of Health* 169; visionary plan 169
Richardson, John 42
"Rise of Cemetery Companies in Britain: 1820–1853, The" (Rugg) 38
Robinson, William 54, 165; envisaged for future cemetery 165–166; *God's Acre Beautiful; Or The Cemeteries of the Future* 54, 165, 166; idea 166; promoting wild garden 54; vision of cremation 166; warning 54
Royal Caledonian Asylum 99
Royal Dramatic College 125
Royal Dramatic Society 132
Royal Parks 32
Royal Society 32
Rugg, Julie 38; study on cemetery companies 38–39
Russell Square 9

"Sanitas Sanitatum, Omnia Sanitas" (Health Cures All Health) 74
Scott, George Gilbert 122
Security, Territory, Population. Lectures at the Collège de France, 1977–78 (Foucault) 64
Select Committee 32
self-expression, in funerary architecture 49
Shaftesbury Park Estate 78
Shury, John 19; Plan of London from Actual Survey (1833) 19–20, *19*
Siemens, Friedrich August 164
Single Day Excursions from the Metropolis (Hassell) 60
small-pox hospitals, Highgate 100–102, *102*
Smith, Jeremy 13
Smith, Thomas Southwood 18; with Chadwick, Edwin 18; health issues addressed by 25
socio-cultural context, of nineteenth-century 13–14
Sombart, Werner 39; capitalist enterprise 40; explanation of capitalism 39–40; outline of private entrepreneur 41; theory 40; view 54
Somers Town, population density 110
South Metropolitan Cemetery Company 38
Space of Death, The (Ragon) 30
St. James's Park 32
St. John Crematorium, Woking *131*, 132
St. John's Church in Waterloo 159
St. John's the Evangelist Church 68, *69*; view from Kensal Green Cemetery 70
St. John the Baptist Church, in Woking 122, *123*
St. Martin's Burial Ground, Drury Lane *16*
St. Michael's Church 44, *93*, 104, 110
St. Pancras and Holborn Journal, The 104–105
St. Pancras Infirmary 104–105, 109; bird's-eye view illustration of *107*; plan drawing 105, *106*
St. Pancras Old Churchyard *24*

Tappen, George 99
Thames Junction Railway 67
Thompson, Henry 162; benefits of cremation 163; *Cremation, the Treatment of the Body after Death* 162; Cremation Society of Great Britain 162; necessity of cremation 163
Thomson, David 39; philanthropic nature 39
Townsend, Charles Harrison 141
trade and commerce: connectivity and accessibility 22; rational laws 13
Tubbs, Cyril B.: advise 141; design 134, 140, 141; and Messer 134, 141, 147; scheme 47

utilitarianism 14

Vauxhall Bridge 20
Victoria Cottage Hospital 121, *122*
Victorian cemeteries: architectural language of 34; critical assessment 54–55; future visions 168–171; landscape in 34–36, 55–56; manifestation of local jurisdiction 59; middle classes 55; private 37; *see also* cemetery companies
Victorian City: Images and Realities, The (Marcus) 64

Wakeford, Iain 133; *A Guide to the Industrial History of Woking and its Borough* 133
Wakley, Thomas 41
Walker, George Alfred 15; as doctor 17; exhumation 15–16; as follower of Bentham's Utilitarian thinking 17; *Gatherings from Grave-Yards; Particularly Those of London* 15, 17; health issues addressed by 25; picture of London 17; shocking situation of graveyard 16, *16*
"waste land" 125
Waterloo Station 47
Waterlow, Sidney 75
Waterlow Park 107–108; Highgate Infirmary view from *108*
Watford, Edward 62
West Cemetery, in Highgate 42; entrance to *43*; large-scale development 113; major changes 107; upper-end of *45*; west boundaries of 112–113
Western Gas Company 71; petition against 73–74
West Norwood Cemetery 17
wild garden 54, 165
Willesden Junction 67

Willson, Thomas 9; drawings 13; earthless vertical cemetery 13; metropolitan sepulchre by *10*; pyramid cemetery proposal 13, 18, 25, 26; scheme 12
Wohl, Anthony 14; suggestion by 14–15
Woking Council offices *134*
Woking District Gas Company 133
Woking Invalid Convict Prison 128–129, *128*, 130
Woking residential estates 141–150
Wren, Christopher 11; plan 11; urban vision 22
Wyld, James 60; "The Vicinity of London" historical map by 60, *61*